T0244284

MAKING OUR FUTURE

MAKING
OUR
FUTURE

Visionary Folklore and
Everyday Culture in Appalachia

Emily Hilliard

The University of North Carolina Press
CHAPEL HILL

Manufactured in the United States of America

Designed by Lindsay Starr
Set in Calluna by Copperline Book Services, Inc.

The University of North Carolina Press has been a member of
the Green Press Initiative since 2003.

Cover illustration: © Annie Howe Papercuts

Library of Congress Cataloging-in-Publication Data
Names: Hilliard, Emily, author.
Title: Making our future : visionary folklore and everyday
culture in Appalachia / Emily Hilliard.
Description: Chapel Hill : The University of North Carolina
Press, 2022. | Includes bibliographical references and index.
Identifiers: LCCN 2022017163 | ISBN 9781469671611 (cloth ; alk. paper) |
ISBN 9781469671628 (pbk. ; alk. paper) | ISBN 9781469671635 (ebook)
Subjects: LCSH: West Virginia—Folklore—21st century. |
West Virginia—Social life and customs—21st century.
Classification: LCC GR110.W47 H55 2022 |
DDC 398.209754—dc23/eng/20220509
LC record available at https://lccn.loc.gov/2022017163

Chapter 3 expands on the essay "'The Reason We Make These Deep-Fat-Fried Treats': In Conversation with the Rosettes of Helvetia, West Virginia," which appeared in *The Food We Eat, the Stories We Tell: Contemporary Appalachian Tables*, ed. Elizabeth S. D. Engelhardt with Lora E. Smith (Athens: Ohio University Press, 2019). A version of chapter 4 appeared earlier, in somewhat different form, in the *Oxford American*, issue 114, Southern Literature Issue, Fall 2021. Chapter 6 draws and expands on an essay previously published in "Slaw Abiding Citizens: A Quest for the West Virginia Hot Dog," by Emily Hilliard, with illustrations by Emily Wallace, *Gravy*, Fall 2016.

To the people of West Virginia,
past, present, and future;
and to my grandmother, Georgette,
who is not a West Virginian but
sings the West Virginia song

We're fighting for our future, don't you understand?

—West Virginia labor songwriter Elaine Purkey,
"One Day More"

Contents

Illustrations

PLATES (FOLLOWING PAGE 182)

A Note on Collaborative Ethnographic Methodology and Writing as Public Folklore Praxis

FOR THE FIELDWORK that constitutes the foundation of this book, I employed collaborative ethnographic methodology through open-ended, mutually directed interviews, dialogue during the fieldwork process, and by sharing draft chapters with consultants and then incorporating their feedback. Most of the feedback I received was positive and minimal, but several consultants offered crucial corrections to details I had omitted or misunderstood. Some elaborated on points that they had made during our interviews or updated me on what they've done since our last meeting, both of which helped me to more thoroughly understand their respective work and perspectives. I address the specifics of my engagement with each community in each respective chapter.

Collaborative ethnography may be an underused model, but it has great value and utility for many types of cultural work. It is an especially useful practice in a place like Appalachia, where journalists and cultural workers have extracted stories and cultural resources without community input, benefit, or respect, employing narratives that frame the region's faults as individual failures rather than systemic problems. Collaborative ethnography offers one pathway to address some of the overarching questions of cultural work: How do we tell stories about a place responsibly and equitably? How do we tell the multivocal, shared, overlapping, and at times conflicting stories of our own communities? How do we tell those stories of communities not our own? How do we enter into mutually beneficial relationships with the communities we work with? Rather than presenting the cultural worker's perspective as definitive, collaborative ethnography frames narratives as participatory and equitable dialogues, so that dialogue and equity become both the topic and the method.

Of course, there can be drawbacks and limitations to this methodology, as many ethnographic texts have illuminated. Namely, the collaborative nature of the approach is somewhat in opposition to journalistic practices of objectivity, the work involves a significant time investment and thorough engagement that demands the whole of a person, and with this level of engagement, differences of opinion and opposing perspectives can be hard to untangle and resolve. Issues of equity remain too, particularly around compensation (folklorists or cultural workers are often paid for this work while consultants or interviewees are not) and authority (cultural workers are still generally seen as "experts" and often make the major curatorial decisions). But collaborative ethnography does present a road map for, not to mention a wealth of literature on, deeper, more honest and integrative work that I hope more writers, journalists, scholars, and cultural workers will consider adopting, especially when working with communities not their own.

One goal of this book is to offer examples of how collaborative methodology can be a tool for more public-facing writing and reporting that engages the participation of cultural communities. My engagement with this material in long-form essays oriented toward a general readership is also intended to demonstrate the type of thorough, historically grounded, critical, and community-engaged work that is necessary to responsibly and adequately present cultural heritage in a way that resists essentialist, stereotyped, one-dimensional, and exceptionalist portrayals. Such generalized conceptions can be detrimental to understanding the diverse and nuanced cultural life of a place, and Appalachia has been particularly susceptible to these types of flat, myopic depictions.

The field of public folklore has long engaged questions of cultural representation, dialogue, and equity, and has produced a vast body of work responding to those questions, not only in text but also in public programming such as festivals, panels, and concerts; apprenticeship and grant programs; cultural documentation and community archives projects; media production; and field schools, oral history workshops, and community expert programs that assist local communities in documenting their own culture. Public folklorists, as Mary Hufford notes, "amplify voices in a democratic polity."[1] We model participatory engagement, bearing witness to the collective expressive culture that underrepresented communities are already engaged in, and facilitating the inclusion of those collectivities within broader contexts and conversations. As Gregory Hansen argues in his article "Theorizing Public Folklore: Folklore Work as Systemic Cultural Intervention," public folklorists challenge the distinction between theory and practice in our work as cultural mediators.[2] All public folklore work—programming, published media, and advocacy—is imbued with folklore theory of cultural equity, collaboration, and interpretation. Though this text is focused on the fieldwork, research, and presentational aspect of public folklore, it is my hope that the book contributes to a picture of what folklore is, why it is important, and how the framework of folklore can help us understand, access, and engage with cultural communities—both those we're a part of and those we're not.

With this value in mind, as I wrote the following chapters, I sought to strike a balance between academic monograph and creative nonfiction, ethnography, reported journalism, and cultural criticism. One specific result of this hybridity is in whether I refer to consultants or interviewees by their first or last names. I made this decision on a case-by-case basis, informed by my familiarity with the particular consultant and the length of our fieldwork relationship, the context, and the consultant's preference. Other editorial decisions, such as a more informal tone, were made for the book's intended readership of a broad audience, which I hope will include other folklorists and folklore students, cultural workers and documentarians, journalists, scholars, traditional artists and practitioners, friends and colleagues, and West Virginians. Though I draw on scholarship and concepts situated in folklore, ethnomusicology, literature, cultural studies, food studies, history, feminist theory, Appalachian studies, and Marxist theory, the text is intended to be accessible to those who do not necessarily have an academic background or experience in those subject areas. The book's hybridity is intentional—an example of theory-based praxis and an effort to move beyond academic silos. I hope that this book can become part of the growing body of work that makes public folklore methodology accessible and useful to a diverse public, including the communities of practice I've worked with and others like them.

MAKING OUR FUTURE

Introduction

IT'S THE SUMMER SOLSTICE, and the warmest season is in its full expression here in West Virginia—the lush and green foliage blankets the mountains that really hug you in along this stretch of Route 60. It's also West Virginia Day, the holiday on which the state commemorates its 1863 secession from Virginia and admission to the Union.[1] These days, the occasion is commonly celebrated by engaging in all things West Virginia: eating hot dogs with chili, slaw (if you find yourself below the "slaw line"), mustard, and onions; basking in the hills and rivers in all their summer glory; and, as one meme jests, leaving Mountain Dew and a plate of pepperoni rolls out overnight for Mothman, West Virginia Day's appointed Santa Claus. I'm headed south along the Midland Trail—perhaps my favorite drive in all of the Mountain State—for a hike in the New River Gorge followed by a stop at a local hot dog joint, Burger Carte. I like this drive because it's winding and charming and beautiful, but the landscape and built environment en route also offer a pithy introduction to West Virginia, providing references to and representations of many of the major factors that impact folklife here:

extractive industry, the tourism economy and its particular construction and packaging of place and culture, labor struggle and occupational disaster, natural beauty and environmental destruction. Along this fifty-mile stretch, the past, present, and future of West Virginia are on display.

Leaving Charleston and heading southeast, the road is immediately hedged in between the mountains on the left and the Kanawha River on the right, with the railroad crossing back and forth over the course of the journey. In Malden, I pass the former location of the saltworks where Booker T. Washington worked as a boy.[2] In Belle, smokestacks and cranes stretch up into the sky, competing with the mountains for the view. A group of Black girls with new glittery pink bikes ride by a group of white girls holding signs advertising a yard sale. I drive past cinder-block auto shops and neat former company houses and churches (so many churches!)—Church of Christ, Church of God, Catholic, African Zion Baptist, First Baptist, Memorial Baptist, and the mysterious "House of Non-Judgement." There's an old three-story brick elementary school, Dollar Generals, and a barbecue restaurant, a couple Taco Bells, the beloved West Virginia chain Tudor's Biscuit World, and a Shoney's Buffet with a sign that reads "Reopening Soon." Past Cedar Grove, hand-painted boards advertising a hot dog joint are stapled to telephone poles every few yards and campaign signs are scattered along the berm. In London, the transport system for the Mammoth Coal Processing Plant arches from the hillside over the road to a looming metal tipple, standing guard.

This route is officially designated as historic, and the setting can feel antiquated if you let it. At Kanawha Falls, where the parking lot is flooded after days of rain, families joyfully wade in to collect driftwood and skip rocks. I pass Glen Ferris Inn, where once over a fine lunch I interviewed a woman whose father died of silicosis after working on the Hawk's Nest Tunnel in the early 1930s, an occupational disaster considered to this day to be one of the worst in U.S. history.[3] In Gauley Bridge, I hit the most stunning stretch, where the river widens out like a glacial lake and the Kanawha dumps into the New. Here, rounding the river bend, the obvious signs of industry fade from view and the mountains seem to emerge right out of the water on the other side of the shore, perfectly reflecting their fog-shaded green bodies and blue sky.[4]

This is the gateway to the newly upgraded New River Gorge National Park and Preserve, which until December 2020 was a "National River." The now 73,000-acre and 53-mile-long area became part of the National Park Service in 1978, heralding an adventure tourism industry built on the vestiges of the coal and timber industry.[5] Ghost boomtowns, coke ovens, railroad tunnels, abandoned coal camps, and other cultural artifacts have all been "reclaimed by the forest," according to the park literature.[6] From 1991 to 1993, the American Folklife Center worked with the National Park Service to conduct fieldwork with southern West Virginia cultural communities for a proposed cultural heritage center located within the National River.[7] The team, directed by folklorists Mary Hufford and Rita Moonsammy, conducted interviews with gardeners, hunters, and fishers in the all-Black Oak Hill neighborhood of Harlem Heights, Lebanese foodways practitioners at St. George's Orthodox Cathedral in Charleston, ginseng diggers, a blues musician, quilters, a multiracial bar band, a former railroad crew cook, Italian restaurateurs, and more. The team's vision was a publicly accessible center within the tourist-oriented park that would engage local communities and serve as a resource for them to share local knowledge, both cultural and ecological. The Park Service never acted on the proposal.[8] Today the area draws over a million tourists per year. But within the National Park, on interpretive placards that tell of former mines, the "amazing journey" of pioneers, and "ancient" American Indian artifacts, there are few signs of the diverse and vibrant cultural life of West Virginia communities today.[9]

I HAVE SPENT much of the past six years traveling in and across West Virginia, crisscrossing mountains, hollers, creeks, and rivers along dirt roads and highways on fieldwork trips to interview quilters, fiddlers, striking teachers, gospel singers, miniature makers, independent pro wrestlers, neon sign makers, herbalists, marble collectors, gamers, woodworkers, playwrights, pastors, turkey call makers, and more. I've been welcomed into homes, barns, churches, and workshops, and spent long afternoons around kitchen tables, sharing meals prepared by home cooks of traditional Filipino, north Indian, Greek, Swiss, and the particular amalgam of predominantly Scots-Irish, German, Native American, and African American cuisines now thought of as Appalachian foodways. I've eaten a lot of hot dogs and pepperoni rolls. I've attended a Lebanese Mahrajan Festival, a Baptist singing convention, local independent professional wrestling shows, ramp suppers, and Serbian "chicken blasts," visited a Hare Krishna temple, gone two-stepping, harvested sorghum, and been a guest at a Ramadan fast-breaking dinner. I've toured farms and gardens and studios, with dogs and cats trailing along as their owners shared family stories and personal accounts of their work, artistic inspiration, and, on a few occasions, divine visions. I've been given several dozen fresh eggs, a handmade broom, a hand-hewn wooden bowl, a rug hooking kit, loaves of salt-rising bread, books, plants, and reel-to-reel tapes. Many of the people I've worked with I now call friends. The intimate glimpse I've been offered of this place has been entrusted to me with extreme generosity, openness, and intention.

I moved to West Virginia on Halloween 2015 from Washington, D.C., where I'd been living for four years, working for several cultural heritage organizations and picking up freelance writing gigs on the side. The West Virginia state folklorist position at the West Virginia Humanities Council was posted; I applied, was offered the job, and accepted it without hesitation. It was in many ways a dream job—an opportunity to establish and direct a completely new state folklife program, in a place I'd been interested in since I started visiting regularly four years prior. But the scope of it was also daunting—an entire state, even a small one, is a lot of ground to cover. I also had concerns about my position as someone not from West Virginia or Appalachia. I am a "flatland foreigner" (as West Virginia fiddler Frank George teased when I met him)—a midwesterner who grew up in the inner city of a rust belt town in northern Indiana, surrounded by cornfields and Amish farms. Appalachia and the Midwest are knitted together by histories of extraction, industrialization, and migration—in the first half of the twentieth century, thousands of Appalachians moved north in search of work to industrial towns like mine, bringing their culture with them. Perhaps because of this, and the two regions' similar juxtaposition of industrial and rural spaces, I felt a familiarity in my new home. I had also done some fieldwork in West Virginia before, mainly in the Swiss community of Helvetia. But ultimately, I was an outsider, now charged with documenting and working with local communities to help sustain the cultural heritage of a place with a deep place-based pride and identity. And I was well aware of the state and greater region's history of extraction and exploitation of both natural and cultural resources. Though the Folklife Program's mission would be to document, sustain, present, and support West Virginia cultural heritage and living traditions from within the state to the benefit of its citizens, I questioned how my personal positionality and intentions might be perceived, and what preexisting conceptions of folklore I would encounter.

Defining Folklore

The National Endowment for the Arts (NEA) explains that the folk and traditional arts are "rooted in and reflective of the cultural life of a community," whose members "may share a common ethnic heritage, cultural mores, language, religion, occupation, or geographic region." Across the field of study, definitions of *folklore* and *folklife* are continually posed and contested, but they all differ significantly from mainstream perceptions of folklore as merely myths, legends and tales, inferior or misguided knowledge, or the untrue. When I describe this interpretation of folklore to the people I do fieldwork with, I say that it's the art of everyday life— creative practices we learn by living our lives, passed informally from person-to-person rather than through formal training. Folklore is all of the ways a group expresses itself creatively, manifesting in foodways, dance, music, language, stories, jokes, memes, dress, craft, and material culture. This is a variation of folklorist Dan Ben-Amos's definition of folklore as "artistic communication in small groups."[10] Both definitions emphasize that folklore is concerned not only with capital A "Art" but the many forms of creativity or "expressive culture" that are pervasive in our daily lives, shared between people, and rooted in community and/or place.

I tend to use *folklore* and *folklife* interchangeably, and do so throughout this book, but there is a subtle difference. I find the term *folklife* better suited to signify the full inclusion of often overlapping cultural practices—foodways, faith, language, material culture, and more—as well as the verbal art and narrative typically associated with the layperson's understanding of folklore. While folklore is the discipline and the field, as well as the subject, I've found that the term can be confusing and limiting as it's more likely to be perceived as myths, legends, and the untrue. Because of this, *folklife* feels more accurate in communicating the subject matter that public folklore concerns itself with, while *folklore* is better suited for describing the field and discipline. *Cultural heritage* and *intangible cultural heritage* (ICH) are newer, related terms, intended to reduce the confusion and limitations of the word *folklore*. In 2003, the UN Educational Scientific and Cultural Organization adopted *intangible cultural heritage*, replacing its previous conception of "folklore," and defining ICH as "the practices, representations, expressions, knowledge, skills— as well as the instruments, objects, artefacts and cultural spaces associated therewith—that communities, groups and, in some cases, individuals recognize as part of their cultural heritage. This intangible cultural heritage, transmitted from generation to generation, is constantly recreated by communities and groups in response to their environment, their interaction with nature and their history, and provides them with a sense of identity and continuity, thus promoting respect for cultural diversity and human creativity."[11] For the purposes of this book, I use *cultural heritage* interchangeably with *folklife*.

The type of creative expression that fits under the banner of folklife is also referred to as the "vernacular" or "traditional," characterizing forms that are variable and passed on directly and informally within communities of practice grounded in geographic locality or shared identity.[12] As folklorist Dorothy Noyes notes, folklore deals with residual, emergent, and interstitial cultural expressions that exist on the margins or, conversely, are so embedded and pervasive in the everyday life of a community that they can be barely perceptible by members of that community (that insider's perspective is referred to as "emic," as opposed to the "etic" perspective from outside a cultural group).[13] We all engage with folklore everyday—the in-jokes that emerge among families, the creative twist on an heirloom recipe, a lullaby sung to a child at bedtime, the vocabulary unique to an occupation, the beloved foodways of a certain place, the meme altered and shared among friends. In his book *Everyday Life: A Poetics of Vernacular Practices*, folklorist Roger Abrahams explains defiantly, "Folklore has been treated with little respect by other social science disciplines because it is concerned with ephemeral cultural productions which arise from vernacular impulses operating in small locales. Yet, for folklorists, what evokes wonder is not the transitory quality of folk culture, but rather the creative vigor in these seemingly unpromising sites for cultural production." There is often an unlikely, even subversive quality to folklore, as grassroots, bottom-up collective expressions in tension with totalizing and homogenizing systems, manifesting as "a rejection of capitalist, industrial, and bureaucratic excesses."[14] People can enact folklore anywhere, from the creative arrangement of plants and material assemblage in a tiny urban front yard to the latrinalia in a public bathroom stall. The disparate forms folklore includes, as Mary Hufford writes, are "spoken, sung, danced, cooked, hunted, sewn, cultivated, and built around the cracks of a hegemonic order that is never complete."[15] Indeed, part of the rationalization for the Folklife Preservation Act of 1976 was that with the institutionalization of folklife, namely through the American Folklife Center at the Library of Congress, underrepresented communities could now recognize themselves within the public sphere.

Public Folklore and State Folklife Programs

Though funding for the folk and traditional arts was included in the NEA's initial appropriation when it was founded in 1965, the first state folklife programs were not piloted until 1976, in Maryland and Tennessee.

Those initial programs were charged with conducting fieldwork, building relationships, and making funding and programming resources available to traditional artists and cultural communities, generally situated, according to NEA Folk and Traditional Arts director Cliff Murphy, "in rural, working-class, immigrant, mountain, maritime, and inner-city communities."[16] Beginning in fiscal year 2021, the NEA requires state arts agencies and regional arts organizations to have some iteration of a folklife program, whether in-house or through partnerships with universities, nonprofits, and state humanities councils (as in West Virginia). These programs, most of which are long established, continue to carry and expand on that original charge from the NEA, working to support, sustain, and promote the living traditions and cultural heritage of their home states, with all activities rooted in ethnographic fieldwork and collaboration with local communities.[17] State folklife programs do this through documentary fieldwork, public programming such as festivals, panels, and concerts; grant and apprenticeship programs that support the transmission of cultural traditions to the next generation; cultural documentation and community archives projects; media production; field schools, oral history workshops, and community documenters or scholars programs that assist local communities in documenting their own culture; and more.

Surprisingly, West Virginia had never had an official state folklorist prior to my position, though I was inheriting a long legacy of work by folklorists, documentarians, writers, oral historians, and community experts who have worked with traditional artists and cultural communities in the state, such as Frank and Jane George, W. I. "Bill" Hairston, Michael and Carrie Kline, Patrick Gainer, Ruth Ann Musick, Judy Byers, Ed Cabbell, Mary Hufford, and my closest predecessor, the former Humanities Council board member Gerry Milnes.[18] The Humanities Council had employed folklorists and undertaken folklife projects but had never had a permanent folklorist position, let alone one with a statewide scope, direct program focus, and support from the NEA. In the original grant the council received to seed my position, the work plan was loose, but with the clear directive that the initial focus would be on folklife fieldwork and documentation. This was not only to begin to collect a documentary archive of active traditional artists and cultural communities for posterity but also to establish a baseline that would inform our future programming, helping us understand who is out there, what work, art forms, and practices they are engaged in, and what their needs are. But fieldwork is not merely for the creation of an archive for future use or statistical analysis—to suggest that would diminish the real and specific human interactions that occur under the fieldwork umbrella. At the center of the fieldwork practice is the development of relationships with individuals and communities that make the fieldworker beholden to those constituencies as a representative of an organization, yes, but also as an individual person. To be a public folklorist is to navigate the tensions and, at times, contradictions across varied roles: ethnographer, outsider, insider, cultural broker, community advocate, grant maker, institutional proxy, and friend.

Collaborative Ethnographic Methodology

Public folklore work is, according to folklorists Robert Baron and Nick Spitzer, "inherently collaborative in its engagement with communities . . . [that are] increasingly interested in safeguarding, presenting, and documenting local cultural expressions."[19] This is reflected in folklore's collaborative ethnographic methodology, committed to equity and dialogue between fieldworker and the community or interviewee, referred to as the consultant or collaborator. In this methodology, the fieldworker and consultant are both considered experts in their own experience, and interviews and other fieldwork documentation are approached as a collaboration between equals. Luke Eric Lassiter, author of *The Chicago Guide to Collaborative Ethnography*, an essential primer on the subject, defines this method: "We might sum up collaborative ethnography as an approach to ethnography that *deliberately* and *explicitly* emphasizes collaboration at every point in the ethnographic process, without veiling it—from project conceptualization, to fieldwork, and, especially, through the writing process. Collaborative ethnography invites commentary from our consultants and seeks to make that commentary overtly part of the ethnographic text as it develops. In turn, this negotiation is reintegrated back into the fieldwork process itself."[20] While there can be an inerasable power dynamic between the person holding the microphone and the person speaking into it, and full collaboration is not always possible, an equitable and participatory relationship is the ideal to strive for. This dialogic, collaborative ethic serves as a moral guide, a compass to rely on to constantly check assumptions about individual or community values, and prevent the imposition of a personal or organizational agenda.

In the context of the Folklife Program, we embedded this dialogic and collaborative commitment in our work from the beginning by actively seeking input from the community to guide fieldwork—namely, through our toll-free Folklife Hotline (for all your burning folklore emergencies, we joke); our public interest meetings in communities across the state where we invite dialogue on important local traditions, practitioners, and artists; our approach to interviews as open-ended conversations where the topic of discussion is guided by both parties equally rather than by scripted one-sided questions; and by ensuring that consultants have the opportunity to view and provide feedback on writing or media pieces about them prior to publication. This feedback and conversation then informs current and future fieldwork and programming. The process of collaborative ethnography can be messy and difficult, but it rests and relies on that tension and multivocality as a basis for greater mutual understanding. Ultimately, it puts the folklorist in relationship with the consultant or consultant community they're working with, so that while perspectives and goals may be different, the work builds from a place of mutual benefit and understanding.

I leaned on collaborative ethnography as a support through my initial concerns about how I, and my intentions, may be perceived. My fieldwork, conversations with other public folklorists and scholars, and research into the culture and history of West Virginia taught me that there are many ways of being an outsider—social boundary lines can be drawn across class, gender, race, ethnicity, folk group, and community both local and small, and large and cosmopolitan. Although I've been ribbed for being a "flatland foreigner," I've found that most people I work with don't seem to care about my regional origins. The few who have commented on my "outsider" status have been concerned not that I'm a midwesterner by birth but rather that I am a representative of an institution and a city person from the state capital who made the long drive to interview them. Though there is a history of exploitation and extraction of cultural and natural resources in Appalachia by outsiders, wealthy elites native to the region have also been guilty of this.[21] Historically and presently, the insider/outsider narrative in Appalachia has been used to obscure class disparity or exploitive behavior by those from the region. Further, I've experienced directly that ethnographers always work from varying and shifting etic and emic positions; our duty is to do so ethically and equitably. Ultimately, the folklorist asks not to direct or control the conversation but to be invited into conversations that are already happening, between the individual practitioner, the community of practice, and the creative expression.

West Virginia Folklore: Combating the
Anachronistic and Monocultural Narratives

When I give my shorthand definition of folklore to the public and the practitioners I work with, I tend to omit the concept of "tradition," as I've found it can be misleading if not fully explained, limiting the concept to only those forms commonly thought of as "traditional," rather than encompassing marginalized and emergent forms (Dan Ben-Amos is also critiqued for decentering the idea of "tradition" in his own terse definition of folklore as "artistic communication in small groups"). But *tradition* is a central, though contested, keyword in the field. In *The Dynamics of Folklore*, Barre Toelken writes that folklore is both conservative and dynamic. Traditions die, reconstitute, and are born anew constantly, but in order for them to sustain themselves, there must be both elements of the form that remain static and elements that evolve. Past and present arts and humanities organizations, funders, publications, and individual cultural brokers—those I've been a part of included—have played significant roles in shaping West Virginia's traditional arts and culture, influencing, for better or for worse, which genres and practitioners are written about, celebrated, marketed, and presented to the public for education, participation, and consumption. In surveying past and current literature, media, and archival collections, I encountered healthy documentation of the residual and conservative aspects of West Virginia folklife, particularly those pertaining to white Scots-Irish and German heritage, but the record was more lacking in evidence of the breadth of cultural diversity, emergent traditions, and dynamic elements of vernacular culture—how established traditions could evolve and be reinterpreted through a new lens, how cultural traditions blend and become amalgams, and how vernacular culture and mass culture intersect in hybridized forms.[22] In some written articles, media pieces, and exhibit text presenting the folklore of the state, I noticed a tendency to essentialize what it meant to be "Appalachian" or "West Virginian" to only the practices and experiences of a select few, generally white populations, engaged in residual or long-standing traditions.

With this newly institutionalized commitment to the state's cultural heritage, we had the opportunity to consider what a folklife program should look like today. We asked, What will we borrow from long-standing state folklife programs and what might we shed? How can we share an equitable, dynamic, and innovative vision of folklife through the type of communities we engage with, how we use media, and how we support practitioners in navigating the specific challenges they face as traditional artists today? How can we assist West Virginia communities so that they are able to continue to practice their expressive traditions, especially those that resist (actively or passively) commodification for local or tourist consumption? How can we center voices that have historically been marginalized or erased from the record altogether? While curatorial choices are an essential aspect of this work too, particularly in coverage of an entire state, I realized I also needed to be aware of how priorities and biases can inevitably impact fieldwork, knowing that idealistic and aspirational visions can be just as misleading—even as destructive—as those that are regressive and repressive. Above all, I made it a priority that the Folklife Program recognize emergent traditions alongside the long-established, and highlight the contributions of populations that have often been ignored in portrayals of the cultural makeup of West Virginia.

The veneration of white Anglo-Saxon traditions as the true culture of the Mountain State, whether directly or indirectly, can dangerously approach gross nationalism. As we witnessed in 2017 through the disturbing white nationalist rally in Pikeville, Kentucky, just across the state border from West Virginia, that problematic narrative, rooted in white supremacy, can be heinously appropriated by outside hate groups invested in homogenous white "purity."[23] Statistically, West Virginia is largely white; in the 2020 United States Census (which has, it is important to note, historically undercounted Black and other people of color) the state's racial makeup was reported as 89.8 percent white, 3.7 percent Black or African American (about 66,000 people), 1.9 percent Hispanic or Latino, 0.8 percent Asian, 0.2 percent American Indian, 0.3 percent some other race, and 4.1 percent two or more races.[24] These statistics also don't communicate the diverse cultural traditions that have existed in West Virginia for decades or that may no longer be substantial in terms of the number of practitioners but have left and continue to leave indelible marks on the culture of the place. Though there are currently no federal or state recognized Indigenous tribes in the state, Shawnee, Cherokee, Delaware and Saponi, and Mingo people were present in what is now West Virginia, through at least the eighteenth century.[25] In the early twentieth century, laborers from all over the world and African Americans from the Deep South moved to West Virginia to work in the coal mines, logging operations, and other industries. In her book *Gone Home: Race and Roots through Appalachia*, Karida Brown notes that from 1900 to 1940, the Black population in central Appalachia nearly tripled, going from about 40,000 residents to 115,000, the overwhelming majority of whom lived in West Virginia. Much of that population has since left the region, both physically and in representations of the place, resulting in what Brown calls a "double erasure," writing, "In response to this double erasure, this group of black people, who now live in diaspora throughout the United States, have adopted a set of practices, repertoires, and rituals to relocate and re-place themselves back in those mountains."[26] Those diasporic communities of Appalachian migrants of various races and ethnic groups often remain connected to their families and home communities in West Virginia and return regularly for family reunions and cultural events.

Further, folklife does not move along statistical lines, and percentage points are not expressions of cultural importance. Vernacular culture can be the most vibrant in small, marginalized communities invested in sustaining their cultural heritage, and migrant, immigrant, and refugee populations often hold onto their community traditions in resistance to assimilation and homogenization by the dominant culture. Today there are still actively practiced African American, Serbian, Lebanese, Italian, Spanish, Swiss, Greek, and Polish traditions, among others, celebrated now in both mixed multiethnic communities and those more homogenous. West Virginia is also home to newer Syrian, Haitian, and Burmese refugees and a quickly growing Latinx population. A new Hindu Temple opened in Dunbar in 2017, and the Islamic Center in Charleston, a multiracial and multiethnic faith community, has over 400 active members. It is important to note that while West Virginia is declining in population overall, notably among its white population, communities of color in the state are growing.[27]

The field of public folklore, which works in collaboration with cultural communities as they exist today, demands that folklore be approached as grassroots contemporary cultural practice, making outdated interpretations untenable.[28] West Virginia folklife has never been singular nor stuck in time, despite persistent stereotypes of the state and region of Appalachia as "yesterday's people," "our contemporary ancestors," or "a forgotten land" that tip the portrayal of folklore too far into the category of the romanticized, nostalgic glance backward to a time that never actually existed.[29] When were the "good old days" exactly? What historical period does that actually refer to and for whom were the days good? Cultural theorist Raymond Williams warns of this fallacy in *The Country and the*

City, his survey of the British cultural imaginary through its literature: "But there is still a crisis of perspective. When we moved back in time, consistently directed to an earlier and happier rural England, we could find no place, no period in which we could seriously rest."[30] This type of romanticism can serve to obscure the material reality of structural poverty, not to mention systemic racism and heteropatriarchy. There is a natural tendency in that nostalgic impulse, though—when the unrest of the present and uncertainty of the future looms ahead, the imaginary idyllic past of a region, state, or community can offer a fantasy of stability. As land and human life in West Virginia is perpetually threatened by overlapping and interlocking economic, social, and environmental crises, a sense of permanence through heritage and a generational rootedness in place can seem grounding.[31] These oppressive forces leave the people and communities they act upon with few good options.

But this romanticization of the past can be particularly dangerous in a place like West Virginia, not only because that narrative, simplified by outside media, and sometimes internalized from within, can lead to xenophobia and a resistance to productive change but also because the presentation of Appalachian culture as existing only in the past is a rhetoric that has been taken advantage of by coal companies and other extractive industry encroaching on the state to "develop" the land and "improve" its people in the name of progress. Mary Hufford describes the phenomenon:

> Mountaintop removal mining is rationalized through operations that belittle the culture of the mountains, stigmatizing "mountain ways" of speaking and relating to the land as a sign of economic backwardness and cultural deprivation. A culture that industry reduces partly by making itself materially huge is officially contained by the state, often romantically, in themed worlds of coal heritage and pre-industrial domesticity. Marketing craft, music, and storytelling as "tradition" and producing new landscapes as "viewsheds." Fixing Appalachian culture in the past, these sites contribute to perceptions of Appalachia as a site of "permanent outdatedness."[32]

The narrative of West Virginia and the greater Appalachian region as an isolated cultural anachronism has long provided justification for extractive industry that may offer jobs in the short term but leaves environmental, community, and human devastation in its wake. Privatization and enclosure have always perpetuated and benefited from depictions of West Virginia culture as antiquated, while disrupting the commons from which that culture generates.[33] In late nineteenth-century West Virginia, that manifested through the dispossession of agrarian farmers from the land they worked by capitalist absentee landowners who effectively pushed them off of their self-sustaining livelihood of subsistence home-steading and into timber and coal camps and other wage work for life-threatening extractive industry.

Hufford ties this disenfranchisement directly to the packaging of Appalachian folklore as commodity, citing folklorist Robert Cantwell, who points out that the very founding of the field of folklore in the eigh-teenth century coincided with the British Parliament's enclosure of the commons.[34] The creation of the discipline was prompted partially in anticipation of all the cultural aspects—the civic commons, intrinsic to the environmental commons of air, land, and water—that would be lost due to the breakup of communal land. But there was also a complicity with that destruction, in both England and Appalachia.[35] The develop-ment of a constructed narrative of cultural heritage facilitated the dis-placement of Appalachian people in the creation of Shenandoah National Park in the 1930s and beginning the decade prior, the commodification of their handmade goods for consumption by wealthy urbanites. In their desire for "the authentic," these cultural tourists from the East Coast sought out folk objects made by Appalachians. The irony was that many of these pieces were mass produced for tourist consumption, and not in regular use by their makers.[36] Historian Steven Stoll notes that the hand-made objects only "increased in cultural value as industrial capitalism undermined their environmental and social basis. . . . They gained allure from the destruction of the culture that created them."[37] The destruction of the commons in West Virginia, as in England, was both civic and envi-ronmental, and relied on a devaluation of local knowledge and a portrayal of its culture as backward, antimodern, and in opposition to progress, while pushing people into debilitating and all-consuming low-wage work, where they would not only not have control over their own means of pro-duction but also would be trapped in a cycle of servitude to the company. Meanwhile, the very agrarian lifestyle they left was being packaged and sold to wealthy tourists at national parks and artisan markets.

The devastation of land and community continued through coal's boom-and-bust cycle. Large energy corporations, many of whose oper-ations were headquartered outside of local counties or even the state, forced many families off their land through the Broad Form Deed, which severed mineral rights from surface rights, resulting in mass outmigration, uprooting families and communities.[38] Mountaintop-removal mining contaminated the water supply and permanently scarred the land. Forced depopulation by industry has always been in the best interest of the industry itself, clearing land for future "development" while eliminating inhabitants who might object.[39] Hufford writes, "Consequently, residents do not view the closing of the mountains in the 1990s as the simple closing off of private property; the closings are widely experienced as pressure to empty out the valleys."[40] Appalachian cultural heritage was then similarly detached from its function as a collective community resource and packaged and marketed as some old-timey relic. Historian Ron Eller says of the post–World War II era, "The modernization of the mountains required further integration of the region into the global marketplace and the subsequent weakening of local, producer-based economies. Although some aspects of local cultures were packaged and commodified for export, local community ties gave way to new, market-oriented identities, and in some places local residents themselves were displaced by newcomers tied to the land only by aesthetic and consumer values."[41] Continuing to present vernacular culture in West Virginia today as antiquated feels like a trap, set to perpetuate these cycles that sever common assets—both environmental and cultural—from local communities, and obscure the presence of new populations and dynamic cultural life.

The Book

Through the new work of the West Virginia Folklife Program, I aimed to counteract the persistent narratives of an anachronistic monoculture by approaching folklife in West Virginia as an evolving commons of local knowledge, resisting an essentializing and narrow view of Appalachian or West Virginia culture, and presenting West Virginia traditions as part of, rather than apart from, contemporary life. This did not mean that we would omit more visible and centuries-old traditions like old-time music, quilting, salt-rising bread, seed saving, or blacksmithing, but rather than situating them as static relics, reproductions, or reenactments, we would explore how these traditions have evolved within a modern context, reveal their complex multiracial roots when present, and consider how they have persisted, at times in opposition to trends and values of the mainstream. As the state folklorist, I wanted to be attuned and responsive to the sites and communities where folklife is actually being generated and shared in West Virginia today—the wrestling ring and the old-time festival, the Facebook group and the mosque, the English for speakers of other languages (ESOL) class and the dance hall.

That approach extends to this book. Where West Virginia culture has often been misrepresented as an anachronistic holdover in the popular imagination, so too has the scope of folklore. In fact, though, folklore theory and practice offer us a valuable framework through which we can understand contemporary culture, as it's being created and leveraged by communities in the current moment. In his 1995 essay "Tradition," folklorist Henry Glassie writes, "Tradition is the creation of the future out of the past."[42] Contemporary communities are the change agents of this creation, molding culture out of the past and pushing it into the future. *Making Our Future: Visionary Folklore and Everyday Culture in Appalachia* dwells in the space between—the space of today—taking into account the current cultural and economic factors that influence how individuals and communities transmit and reshape West Virginia's diverse and varied folklife out of yesterday and into tomorrow, and revealing the power and possibility within that remaking. Ultimately the unifying framework of this book is one of temporality, which warns of the dangers of fixing West Virginia vernacular culture in the past, attempts to meet and examine that culture as it exists today, and in doing so, models a folkloric approach for future storytelling and community-engaged cultural work. This modeling is not only in collaborative ethnographic methodology and the specific inquiries of the field of folklore related to transmission and evolution of folklife but also in the long-form narrative I employ, which contextualizes specific cultural forms within their community of practice, grounds them within their historical context, and examines how they are being leveraged and acted upon by individuals and communities. In doing so, I hope to demonstrate the public intellectual practice of folklore, which values, illuminates, and opens space for the forms of collective imagination that already exist among local communities.

Studying the way contemporary folklife functions in a specific place requires bringing together and drawing connections across some of the seemingly disparate topics that are included under folklore's umbrella. As folklorist Valdimar Hafstein said in a 2021 American Folklore Society panel on heritage, folklore, and the public sphere, "Cultural heritage is a novel category of things, lumped together, in innovative ways under its rubric. Buildings, monuments, swords, songs, jewelry, visual patterns, religious paraphernalia, literature, healing dances, wood carving traditions—things, in other words, that have nothing in common except for the fact that we see them through the same lens as cultural heritage, and act on them through the same means."[43] Folklore is a unifying concept that puts various cultural forms in conversation and asks us to identify the through lines across them, consider how each is part of the aesthetics of everyday life, and highlight how these forms are acted on and shaped by collectivities. *Making Our Future* operates within that conception, examining how communities in West Virginia engage with disparate forms of folklore—the collective counternarrative of a community museum, women's nonprofessional songwriting in country and gospel traditions, traditional Swiss foodways and material culture, the sense of place derived from the writings of Breece D'J Pancake, the expressive culture of the West Virginia teachers' strike portrayed in memes and protest signs, the amalgam of the popular and the vernacular embodied by the West Virginia hot dog, the dialogic storytelling of local independent pro wrestling, and the postapocalyptic West Virginia rendered and shaped by players in the video game *Fallout 76*—considers why those forms are meaningful, accounts for them, and identifies common threads across them, all as part of the makeup of modern folklife in West Virginia.

Recently, in discussing a proposal for a fieldwork project, a historian colleague asked me, "What are the questions and approaches your field brings to this?" It's a simple but very good question, one that folklorists have not answered sufficiently to audiences outside of our own field. Of course, the answer can—and has—filled many volumes, more thoroughly and eloquently than I will here. But these are the questions and specific approaches I'm bringing to the examination of culture, community, and public folklore that readers should look for across the following chapters: In each of these examples, how is expressive culture evolving through the actions of artists, practitioners, and cultural communities, as well as through the impact of outside forces—folklorists and cultural workers included? How is folklife being transmitted across time and space, between people and across generations? How are communities using those cultural forms to negotiate and affirm identity? What is the role of expressive culture within historical moments? Though public folklorists draw from the historical record to situate contemporary folk culture and engage conceptions of heritage, as I do in the following chapters, we are not historians; rather, we examine how folklife responds to history and its immediate surroundings in its contemporary manifestations (and we document that for the future). How is vernacular, grassroots culture engaging and augmenting more formal and institutionalized mass and popular culture and what function do those hybridized forms have within their cultural community? (This is particularly pertinent to the later chapters on hot dogs, wrestling, and *Fallout 76*.) What patterns can we identify across what may at first glance appear to be the work of a singular artist, and how can we contextualize that work within a specific tradition of a community and/or place? And what is the role of the public folklorist in these engagements with communities and culture? What do the position and cultural encounters of the state folklorist allow for? How do collaborative ethnography and folkloric inquiry facilitate a deeper understanding of contemporary cultural traditions? And though this book focuses on the engaged storytelling of these interactions to a broader audience, what is the next step? How do we work across positionalities and question borderlines to further advocate for the sustainability of cultural traditions and the self-determination of communities that practice them?

SCOPE

The chapters of *Making Our Future* draw from significant fieldwork I conducted from roughly 2015 to 2021. The book by no means attempts or claims to be a comprehensive or essentialized picture of contemporary folklife in West Virginia. Rather, each chapter serves as a case study of how a specific community engages with a different form of expressive culture, illustrating how a folkloric approach enables us to understand contemporary expressive culture as it's being shaped, while also offering a model for equitable engagement with cultural communities, across multiple positionalities. To do so, I present these case studies through a long-form narrative, which I believe is necessary to fully contextualize, situate, and engage with each specific cultural form and respective community. The stories I chose to bring together in this book, and the way I chose to tell them, highlight the collective aspect of folklife. Though on a day-to-day level I'm often documenting the work of a singular vernacular artist, practitioner, or community elder whose work is situated within a specific tradition, here I focus on the communities and collectivities of which those individuals are a part, in order to emphasize that even when expressed by an individual artist, folklore stems from community practice and local knowledge passed on between people in place. It is my intention that this brings to the fore the community practices, hybrid forms, and cultural "surround" that can often be ignored because they are not readily commodifiable for local or tourist consumption as marketable products or do not fit within the narrow anachronistic and whitewashed ideal of "mountain" craft or culture.[44] I hope that this specific outlook, rooted in public folklore practice, contributes to ongoing and new efforts to reframe, restore, and leverage culture in West Virginia as a collective community resource—part of the commons that have been so threatened by hegemonic forces.

My fieldwork has occurred during a distinct cultural moment in West Virginia. Population decline due to outmigration and an aging demographic, resource extraction and subsequent environmental degradation, loss of jobs, a shrinking tax base, and an opioid crisis have disrupted the communities from which vernacular culture emerges and is transmitted. In a 1993 piece on her work in southern West Virginia, Hufford writes, "The depopulation of industrial communities and the generalized dispersal of family networks creates a rupture between past and present that current residents and former residents and their descendants are already trying to mend in various ways."[45] This "rupture between past and present" inevitably impacts the viability of expressive culture, as it is being made out of the past and into the future. And yet vibrant cultural traditions persist, adapting, responding, evolving, and resulting in new emergent forms. These vernacular expressions can be a grounding force, linking local communities across time and place.

From its very outset, the discipline of folklore was a historically specific response to widespread societal change, a lens through which people could understand the culture and tradition of everyday life as it was shifting before them. As Hafstein notes, "The field of folklore at its inception was about documenting and annotating through the rear view mirror, the social, economic, and environmental transformations that came to be described as industrialization, urbanization, and modernity."[46] As we enter a new era of rapid change through automation, deindustrialization, privatization, climate change, and other prevailing forces of contemporary life under capitalism, the framework and methodology of folklore—as they have developed since the field's founding—can be valuable tools to help cultural workers and communities alike contextualize, understand, and record how these changes manifest in the cultural sphere, within local communities. This process can be powerful. As Richard Kurin writes, "Conserving culture is a matter of community being empowered to bring forth aesthetic, cognitive, normative, manual understandings in contemporary life—to gain some measure of control over technological, economic, social, and cultural change."[47]

THE CHAPTERS

As West Virginia goes through this economic and cultural transition, disenfranchised communities are leveraging expressive culture and local knowledge as a source of power. Chapter 1 takes us to Scotts Run, West Virginia, the multiethnic, multiracial former coal camp community that was documented by Farm Security Administration (FSA) photographers and which inspired Eleanor Roosevelt's first New Deal homestead. There every Saturday, former residents meet at the museum they founded to recount old stories, shape a counternarrative, and reconstruct a place through collective memory. As a collective working in collaboration with graphic designer and retired West Virginia University professor Eve Faulkes, they demonstrate the power of collaborative community-engaged cultural work and offer an example of "creative placemaking" that is effective because it is both community-generated and prioritizes the quality of life of the local community itself, rather than being aspirationally tourism-driven. In this chapter, I introduce folklorist Dorothy Noyes's concept of a "network," which helps us understand the complex and overlapping relationships of communities. Because the network of the Scotts Run Museum members engages with historical representation in the construction of a counternarrative, it was important to do historical research so I could understand the predominant narrative they are responding to. Through this research, I uncovered a historical example of how conceptions of Appalachian regionalism have reinforced racial stereotypes and white supremacy.

Chapter 2 illuminates how four nonprofessional musicians, through the generic conventions of country and gospel and a long-standing tradition of women's writing, maintain their respective songwriting practices in service of their community, faith, the union, and as a form of personal catharsis and self-documentation. The role expressive culture can play in self-realization is evident across the work of these women. This chapter also demonstrates the importance of public folklore and collaborative ethnographic methodology, in particular for engaging with, contextualizing, and presenting creative practices that are not public-facing, or in this case, can be considered a "public private" practice.

In chapter 3, I examine how ethnographic fieldwork mirrors the evolution of folklife, specifically in that they are both dialogic processes, negotiated at every step through informal conversation. I first went to Helvetia in 2011 and began fieldwork there in 2014, making it the West Virginia community with which I've had the longest relationship. That experience paired with historical research has allowed me to witness how culture—particularly foodways—in Helvetia unfolds. Through the lens of rosettes, fried cookies made for Helvetia's pre-Lenten celebration, Fasnacht, I investigate how a specific localized tradition can be a point of inter- and cross-cultural connection—a good example of how culture in Appalachia can be viewed as connective, rather than singular and insular.

In chapter 4, through a tour of many of the sites and the atmospheric setting that inspired writer Breece D'J Pancake's stories in his hometown of Milton, I consider the notion of sense of place as a form of folklore that entwines narrative, experience, and landscape. Scholar Kent Ryden refers to this particular iteration of folklore as "the invisible landscape," writing, "Folk narrative is a vital and powerful means by which knowledge of the invisible landscape is communicated, expressed, and maintained. In fact, the sense of place—the sense of dwelling in the invisible landscape—is in large part a creation of folklore and is expressed most eloquently as folklore."[48] Experiencing Milton through an embodied experience of Pancake's writing—which itself documents a fading culture—also reveals the cultural, social, and environmental shifts of small-town West Virginia in the forty years since his stories were written. As an experiment to add another layer of narrative to this already storied invisible landscape, I wrote this chapter as a "place essay," which Ryden asserts is a "blood relative of place-based folklore," relayed by a folk narrator—both communicated through the poetics of personal expression, while grounded in place and linked to a collective narrative.[49] I wanted to model how folkloric concepts can undergird creative nonfiction, while not necessarily being framed explicitly as theory or written in an academic style, and thus opening possibilities for new audiences and contexts.

In chapter 5, I examine the 2018–19 West Virginia teachers' strike from a folkloric perspective, revealing how the application of expressive culture as a form of resistance was employed by public school teachers as they organized online and in physical spaces, communicating through clothing, signs, food, chants, songs, and digital memes the importance of their care work in sustaining the everyday life of their communities. The way the expressive and largely ephemeral culture of the strike was evolving and being performed in real time demonstrates the importance of public folklore institutions as entities well-positioned to document these types of actions—which disrupt everyday life in order to sustain it—as they unfold. To witness the teachers' strike as it evolved was to experience the visionary possibilities of expressive culture and its ability to bolster group identity and forge a new reality in resistance to dominant power structures. Through their creative expressions, West Virginia teachers opened the walls of their classrooms to a broad public audience, both in the state and across the country, as they became the model for other public school teachers in other states who warned their legislators, "Don't make us go West Virginia on you." Through the teachers' examples, I am reminded of Marxist scholar Silvia Federici, who writes of how the defense of the communal births a new form of existence, inhabited through new tools and new social bonds, or as folklorist Dorothy Noyes pithily puts it, "Acting in common makes community."[50]

In chapter 6, I explore the immigration, class, gender, and labor history of the beloved West Virginia hot dog (generally identifiable as containing chili or sauce, slaw—depending on geographic location—mustard, and onions). Though hot dogs are a pervasive aspect of West Virginia's cultural heritage, the tradition relies on the precarious economy of non-union low-wage labor in the service industry, generally undertaken by women. With this history and precarity in mind, I examine the particular role that hybridized, commodified forms that combine the popular and the vernacular can play in the cultural surround and built environment of a place. Working as a public folklorist and resident embedded in the cultural life of the state allowed me to witness this phenomenon of the cultural surround; much of my fieldwork regarding the hot dog's role in West Virginia was observational, a result of living in the state and being a part of physical and digital social spaces where hot dogs, hot dog joints, and hot dog opinions are prevalent. From this, I encourage communities and cultural workers to pay greater attention to common, pervasive culture forms that may be susceptible to invisibility because they are deemed too trivial, ubiquitous, or inconsequential.

Independent professional wrestling is another expressive tradition that can be trivialized because of its demarcation as a contrived and working-class entertainment, but wrestling has a long history in West Virginia, predating the state's founding. In chapter 7, I review the roots of the sport in West Virginia, which emerged out of nineteenth-century carnival and vaudeville performance and constituted an important part of the first live television programming in the state. Through fieldwork with the All Star Wrestling (ASW) promotion in Madison, West Virginia, I argue that independent pro wrestling's current iteration in the Mountain State is a vernacular form where wrestlers, who assume the role of storytellers and modern day folk heroes, perform in direct and instantaneous dialogue with their live local audiences. The content and themes of these carnivalesque shows enact popular tropes and engage with current events in a mishmash of contradicting social and political opinions on race, class, and gender.

In the final chapter, in which I discuss *Fallout 76*, the multiplayer video game set in a postapocalyptic West Virginia in the year 2102, I consider how the game and a network of its players engage with folklife to various ends. I argue that the game developers' retrofuture virtual rendering of West Virginia serves as a canvas on which they project overarching anxieties of late capitalism, and I examine similarities of that rendering with other historical examples of the narrativization of Appalachia, as well as the potential implications of that vision. On a user level, *Fallout 76* players inhabit the imaginary of a virtual postapocalyptic West Virginia to create their own vernacular culture in a digital space, which maps onto physical locations in West Virginia and codifies a narrative about the state's culture, folklore, history, landscape, and aesthetic. In turn, gamers are enacting their virtual experiences in *Fallout 76*'s West Virginia, in their real-world counterparts, foregrounding questions of the potential benefits and negative impacts cultural heritage tourism brings to West Virginia communities.

In the face of enclosure and privatization, which destabilize communities and force them to market and commodify their cultural heritage, as well as deindustrialization and environmental disaster, which can break up place-based communities from which folklore is created, resistance and self-determination can be found by reaffirming the common and collective, and redeploying that back on the destructive and deracinating forces. As folklorist and activist Kay Turner asserted in her 2017 presidential address to the American Folklore Society, collectively owned narratives offer a counterpoint to the singular and reductive "me" story that capitalism favors. These shared narratives "allow the willing suspension of disbelief to stimulate imaginative identifications and attachments."[51] In a place where depopulation and disenfranchisement are not just byproducts but also strategic objectives of industrial extractive capitalism, expressive culture that is rooted in community and place is subversive.

As Frank Proschan writes, "Social functions and deepest meanings of folk traditions are often displayed most clearly and compellingly at times of social stress."[52] There's not a better place to examine how that works than West Virginia. Long approached effectively as a "sacrifice zone" by governmental and corporate entities, West Virginia communities have experienced the violence of industrial corporate greed, bearing the brunt of the environmental and social disintegration it brings. The localities, groups, and social networks that live here have adapted and re-formed in response, through outright rejections of austerity, perpetual performances of counternarratives, and gatherings around expressive culture. Those expressions, which bolster community identity and affirm shared values, can be a powerful tool in collective struggle.

The challenges West Virginia faces are not unique to the state. Environmental hazards and climate change, postindustrial fallout, a disintegrating social safety net, loss of land and community, corporate malfeasance, structural racism, and a widening gap between the rich and poor are structural problems faced by the entire country; their impact can just be more glaringly obvious in Appalachia.[53] What I hope this book reveals is not only the power but also the possibility of folklife, as well as communities' and cultural workers' engagement with it—not merely as a source of counteractive resistance but also as a productive, creative, and visionary force. As communication studies scholars Kent Ono and John Sloop state, "Vernacular discourse does not exist only as counter hegemonic, but also as affirmative, articulating a sense of community that does not function solely as oppositional to dominant ideologies."[54] Perhaps the struggles, responses, and creative possibilities of West Virginia communities, developed in some cases in the direst of conditions, can offer a model for other places and futures.

In my conclusion, I turn from a focus on the present formation of cultural traditions to the future, considering how communities and cultural workers can adopt a visionary outlook. I ask: What can we do today that will enable communities in the future to share local collective knowledge and be self-determining in their approach to their folklife traditions? And reflexively, how can cultural expression bolster collective identity and self-determination? I hope that as cultural workers and community members, we not only question but also act on those visions in our work.

In presenting this critical picture of West Virginia folklife as I've encountered it, I also aim to convey to the reader a sense of the work of a public folklorist, particularly the dialogic nature of the collaborative ethnographic fieldwork process, from interview to relationship-building, to the meaningful presentation of that shared story in the world. The conversation among people and communities I write about was already in progress; through fieldwork, I asked to enter the conversation, to be oriented to it, and become part of it, sometimes minimally, other times centrally. The people I worked with generously invited me in. Though the focus of this book is on the communities themselves, I hope the following chapters also communicate what it means to be entrusted with these stories, to bear that responsibility, and to develop powerful relationships across positionalities. Through writing this book, I've come to understand that the nature of my work as a public folklorist is to offer my assistance to local communities in recognizing themselves as collectivities with some shared identity and history (even if contested), communities that, through shared creative expression, can together realize the power of self-determination in making their future.

CHAPTER 1

We All Own It

The Interracial, Intergenerational
Community Counternarrative of
the Scotts Run Museum

IT'S SATURDAY MORNING in Scotts Run, a five-mile holler in Monongalia County's Cass District.[1] Hills circle the low valley like a wall. It's a stone's throw across the river from Morgantown, home of the state's largest university, but the distance can feel much further. Today half a dozen cars are parked around a small cement block building in the otherwise quiet, now unincorporated community of Osage. That former mechanic's garage is now the Scotts Run Museum and History Trail, marked by a blue and orange sign with simple illustrations of a banjo, a pick and shovel, and a nugget of coal (see fig. 1.1). The names of the thirteen communities that compose Scotts Run circle the design: Tropf Hill, Bertha Hill, Miller Hill, Pursglove, Chaplin, New Hill, Osage, Liberty, Davis, Shriver, Cassville, Bunker, and Jere. Underneath is a smaller sign with the same colors and degree of permanence. It reads,

and the Coffee Shop
Where History Lives
Saturdays 10–2

Inside the museum, shelves are lined with artifacts typical of a small-town history museum in the coalfields. There are aprons and old country LPs, miners' buckets and helmets, an old coal-fired range and stacks and stacks of books. But the Scotts Run Museum is also unusual: the design used on all the exhibit walls, art books, maps, brochures, posters, even a CD, is strikingly cohesive and freshly modern. Portraits of Franklin Delano and Eleanor Roosevelt hang prominently on the wall. Four tables in the center of the museum, covered with tablecloths, placemats, and cloth napkins, are set as if for a fine luncheon. And, perhaps most unusual, the museum is full of people sitting and talking at these tables, as museum Executive Director Mary Jane Coulter stands at a kitchen counter, making coffee and preparing plates of crackers and cheese, fruit, and pastries for each guest. The people sitting at the tables are not tourists on a weekend drive come to learn about the history of this community but rather friends who grew up here, gathering to see each other, recount memories, and plan for Scotts Run's future. They are the embodiment of the living history advertised on the Coffee Shop sign (see plate 1.1).

Among the Coffee Shop regulars are Lou Birurakis, a ninety-four-year-old amateur historian, writer, and former West Virginia University (WVU) football player of Cretan heritage who has devoted a room in his house to the extensive archival research he's done on Scotts Run; Sarah Boyd Little, ninety-seven, the museum president and a lifelong gospel singer from Osage whose choir from the all-Black Monongalia High School sang for President Roosevelt at the White House in 1942; Al Anderson, eighty-four, a Black soul singer, bandleader, shoe repair man, business owner, and the sentinel of Osage (see plate 1.2); George Sarris, eighty, a Liberty native whose Cretan father ran an Osage restaurant that catered to the Black community; Charlene Marshall, eighty-seven, an Osage native who was the first African American woman mayor of Morgantown and in the state of West Virginia; Mary Jane Coulter, seventy-one, white, who has lived in Osage her entire life and is the executive director of the museum and the Coffee Shop host; and Eve Faulkes, sixty-six, white, a retired WVU art and design professor originally from South Charleston who helped revive the museum in 2011 and is responsible for its cohesive design aesthetic. There are always other Scotts Run natives, family and friends, as well as occasional tourists, students, or documentarians like me stopping by from out of town.

I first learned of Sarah Boyd Little through West Virginia photographers Betty Rivard and Mark Crabtree. Mark put me in touch with Eve

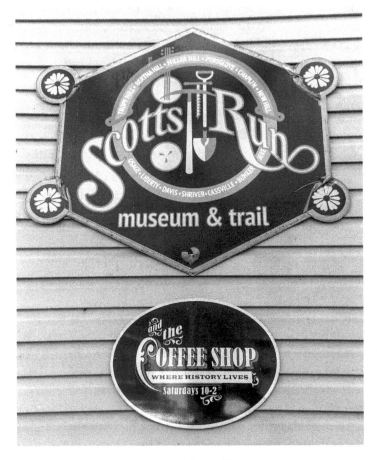

FIGURE 1.1. Scotts Run Museum and Coffee Shop signs, Scotts Run,
West Virginia, February 18, 2019. Photo by the author.

Faulkes, who works closely with Sarah and often drives her to events, and
we scheduled an interview with her and Sarah at Eve's Morgantown home
in March 2018 (see plate 1.3). In our interview, Sarah described the museum
as a gathering place, where the men sit at the "boy's table," recounting
their more salacious memories of Osage, as kids peeking into the speak-
easies and catching wind of the rumors that circulated in the community.
With so many of the social spaces—homes, churches, stores, and speak-
easies—now gone in Scotts Run, the museum has become the communal
hub, where she suggested I meet other community members. Almost a
year later in February 2019, I started attending the Saturday Coffee Shop
gatherings at the museum, making the drive up from Charleston nearly

every Saturday for four months to talk with regulars and newcomers over coffee and plates of snacks—always lovingly prepared by Mary Jane. I interviewed some regulars—Lou Birurakis and Charli Shea Fortney-Heiskell, the twelve-year-old granddaughter of Mary Jane Coulter—at the museum during those events, and made other trips to interview Charlene Marshall, Al Anderson, George Sarris, Eve Faulkes, and Mary Jane Coulter in their homes or places of work. This chapter draws on those experiences at the museum, interviews with Coffee Shop regulars, and historical research to understand the past that the regulars are drawing from in their creative remaking of their Scotts Run community.

In folklorist Dorothy Noyes's classic essay, "Group," and the follow-up, "The Social Base of Folklore," she explains the concept of a "network"—an alternative to the notion of the more formalized and cohesive "group" or "imagined collectivity" of a community—as the connective collective that forms "the social base of cultural practices."[2] It is useful to apply here to understand the social structure of the Scotts Run Museum's Coffee Shop regulars (as I'll refer to them). They constitute a dense, multiplex, stable social network, in that the members have known each other all of their lives, have multiple relational ties to each other (some are also siblings, neighbors, bandmates, landlord and tenant, or customer and proprietor, for instance), live in proximity (though most no longer live in Scotts Run), and gather regularly. They are bound by place and memory, motivated by a common need to transmit a counternarrative about the place they are from. They have "performed," in the folkloric sense of the word, this counternarrative through multiple forms of expression: in song, art books, a CD, a community garden, and by merely gathering each week—an insistence on their own existence. The inscription "Where History Lives" on the Coffee Shop sign can be read as a challenge to the version of Scotts Run interpreted from the FSA photographs, mentioned briefly in history books of more notable places or people, written as if this place is dead and gone, or absent from the narrative altogether. But the community centered around the Scotts Run Museum is alive and well, with a lot of history still to reckon with.

Mother Eleanor, Father Scotts Run, Child Arthurdale

Though coal companies had already begun to acquire mineral rights in Scotts Run by the late nineteenth century, the holler at that time was largely inhabited by white, American-born subsistence farm families. In 1880, farmers and farmworkers accounted for 66 percent of the heads of household in the Cass District; by 1920, after World War I precipitated the coal boom, the numbers had essentially flipped, with coal mining accounting for 63 percent of labor and farming reduced to 21 percent. As coal companies developed their extractive operations, they quickly realized there was not enough of a resident labor pool in Scotts Run, so they imported laborers—immigrants from Europe and Black migrants from the Deep South, shifting the racial and ethnic makeup of the area dramatically. The 1920 census identified nineteen different ethnic nationalities among Scotts Run residents: Austrian, Bohemian, Canadian, Croatian, English, Finnish, Greek, Hungarian, Italian, Irish, Lithuanian, Polish, Romanian, Russian, Scottish, Serbian, Slovenian, Ukrainian, and Welsh. The population was 60 percent foreign-born, 93 percent of them southern or eastern European, with American-born whites and Blacks each composing about 20 percent of the population.[3] As local whites had been pushed off their land through enclosure by the coal companies, and immigrants and migrants were imported—not just for labor but as part of the coal companies' imposition of a strategy they called a "judicious mixture," thinking that the uprootedness of the immigrants and migrants, paired with cultural and linguistic barriers, would make organizing among workers difficult—Scotts Run residents became subject ever after to the boom-and-bust economy of the coal industry.[4] By the mid-1920s, multiple companies were operating a total of thirty-six mines and owned 75 percent of taxable land in the five-mile holler.[5] In 1931, at the tail end of the seven-year Northern Mine War (1924–31), which included a series of strikes in the northern West Virginia coal fields, Scotts Run miners went on strike against further wage cuts. After a month, coal companies in Scotts Run recognized the United Mine Workers of America (UMWA), largely out of fear of the more communistic National Miners Union, which organized the strike. The Great Depression and years of precarious work had left the Scotts Run community impoverished, many families deprived of their means of subsistence.

Lou Birurakis was seven years old in 1933 when Eleanor Roosevelt visited his hometown of Liberty. What he doesn't remember, though, is the First Lady stopping by his family's home.

> My neighbor who lived across the street . . . said he and his mother
> were sitting on the porch on a swing . . . and they saw Mrs. Roosevelt
> drive up to the house. Apparently somebody had told her that my
> mother was baking bread in an outside oven. So he said they saw

Mrs. Roosevelt go up our steps, stay a few minutes, and then come back down and then go on up through Scotts Run. And like I said, I didn't hear about this. I didn't hear it from my mother because when I wrote the story, I put in my story that my mother gave her a loaf of bread and Mrs. Roosevelt left and went on up. But I doubt it because I don't think they could correspond because Mrs. Roosevelt couldn't speak Greek and my mother couldn't speak English, so I think they just shook hands and parted.[6]

Sarah Boyd Little also remembers Roosevelt from the 1936 dedication of Monongalia High, the Black high school that Little attended outside of Scotts Run. "She was a stately woman," Little said. "She wasn't pretty, but she was very elegant in her speech."[7] When I asked Mary Jane's twelve-year-old granddaughter, Charli Shea, to tell me about Osage, the former First Lady was among the first things she mentioned. "A long time ago there were a bunch of trains that would just run through Osage, and Eleanor Roosevelt came here a long time ago and there were not many buildings and most of the buildings got torn down in Osage and got rebuilt."[8] Mrs. Roosevelt's presence in Scotts Run is elementary knowledge among this local network.

Eleanor Roosevelt's legacy is deeply entwined with the history of Scotts Run, but her impact on the place is complicated, and it's simultaneously celebrated and criticized by Coffee Shop regulars. Roosevelt first toured Scotts Run in August 1933 after her companion, Associated Press journalist Lorena Hickok, wrote to her of the conditions in the district: "Scott's Run, a coal-mining community, not far from Morgantown, was the worst place I'd ever seen. In a gutter, along the main street through the town, there was stagnant, filthy water, which the inhabitants used for drinking, cooking, washing, and everything else imaginable. On either side of the street were ramshackle houses, black with coal dust, which most Americans would not have considered fit for pigs. And in those houses every night children went to sleep hungry, on piles of bug-infested rags, spread out on the floor. There were rats in those houses."[9]

Intent on seeing the place with her own eyes, Eleanor Roosevelt made a trip accompanied by Hickok and hosted by the American Friends Service Committee, which had already been engaged in relief work in the area. As she writes in her autobiography, "I came to know very well a stream near Morgantown called Scott's Run, or Bloody Run, because of the violent strikes that once occurred in the mines there. . . . I took many people to see this village of Jere, West Virginia, along Scott's Run, for it was a good example of what absentee ownership could do as far as human beings were concerned."[10] Her visit eventually inspired the attention of photographers from the Resettlement Administration (later renamed the Farm Security Administration), including Walker Evans, Lewis Hine, Marion Post Wolcott, and Ben Shahn, in 1935 and 1938.[11] Historian Ronald L. Lewis writes, "They [their photographs] heightened the nation's consciousness about Scotts Run, and while it became easier for social agencies to justify their work and to raise scarce resources for the relief effort, the symbol also became a fixture in the iconography of the popular imagination."[12] While you may have never been to Scotts Run or known its people, you have likely seen its faces from these iconic images—Black and white miners standing in line together for their payday checks; men smiling at the camera in their Saturday best at Osage's bar, the Spot; and children sitting barefoot in the newsprint-wallpapered kitchen of a company house. The people of Scotts Run effectively became national poster children for poverty spurred by the Great Depression. While Scotts Run did have poor living conditions, Lewis points out that its proximity to Morgantown and relative accessibility by bus, car, trolley, train, or public ferry made it a prime target for media attention and relief work, compared to other areas of the state impoverished by the coal industry. Due to cost, language barriers, and racism, transportation amenities were largely prohibitive for Scotts Run residents, however, contributing to a condition that Lewis describes as more "stranded" than "isolated."

After her visit to Scotts Run, Mrs. Roosevelt grew concerned that the economic and social conditions in the holler would lead to a communist revolution. In a September 1933 column for *Women's Democratic News*, she writes, "It is misery that drives people to the point where they are willing to overthrow anything simply because life as it is is not worth living any longer."[13] She became interested in a nearby subsistence community planned to relieve mining families from the Scotts Run area. Her husband, FDR, shared this interest and attached the Division of Subsistence Homesteads to the National Industrial Recovery Act; the Reedsville Experimental Community, known as Arthurdale, would be its first project. While Arthurdale was, in the Roosevelts' minds, a solution to avoid communistic unrest, the project was critiqued by conservatives and other Democrats as itself a communist enterprise. In truth, the community still operated within a capitalist economy, bound to both wages from private industry and subsistence from gardens that individual families were required to tend, while also relying heavily on government assistance. Arthurdale offered residents a loan for their home, land, farming equipment, and livestock—and thirty years to pay it back.[14] A total of 165 families, 110 of them from Scotts Run, were relocated to the new planned community, fifteen miles away over the Preston County line. But more than 70 percent of the 3,000 families in Scotts Run were not eligible for acceptance into Arthurdale. Though 200 African Americans applied upon encouragement from Mrs. Roosevelt, Black and foreign-born people were excluded following complaints by locals in nearby Reedsville.[15] Even among the American-born white families in Scotts Run, only the more affluent families were relocated. Rev. Franklin Trubee, a Presbyterian minister and missionary to Scotts Run during the Great Depression, says, "What they did was take the most ambitious, those you could tell had ambition. The last fifty families had only been gone a short time so I took a good look at the houses they moved out of and it was pretty obvious that they took those people who were best-off."[16] They also excluded applicants based on perceived political affiliations, namely those considered "radical agitators."[17] Families were required to complete an eight-page application and were chosen by social workers who "checked applicants' neatness, posture, church affiliation, debts, and attitudes."[18] By handpicking their ideal residents, the relief workers of Arthurdale thought they would ensure the success of the community, but the exclusions throw into question how much relief they were actually providing.

As Arthurdale began to develop its educational and cultural programs, the white Scots-Irish and Germanic population that had been chosen to inhabit the homestead presented an opportunity in the eyes of Fletcher Collins, a folk song collector and Yale University instructor who worked under Elsie Ripley Clapp, the school and community affairs director of Arthurdale. Influenced by a growing emphasis among scholars on regionalism and its quest for the true essence of American culture, Clapp tasked Collins to determine what constituted the "rural culture" she and her faculty promised to develop at the homestead, and how best to implement it programmatically. Collins identifies the Scots-Irish rural culture as "Balladry . . . Lyric folk song, Square-dances, Fiddle-music, The craft of making musical instruments, particularly fiddles, Folklore, much of it widespread in the cultural history of the race."[19] He reported that Arthurdale residents' cultural traditions "were in need of assistance," remarking that they sang both "artistic ballad and modern fake" with "equal ardor" and that "the homesteaders' knowledge of ballads was decidedly

rusty, smeared with coal dust."[20] Collins dangerously felt that the success his team had in cultivating these traditions could provide a model
for the promotion of a national Scots-Irish cultural revival, if "homo-
geneity on a regional or national scale can follow."[21] But it wasn't just
coal dust he wanted to wash from the homesteaders' culture. His vision
hinged entirely on a spurious cultural purity—both in the regulation of
the homesteaders' traditions to foster only what they could trace back
to England and shed what they may have learned from "the radio, the
movies, and bourgeois cultural standards," "urban deracinations," and
any other opportunities for cultural hybridization—and in the construction of Arthurdale itself as a homogenous white ethnic community.[22]
Though balladry, fiddling, and square dancing may have been part of the
homesteaders' cultural heritage, the imposition by Collins from above to
curate, purify, and leverage these traditions to promote a nationalistic
white culture is troublesome. The supposition that these traditions were
of pure Scots-Irish origin also ignores the other cultural influences, particularly African American and Native American, that shaped how these
forms evolved in the early United States.

This model of cultural revival by elite, often (but not always) outside forces was not new in the mountains. As scholar David Whisnant
chronicles in *All That Is Native and Fine*, the culture industry in Appalachia boomed well before the coal industry, as seen in the circa 1895 estab-
lishment of Sarah Chestus's Log Cabin Settlement in Asheville, North
Carolina, and Fireside Industries in Berea, Kentucky, and in the founding
of Hindman and Pine Mountain Settlement Schools in eastern Kentucky
in 1902 and 1913, respectively. But the motives of those working in cultural programming at Arthurdale are worth mentioning here because it
is part of the history of, as Whisnant says, "manipulative cultural intervention" in the region and offers a point of comparison to how culture
developed in Scotts Run, evident in its current iteration in the Scotts
Run Museum community.[23] Though Scotts Run was also subject to such
interventions through the Friends Service, Settlement School, and Mountaineer Craftsmen Cooperative, what evolved and is now displayed at the
museum shows evidence of a diverse, communal expressive culture that
occurred in addition to, outside, or in spite of efforts from those intent
on reviving and manipulating what they saw as "correct" traditions for
their own agendas.

Eleanor Roosevelt's visage and name are peppered throughout the
Scotts Run Museum materials: her portrait hangs on the exhibit wall,

her photograph is one of nine images on the *Songs of Scotts Run Museum and Trail* CD, and no history of the district goes without mention of her visits. Having a Roosevelt story is indeed one marker of identity in the network of Coffee Shop regulars. The character of Mrs. Roosevelt, who visited Scotts Run at least a dozen times from 1933 to 1943 and supported some social service programs there, links the story of the holler to a more widely known history. In the stories of Scotts Run natives, however, her function is generally to validate their own narratives, rather than necessarily to celebrate hers.[24] George Sarris, eighty, who was too young to remember Mrs. Roosevelt's visits, says he gives the First Lady credit for her concern for the area, but he is critical of the selection process for Arthurdale. "I heard those stories and at first I was really a Roosevelt fan because of what they did, but then when I got to thinking about the way they selected the people, and I read some place that the foreigners were thought of less than the Blacks, and the poor Blacks—you know how they were discriminated. So when I put all of that together, then I get upset with the Roosevelts."[25] Other Coffee Shop regulars mention Eleanor Roosevelt to highlight the role their community played in the founding of Arthurdale. Lou Birurakis credits Scotts Run as the father of the subsistence community. "After she came up through Scotts Run, that was her new husband. . . . So I think she eventually married Scotts Run and then the offspring was Arthurdale, which is still working as a historical site, very well."[26] Al Anderson, ever the ardent Scotts Run defender, argued, "People should remember that we made Arthurdale possible for those fortunate ones."[27] Scotts Run's relative absence from the dominant narrative regarding Eleanor Roosevelt and Arthurdale is still a point of contention in the community, an important aspect of, even an inspirational force for, their vernacular counternarrative.

Though the visits from Mrs. Roosevelt and the FSA photographers happened over eighty years ago, when most of the regulars were babies or not yet born, that time period is still present and vivid in their lives. While in the Library of Congress online digital archive no names of subjects are listed in the Scotts Run photographs by Evans, Hine, Post Wolcott, and Shahn, many of the regulars can identify relatives and neighbors among them. One of the scrapbooks at the museum has a few dozen of the photos printed, with individuals labeled "Wink Riggleman or Pete Lungader," "Bradley Johnson Family," or "Ms. Mary Shelton." Sarah Boyd Little's sister Willa Boyd Gibson is pictured in the Walker Evans photo, *Women Selling Ice Cream and Cake, Scotts Run, West Virginia* (see fig. 1.2).[28]

FIGURE 1.2. Sarah Boyd Little's sister Willa "Bill" Boyd Gibson (center) and Gibson's mother-in-law, as photographed by Walker Evans, 1935. *Women Selling Ice Cream and Cake, Scotts Run, West Virginia.* Library of Congress, Prints & Photographs Division, Farm Security Administration / Office of War Information Black-and-White Negatives.

"Oh yeah, that's my sister . . . Willa, that we called Bill," she says, reflecting. "And that's her mother-in-law there. They had been at Osage selling cake or whatever, for the church." Sarah told us that Willa had "died of a broken heart" not long after her husband died in a mine accident. The perceptions of Scotts Run that were the result, in part, of Roosevelt's work and these photographs feel personal, because they are. On one Saturday, I was sitting at a table with George Sarris and John Propst, a retired schoolteacher and Scotts Run native, who passed away at age ninety-two in November 2019. John was reading from *A Taste of History—with Ethnic Flavor,* a spiral-bound community cookbook with recipes collected from Scotts Run families, published in 1982. In the book, a section of Eleanor Roosevelt's autobiography is reprinted. He read out loud, "Most of the people living along the Run, which flows in to a broader stream below, worked no more than two or three days a week. Some of the children were subnormal, and I often wondered how any of them grew up."[29] He laughed and rolled his eyes but was clearly perturbed, slapping the book down on the table, "We're right here, if you're wondering!" George replied, "I never did like the Roosevelts," and pointed to the portrait of her behind me. "But I have to look at them all the time!" Though others defend Mrs. Roosevelt, seeing her intentions as honorable, and some may view the FSA photographs as a source of pride, regulars cannot escape these widely disseminated, now historical and often pejorative depictions of their home.

Those children Roosevelt describes grew up and became teachers, musicians, construction workers, museum directors, mayors, and state delegates. They had children of their own. But in the popular imagination, Scotts Run is still the subnormal child, a sacrificial symbol of the greed of the coal industry, arrested in time as if after the FSA photographers left, Arthurdale was born, and the First Lady stopped visiting, Scotts Run ceased to be a place. Those children, the Coffee Shop regulars, are evidence of something else that happened—and is still happening—in Scotts Run. It may not be normal, but it's far from subnormal. Though for the most part Scotts Run lacked the comfortable housing with indoor plumbing, modern amenities, cooperative programs, and social safety net that Arthurdale provided, the communal aspect that Mrs. Roosevelt hoped to implement through government backing already existed in Scotts Run. It was grassroots rather than government-sanctioned, and multiracial, multiethnic, and multilingual, rather than restricted to white English speakers, deemed "best-off."

"If It Wasn't for Osage and Scotts Run": Performing a Collective Counternarrative

Through collective (and sometimes collectively contested) memory, Coffee Shop regulars have developed a counternarrative that they regularly perform for each other and whoever else is there. The intention to offer a different, insiders' perspective of Scotts Run infuses all work of the museum. The liner notes of the *Songs of Scotts Run* CD state, "Some of these songs set the facts straight and some just ask you to listen and feel the power in the words just as we have in the singing and the living." Regulars want it to be known that their home was a safe, well-kept, and vibrant community. Mary Jane Coulter said, "We had grocery stores and plenty of beer gardens—they called them beer gardens then. And clothing stores . . . pawn shops. Osage even had two theaters and a bowling alley at one time. It was a booming coal camp area. . . . I always thought it was great to have all of this—it was like living in a little city." In all of Scotts

Run, no one locked doors, neighbors were treated like family—for better or for worse. Charlene says, "Some people who didn't live there would act like, 'Oh, that's the scariest place to go' or something like that. And I would babysit for people in town and I guess if they would take me back home and let me out of the car it'd be two or three o'clock in the morning, I would just scoot up on that hill. I was never afraid." George describes feeling more secure when growing up in Scotts Run than in his current suburban Morgantown development. "It was a real nice community, it was real clean, everyone kept up their yards or houses. Everyone helped each other out. We didn't even have locks on our doors or our windows. And today I live in a pretty nice development, and we keep our doors locked twenty-four hours a day." George and other regulars often joke that there was nothing worth stealing, but these stories are indicative of the network of social relations that existed in Scotts Run. Sarah recalls, "If we would be out late or something we'd just go to [the neighbors'] house and my sister's house or wherever the door was open . . . we'd just go in there and go on the couch and go to sleep. Nobody locked the doors and that's the way we did [it]. They'd come downstairs and say, 'Oh what-cha doing?'. . . And then my neighbor, we'd do like that if I needed coffee and cream, I'd just go in her house and get it and she did the same—that's how we lived."[30]

Mary Jane describes a system of sharing, where lines were fluid between private and public property. "You could go in anyone's house and you were welcome," and were offered "soup beans, pinto beans, and always homemade bread or pepperoni rolls."[31] Sarah recalls that "it was just so much love, you know, it really was. And when something happened to a family everybody would just pitch in—they would just come and cook the meals or they would bring them a pot of this, a pot of that, a pot of that, or make two cakes and the pies and bread and they would bathe the kids."[32] Of course, Scotts Run wasn't a utopia. George remembers fights that would break out at his uncle's bar above his father's store, and Mary Jane recounts how she and her friend Louise would peek through the Osage beer garden windows when they were kids. "We'd catch a lot of good fights and arguments over dice games," she said, smiling. Many of the regulars will tell you, though, that the instigators were people from Morgantown and elsewhere who came to Osage to make trouble. Poverty was persistent, and men frequently died in the mines. But Scotts Run did have its own social order. Though subject to the oppressive and dangerous working and living conditions created by the coal companies, the people of Scotts Run established their own system within this structure—a commons that relied on mutual sharing of food, space, and familial relations—across race and ethnicity.

"The legacy is that integration happened in Scotts Run long before the Civil Rights era in US History," reads the description on the museum website. The integration of Scotts Run is a common topic of conversation at the Coffee Shop and another marker of identity—even a source of pride—among the regulars. While most coal camps in West Virginia were segregated by the companies, in Scotts Run, African Americans, immigrants, and American-born whites all lived together in the same areas, though there were some neighborhood concentrations of certain races or ethnic groups. In Scotts Run, with foreign-born residents of nineteen different ethnic groups composing 60 percent of the population, and 20 percent each of American-born whites and Blacks making up the rest, the notion of who was considered a minority was different than it was just five miles away in Morgantown. Coffee Shop regulars recount stories of interracial friendships—families taking in children of another race when their parents became overwhelmed by poverty or passed away and Black and white children playing together unaware of racial differences. The regulars frequently express their fraternity across race. Charlene Marshall tells a story of the friendship between her sister and John Propst's sister:

> Years ago you would have photographers going through the mining camps to take pictures . . . and there was one of my sisters and John's sister. . . . John's sister had on an apron, like a pinafore, you just put your arms through it and it fastens in the back. And they're standing there with their arms around each other and they're probably about, I don't know, five, six years old, something like that. And that just shows how everybody was friends. So evidently the story goes, when the photo came back, John's mother . . . said, "Mary Lou, now which one are you?" And then she said, "Mother, don't you recognize me with my apron on?" His mother and my family—I got a big kick out of that.[33]

Scotts Run was not completely devoid of racial tension or untouched by systemic racism, however. Charlene also remembers a neighborhood of more affluent homes where Black people were not allowed to live by unspoken rule. "We never thought about it being segregated, but . . . I think to a certain extent, there was some segregation because I can think of several places . . . that I never knew African Americans to live in. But for the most part, in the coal camps, everybody just, you know, you maybe had Black, white, whatever, living there."[34] The schools were still segregated until 1954, and a few families were overtly, even violently racist, though that was not the norm. Sarah Little commented, "Most of the time we didn't have no issues with Blacks or whites. There was always a few, you know, you always had that somebody. Like this one family, they was KKK. We knew that. But the white people didn't like them either because they saw how they treated us, so they didn't like them either for how they behaved! So they wasn't liked by the Blacks or the whites!"[35] Racist attitudes among community members were not acceptable and were grounds for exclusion in a community where cultural difference was more common than not. Again and again, Scotts Run residents speak of how their geographic proximity and shared economic condition was the most important binding force. Al Anderson was the only Black member of the R&B group the Fabians, and the only member from Scotts Run. All the other musicians, including the sheriff's son, were from across the river in Morgantown. "I'm from Osage, you know. And actually it was like— even if it was a white guy from Osage, and those guys [the Fabians] from Morgantown, it would have been like a little bit of a slant."[36] Negative perceptions of Scotts Run, particularly Osage, with its beer gardens and night clubs and vibrant Black population, hinged on both race and class. Al said, "I think the stigma started there, that you see all these people, and a large Black population as well—but a lot of times people thought it was mostly all Black people in Osage. But it was quite the contrary to that. And there was every mixture of person was in Osage, but when you see a lot of Black folks, it's like a Black town, you know?"

In the past few decades, it's been unclear if Osage was even still a town at all. In the late 1960s, the state put the Interstate 79 interchange through, resulting in the destruction of homes through eminent domain, including those inhabited by Al's father and Charlene's mother.[37] Al sees this as the first step in a plan to get rid of Osage. "I'm sure they could have found the road without taking down all these houses in Osage. And I think it started right there. Okay. 'We gotta get rid of Osage.'. . . . I mean everybody has to leave."[38] In 1994, facing debt and a lack of residents interested in serving on the city council, the town voted 49–24 to dissolve. Al disputes that Osage was never officially unincorporated though, as West Virginia law requires a municipality to be free of debt in order to disband. As of 2006, the town was still listed as a municipality on the West

Virginia secretary of state's website, but its status has been contested. As an unincorporated entity, Osage is now unable to receive coal severance taxes and is more vulnerable to annexation by surrounding towns. When the University Town Center Mall was built along the interstate in 2005, it was given to Granville and not Osage. And in 2013, Scotts Run lost its public service district (PSD).[39] Mary Jane laments, "I say the PSD was a heartbeat, and we lost that. It just seems like it has just been stripped from you know, its identity, completely. It's sad." Al sees these actions as attempts to erase the place that provided coal and subsequently wealth for the surrounding area—a microcosm of the extraction prevalent across Appalachia, depleting the source while benefiting the recipient—amplified by racism and classism. He tries to communicate this during his frequent guest lectures at WVU. "I said, 'Well guys, if it wasn't for Osage and Scotts Run, you wouldn't be sitting in these nice seats you just sat [in] over here at the university.' . . . I said, 'You got about 6,000 students here, you probably wouldn't have many more than that if it wasn't for the coal mine that came outta here to help build that university that you have here.' And I always relate that to them to let them understand that, if it wasn't for Osage and Scotts Run you know, that really paved the way."[40] These more recent events threatening the area have only emphasized the need for the museum to "be the heartbeat," as Mary Jane says.

A Place for Remembering, Preserving, Communing

Dorothy Noyes writes of how dense, multiplex networks like that of the Coffee Shop regulars are characteristic of working-class communities, which are dependent on proximity and frequent interaction for community-based respect, recognition, and support. When these networks are disrupted geographically, in cases of urban renewal or otherwise, and individuals are relocated, "people are inclined to become more interested in impersonal respect and recognition through the signs of status—education and consumer goods."[41] Though many of the Coffee Shop regulars did move to Morgantown, the suburbs, or points beyond either by choice or through eminent domain and went to college, joined the military, and took jobs as teachers, business people, craftspeople, or politicians, they retained their personal ties of respect and integrity in the Scotts Run community. Charlene remembers her first TV news interview as mayor of Morgantown: "I let him know right away—I said I've lived in Morgantown most of my life, but I was born and raised in Osage. Because

I didn't want anyone to think, she's not gonna say she's from Osage, but that's the first thing I said!" The museum has been crucial in upholding the value of community relationships over monetary wealth. Its website states, "Many personal stories attest to happiness unconnected to financial success, lessons from which we can learn a thing or two." It continues, "Come explore some of this heritage and wisdom in our Museum and Trail which begins in Osage and leads you through the communities of Scotts Run." This "wisdom" is the members' heritage and the message the museum hopes to transmit.

The Scotts Run Museum formed in response to the threat of nonexistence, and this action bolstered the network itself.[42] Noyes writes, "We might turn the problem around, however, and instead of defining this network type as the structure of the traditional community, define it as the product of a desire for tradition, a closing of ranks in conditions of threat."[43] When Coffee Shop regulars envisioned the new museum space and began their Saturday gatherings, they were rediscovering those relational ties, reviving the dense, multiplex network that they knew in Scotts Run as children, and restoring its physical home base. In doing so they reaffirmed their existence and developed their own expressive culture, a form of resistance against obliteration. The network, like Scotts Run, is multiracial and multiethnic, operating more like family than friends. As Eve Faulkes explains, "They look at life—at reality—as this is what we got, and we're gonna make the most of it. And like any family, you know, they have squabbles, they've done each other wrong different times, but they're forgiving and they're looking at the big picture."[44] The characteristics of the network mirror those that they grew up with—welcoming, communal, familial, interracial, and intergenerational. The Coffee Shop runs by donation, though no one is required to donate, and the museum is seen as communally owned—when someone introduced Mary Jane to me as the owner, she countered, "No, we all own it." This revived network is a social location from which their community culture forms. This is evident in the Coffee Shop regulars' verbal art, with shared phrases and stories that coalesced as they developed their communal counternarrative. Charlene explains how this narrative formed and is in a constant state of collective reshaping: "I think it has brought a lot of people together and then just to sit there and reminisce, there's always something there that maybe someone will mention. You'll think, oh wait a minute! And they'll refresh your memory about something, and then as you discuss it and everybody tells their side of it, and brings something to the conversation, it brings back a lot of memories or reminds you of something that maybe you had forgotten about, so it's just great to go."[45]

The Coffee Shop members' expressive culture exists in other forms, too. In 2000 Al, the Thomas family, Miss Sarah, and other Boyd family members started the Flying Colors, a multiracial gospel group that formed when the Scotts Run population became so sparse there was little attendance at funerals; they wanted to be able to offer everyone a big musical send-off. The group is featured on the *Songs of Scotts Run* CD, which the museum produced in 2017, and includes other Coffee Shop regulars singing gospel, folk, old-time rock 'n' roll, and country, along with two original songs about Scotts Run composed and sung by Morgantown songwriter Chris Haddox. The liner notes state, "Gospel has been very important to the community as a source of protection, since Lord knows, help wasn't coming from the mine owners."[46] Eve Faulkes often incorporates the museum into her WVU art and design classes, where students have worked collaboratively with Coffee Shop regulars and other Scotts Run natives to design a community garden and paint a mural across the street from the museum, clean coal-dust-covered store fronts, and create art books to tell individual and collective stories from the area. The museum puts on an annual street fair that serves as a homecoming for former residents and has held fundraiser spaghetti dinners, dances, and a concert at the Metropolitan Theater. Mary Jane hosts regular holiday dinners for regulars. The network of Scotts Run demonstrates how expressive culture—particularly a performance of community—can leverage power and create solidarity. Silvia Federici writes of this phenomenon of communities reforming and reenforcing their bonds and finding new forms of subversive creative expression when communal space and prosperity is threatened: "It is impossible, in fact, to defend existing communal rights without creating a new reality, in the sense of new strategies, new alliances, and new forms of social organization. A mine is opened threatening the air that people breathe and the water that everyone drinks . . . immediately new lines are drawn."[47] By acting in community, the Scotts Run Coffee Shop network bolsters its collective power and identity.

"Wasn't a Stranger in Osage"

One Saturday morning, after I'd been coming to the Coffee Shop for a few weeks, I pulled up to the museum and found the lot empty, with a sign on the door.

Closed March 9, 2019
Due to a Community Death
Join us at Euro Suites Hotel
Memorial for our Dear Friend
Jerry Huey
1:00–4:00
501 Chestnut Ridge Road
Morgantown, WV
See you next Saturday

I had only met Jerry once, briefly, the week before. He was relatively young—fifty-two—white, with long dark hair and a cap, shy and smiley. I didn't know if I should go to the memorial, having not really known him, but I'd made the two-and-a-half-hour trip from Charleston that morning and brought a cake. I could at least stop by, pay my respects, and leave an offering. In the hallway on the second floor of the hotel, Jerry's adopted family was setting up a catered barbeque lunch with a potluck of desserts and sides. As I set the cake down on a table, one of them came over to ask if I was Jerry's family, in from out of town. I found the core Coffee Shop group in the adjacent banquet room: Mary Jane and her brother David, her daughter, and granddaughter Dani Rease (twin sister of Charli Shea), George, Al, Eve, Lou, and others I didn't know, including Dolly King (another Coffee Shop regular I hadn't yet met), Sherri Harris, the Coles family, and Jerry's aunt and another relative from out of state. The group of attendees was diverse, about equally Black and white, young and old. I learned that Jerry was everyone's handyman and had died of a heart attack after working storm cleanup in several yards, including George's. He wasn't from Osage originally and hadn't lived there very long. He'd recently been living with Nancy Coles's family but did work for George and others in Morgantown. He didn't drive because of too many DUIs, and was open about that. He was in everyone's home often and relied on the network for rides, so people knew him well and, in turn, depended on his skills and his friendship. We ate lunch, and then everyone who knew him got up and said something. Dolly said he came to visit her every day of the three weeks she was in the hospital, telling people he was her son. She called him her soulmate, then worried that might suggest a roman-tic connotation and dialed it back: "Well, just a good friend." Everyone laughed. Al sang an energetic duet of "Down by the Riverside" with Dani Rease. Several people repeated a phrase that seemed to carry a lot of weight and respect among the group: "Jerry wasn't a stranger in Osage." Jerry's central role in the network demonstrated that its membership is more defined by a shared value system and a physical present than a nostalgic past. Newcomers like Jerry or Eve are welcome if they show up, contribute, and are not a stranger to Osage.

Succeeding in a Diverse and Interdependent World

Though rooted in its shared history, the network of Coffee Shop regulars and community surrounding Scotts Run Museum is also forward-thinking, committed to the future of their home. The museum website outlines their collectively drafted vision:

> A clean, safe place, free of potential environmental hazards associated with truck traffic and surface water run off that can cause flooding.

> Attractive community recreation, education and arts center, integrated with the park, offering indoor and outdoor activities and events.

> Coal heritage is remembered by having a coal mining museum that represents coal heritage, the New Deal, the Scotts Run Settlement House Movement and the Shack Neighborhood House. A coal trail linked to historical mine sites and memorials at mine tragedy sites.

> New development and buildings evoke architectural character of the predominant architecture during the Scotts Run coal booming era.

> A prosperous community that offers diverse employment opportunities; small business owners employ cashiers, cosmetologists, cooks, day care providers, cleaning persons, managers and professionals. The business owners are engaged with the community.

> A community that is self-governing with a town hall and law enforcement.

> A community with decent and affordable housing.[48]

Their desires are basic, illustrating the healthy community we all should be entitled to, but their vision is like a blueprint with sketches overlaid on top of what the community currently lacks. Mary Jane speaks of the fly ash and coal trucks that scatter debris on their homes and pollute the air, the buildings—owned by wealthy Morgantown landlords—that have collapsed into the street, the trash that runs down the creek after a downpour, the fifty-six miners killed in an explosion at Osage in 1942 who, at the time of our interview, had still not been memorialized by the state, county, or coal industry.[49] When I ask her what her personal vision is for Scotts Run, she alludes to a historically preserved town with bustling shops, then stops herself. "I would love to see that but that's not gonna happen in my lifetime I know." She laughs. "That's really stretching my vision." Reconsidering something more immediately attainable, she then answers assuredly, "My vision would be low-income housing for seniors and for families." She notes that low-income housing access would assist current residents of Scotts Run, even Coffee Shop regulars, as well as other residents across the county who are pushed out of the rental market by West Virginia University student demand.

Though it needs more support to remain sustainable, the museum that celebrates the history of Scotts Run is the one tangible outcome of this group's collective vision. The network it created may be the cornerstone for developing the rest. Mary Jane, Eve, Lou, George, and Sarah inherently understand that the most crucial aspect of "creative placemaking," a catchphrase in the arts and economic development sector, is to center the well-being of local residents rather than focus on attracting tourists. When a community has prioritized housing, public safety, transportation, infrastructure and jobs for locals, and in doing so, has developed a strong sense of its own identity, tourism can follow, with parameters set by the community. Through their continual recounting, the Coffee Shop regulars have constructed a collective memory, performing it so often that it's become a reflection of Scotts Run back to itself. What they see in the mirror boosts their collective self-image, reifies their story, and validates their desires for a healthy community. By highlighting a historical past, they have created a new community in the present, with a line on the future.

The museum's mission statement fleshes out the simple slogan "Where History Lives," on the Coffee Shop sign, communicating the specific lessons those who embody that living history have to share and seek themselves: "Our mission is to educate ourselves and future generations about the culture, values, resilient relationships and social bonding of historic Scotts Run that meant survival in coal camp life, to save history through storytelling in multiple media of residents' experiences that add to published accounts, to provide a place for remembering, preserving, communing and for open discussion within a museum setting, to provide outreach through events and programs—alone or partnering with other organizations, to translate such experiences for succeeding in a diverse and interdependent world."[50] If the Coffee Shop regulars know anything, it's how to succeed in a diverse and interdependent world, both as individuals and as a collective with commonly shared resources. With Eve Faulkes collaborating with museum regulars—contributing designs to showcase their work, facilitating platforms for them as speakers and performers in academic and public spheres, and helping them document their stories through art books, exhibits, and museum promotional materials—this network models the power of community-engaged cultural work. Moving forward, Eve has asked if I might contribute to a new book she is working on with the Coffee Shop regulars and her students, a book that will highlight their ten-year collaboration, the community's history, and the museum's mission. Ultimately, this network centered on the Scotts Run Museum knows how expressive culture is shared, how to cultivate it, and how to leverage its power. It's not in the traditional forms imposed from above, and it's not motivated by nostalgia for a cultural purity that never was. Instead, it's constantly reshaped in community by equals, built on a common identity. It's honest about its past. It's multivocal, multiracial, multiethnic, and multigenerational. And it is a productive and subversive tool against erasure.

CHAPTER 2

So I May Write of All These Things

The Individual and the Collective in the Songwriting of
Shirley Campbell, Ella Hanshaw, Cora Hairston,
and Elaine Purkey

For Shirley (1949–2021), Ella (1934–2020),
and Elaine (1949–2020)

"I COULD STILL WRITE you a poem about anytime, you know. It's almost unbelievable. I woke up one night singing a song that I wrote. . . . I don't know where that comes from. But I've heard other people say that. That it just comes from something, somewhere, I don't know." Shirley Campbell told me this the first time we met. I had been acquainted with her son Jerimy Campbell through his cousins, musicians Zane and Hugh Campbell, when I lived in Washington, D.C. They are all nephews of musician Ola Belle (Campbell) Reed, who with her husband and brother established an Appalachian migrant country music community on the Maryland-Pennsylvania border after the Great Depression.[1] I didn't know of Jerimy's mother, Shirley, who had been married to Ola Belle's brother Herbert, until I moved to Charleston and received an email from Jerimy, telling me that his mother was a songwriter from West Virginia who had songs recorded by country stars Grandpa Jones and Ernest Tubb. Jerimy said she was living in Charleston and asked if I would be interested in interviewing her. I wrote back excitedly to tell him that yes, I was indeed very interested, and I called Shirley the next day to set up an interview.

When Shirley showed up at the Humanities Council on a March afternoon in 2016, she brought with her an armload of three-ring notebooks full of hundreds of her songs and poems—typed, dated, and alphabetized—spanning the period from 1965 to 2000. She had short gray hair with a wave, small hoop earrings, wire-frame glasses, and walked slowly, with a cane. She was immediately open and very funny. We spent that first hour talking through details and circumstances of her life—the song of hers that Jones recorded and the one she said Tubb stole, her tormented childhood with a mentally ill mother and talented yet abusive father, her writing practice, her current singing audience (her dogs and cats), and the wild coincidences (as she said, "irony") that seemed to just happen to her. And we read aloud from her notebooks. As we leafed through the yellowed typewritten pages one by one, I was struck not only by her prolificity but also at how Shirley had entextualized her life experiences in song and poetry, asserting and defining her identity within the context of her relationships. The materiality of her notebooks also seemed important to her as physical objects that demonstrated the extent of her creative work.

Shirley's writing and record-keeping practice is strikingly similar to that of East Kentucky banjo player and songwriter Nora Carpenter, whose collection I studied in 2014 at the Berea College Appalachian Sound Archives.[2] Like Shirley, Nora also kept meticulously organized notebooks of typed and dated song lyrics, though hers were a mixture of originals, traditional tunes, and popular songs. But Nora passed away in 1975, so was no longer around to answer my queries about her writerly motivations, process, stories, and subjects. I couldn't inquire about her inspiration or thoughts on gender roles (Nora seemingly defied those of her era, as a business owner, band leader, radio personality, and known crack shot who briefly served as town sheriff) or domestic life, or if she had indeed met Alan Lomax when he passed through her town in 1937, recording her musical partners, but not her.[3] Shirley's and Nora's respective stories and writing were unique, of course, and they were from different eras, classes, and states—but I recognized similar conventions in their work, both part of a tradition of women's writing and self-documentation in Appalachia. This traditional practice is most fully explored in folklorist Patricia

Sawin's *Listening for a Life: A Dialogic Ethnography of Bessie Eldreth through Her Songs and Stories*, both a portrait and an ethnography of North Carolina traditional singer Bessie Eldreth "that understands the creation of a self as a recursive and dialogic process."[4] Through conversations with Eldreth about her documented and performed repertoire of stories, jokes, and popular, traditional, and original songs, Sawin examines how Eldreth negotiates and constructs a gendered self within the context of a patriarchal, working-class culture in the mountain South.

Over the past six years, I've worked with several other women songwriters in West Virginia who write not for professional performance or publishing royalties but rather as a personal pursuit. As far as I'm aware, Shirley Campbell, Ella Hanshaw, Cora Hairston, and Elaine Purkey didn't know each other, but they all work within an often invisible tradition of nonprofessional women's songwriting in Appalachia, tied to the mass popularization of country and gospel; familial music and home-based creative traditions including women's vernacular poetry, ballad singing, and diaristic practices; as well as domestic record-keeping. Though the four women's writing processes, end goals, and relationships with performance, recordings, and self-documentation differ, there are commonalities in their backgrounds and practices: they all come from musical, working-class families in southern West Virginia; they are all mothers; they all write outside of a commercial music industry; and they are all subject to a patriarchal culture that limits women's creative outlets. Though their creative practice draws from the conventions and canon of mass music genres popular in their respective working-class communities, their work largely exists outside of a commodity exchange. Their songs are not commercial products but rather are part of a creative practice of everyday life that approaches music as a social and participatory form, even when their writing is a solitary endeavor. Their work—and how they have employed it to define an identity, entextualize experience, create a tangible record, and carve out a space for themselves within their respective relational roles—is the subject of this chapter.

With the exception of Elaine Purkey, whose songwriting has always been oriented toward public performance, I was told about these women and their work by their respective family or community members. The creative practice of these songwriters is personal—for most of them, tied to domestic space or existing solely within their communities of family, friends, church, or union. Because of this, relationship building through collaborative ethnography was crucial in order to access their work and facilitate our discussions of their motivations, inspirations, and creative practice. The women's self-reporting and reflection during our interviews are the primary sources for this chapter. The collaborative ethnographic process has also facilitated my own understanding of their work through their contextualization, illuminating the past utterances they are responding to through poem and song. For Shirley's writing, which is the most autobiographical and privately oriented, conversations that recontextualized her songs and poems within a narrative of her life's experiences seem to be part of their intended performance. She commented that the ethnographic dialogue with me advanced her own self-discovery that she was already engaged in through writing, saying, "It's true too sometimes if you understand what made you write what you wrote, it's even more fascinating, isn't it?" I'm ever grateful to Shirley, Ella, Cora, and Elaine for their trust, generosity, and willingness to share their work and often intimate details of their lives with me. I greatly admire them as talented writers and musicians and our work together has reaffirmed my belief in the importance of collaborative ethnography, particularly in accessing practices that are not readily public.

In the fall of 2020, as I was finishing this manuscript, I learned from Ella Hanshaw's granddaughter Kelly Kerney that Ella had passed away after another battle with cancer. In September of that same year, Elaine Purkey died of COVID-19 after being on a ventilator for two weeks. In January 2021, Shirley Campbell passed away suddenly at home. The loss of these women was tremendous, for their families and communities, and for me personally. In their sharing of their creative work and personal experiences, we had formed close bonds, and I was looking forward to working more with each of them. I wish we could have been in dialogue after I'd finished a draft of this chapter, though I'm especially grateful I was able to spend the time with them I did. I'm thankful for their respective family members who read drafts and offered feedback in Shirley's, Ella's, and Elaine's stead. For the purposes of this chapter, when I write about their writing practices in conversation with Cora Hairston's, I will use the present tense, as Cora's work is ongoing and Shirley's, Ella's, and Elaine's lives on through their songs and poems.

Shirley White Campbell

Shirley Anita White Campbell was born into a Methodist family in Pinch, West Virginia, in 1949. Her aunt Florence White played the banjo, and her father was a guitar player, singer, and songwriter, though he was incarcerated at the West Virginia State Penitentiary in Moundsville until Shirley was eleven. She started writing songs around age eight, much to the dismay of her mother, who saw songwriting as a hobby too closely resembling the wayward ways of Shirley's father. Shirley's grandmother Sarah Jane Jarrett, who had been her primary caretaker, passed away shortly after her father returned, and life with her father and her mentally ill mother was tumultuous and traumatic. Shirley's father was abusive to her and her mother and constantly uprooted the family.

When Shirley was a teenager, her father, Jack White, took some of his and Shirley's songs to Nashville, pitching them on Music Row. Grandpa Jones had previously recorded Jack's song "My Darling's Not My Darling Anymore." Shirley said the men maintained a relationship and Grandpa Jones visited him when he was in prison. On this occasion, though, Jones was interested in one of Shirley's songs, "Castles in the Air," which he eventually performed on a live album, *Grandpa Jones Live*, released in 1969.[5] Shirley is credited on the album as "Shirley White." She said Ernest Tubb also took one of her songs from her father but neither credited nor compensated her. "We were all standing in Campbell's Corner [the general store that Ola Belle Reed's family ran] one day and Ernest came across the radio and everybody in Campbell's Corner knew that was my song. . . . I don't even know how to explain it. I was so shocked."[6] Between the actions of her father and Tubb, Shirley from a young age experienced men's disregard for her work and life. It was all the more reason to keep writing. Through the internal creative process, Shirley dealt with external negative experience, using the act of writing as a means to reclaim personal dignity and produce tangible evidence of her creativity, experience, and interpretation of the world.

When Shirley was about fifteen, her father took her up to the Maryland-Pennsylvania border where the Campbell and Reed families, themselves Appalachian migrants, broadcast a live country music radio show out of their general store and ran the country music park, New River Ranch. These establishments were important outposts of the Appalachian diaspora in the area. Her father befriended the families through music, and Shirley quickly took a liking to Ola Belle; Ola Belle soon saw that Shirley needed protection. Ola Belle encouraged her songwriting, and according to Shirley, sang and recorded some of her songs like "Lonely I Wait" and "Let Me In." Eventually Ola Belle took her in, and Ola Belle's much older brother, Herbert Campbell, proposed to Shirley, offering his name and a home. They married and had Jerimy in 1967 and a daughter, Carlie, in 1974. Eventually, Shirley moved with her children to Oklahoma City, first landing in a homeless shelter and eventually finding work as a dog groomer. Though she was isolated from a community of musicians like she had in Pennsylvania, her time in Oklahoma was one of her most productive writing periods, perhaps as a result of her solitude as a working single mother in a city where she didn't know anyone.

Though Shirley's work was largely a personal pursuit, the self-creation she engaged in through writing was inherently interactive. Her songwriting was a discursive practice, in conversation with and written to imagined audiences including herself, her family members, children, and romantic partners. In her text, she responds to their past actions and words, as well as to political rhetoric and local and world events. The idea of home—whether with a lover, her children, or as a conceptual ideal—is prevalent in Shirley's lyrics. Elusive when she was a child, the concept of home in her writing is almost always an aspirational apex of stability, the reward after slogging through emotional or material difficulty. In "I Never Dreamed," she writes,

I never dreamed that life could be
Anything but drone.
I never dreamed my little house
Could turn into a home.
I never dreamed the walls would be
Apholstered [sic], all, in love.
I never dreamed the floors would send
Vibrations through the rugs.[7]

Home is a mental and physical refuge, a gendered domestic space of home-cooked food, cookbooks, recipes, decor, and even children's squabbles. She equates food with love and a provider, as in "The Telephone," which mourns for a lost lover,

There could be laughter
And bacon and eggs, and confusion
In the kitchen.
Silence only
Reaks [sic] of lonely
On this bright, Sunday morning.[8]

Her writing exists within this domestic sphere too. She writes, "Spent the night so low and lonely. / Spent the night alone with only / A coffee cup, a notebook, and four walls."[9] Within this gendered realm, Shirley writes from the position of a mother. She expresses doubt regarding her suitability as a parent, worries about repeating her own parents' behavior, and offers earnest prayers for her children's happiness, as in "A Mother's Prayer," pleading, "Let me be a mother that is worthy of her child."[10] She is simultaneously content with and overwhelmed by her role, as seen in "Mom,"

> What more is there to life than the overwhelming responsibility
> for the ultimate outcome of one's children?
> I am left breathless
> By the magnitude of it.[11]

In other pieces, she details events in her children's lives, and playfully riffs on a mother's multitasking,

> Ah, this creature of organization
> With soapsuds on her nose.
> Prompting you to be all that you can be
> While reminding you that you are utterly hopeless.
> We depend upon her for strength, encouragement, and love.
> She hugs and kisses us,
> Exuding the fresh scent of onions.[12]

Alongside the sweet, vulnerable songs are joke rhymes, odes to the beauty of the West Virginia landscape, science fiction poems referencing elaborate alternate universes with made-up words, country parodies, and reverent gospel. While she said it was early rock 'n' roll that initially inspired her to write, the majority of Shirley's secular songs follow popular classic country music in form, style, and topic. Parodies like "There Goes My Big Everything" (see fig. 2.2) and "I'm Proud to Be a Coal Miner's Poodle," a spoof on Loretta Lynn's "Coal Miner's Daughter," make that connection clear. Her early and constant exposure to country music offered Shirley a model of emotional textual form, and she employed its conventions throughout her own writing.

"Old MacDonald" is her lone clear-cut protest song. Dated October 3, 1985, a farm bill year, the song is ostensibly a reaction to decreased agricultural exports, bribes for farmers to idle their fields, and handouts for large industrial farms while small farmers were left to struggle.[13] She advocates tax money for farm subsidies rather than nuclear arms.

They're raping "Old MacDonald,"
Our sustinance [*sic*] of life,
Replacing him with paperwork
And three blind mice.
Not just corn and sweet-peas,
But amber waves of grain
Fall victim to the combine
Of governmental gain.[14]

Other writings call for racial equality, express concern for world events such as the Mexico City earthquake and the Bhopal disaster in India, and question legal reform:

Is anybody watching?
Can anybody see
The wheels of justice turning
Like a rusted, broken key?
Four years for marijuana,
For molestation, three.
Is anybody watching? Can anybody see?[15]

As an extensive body of work, Shirley's songs and poems, most of which were written in the 1970s and 1980s when she was in her twenties and thirties, portray a vulnerable and sensitive, troubled, whimsical and creative, funny, empathetic, religious, observant, and informed narrator. She processes her father's abuse and her relationship with her mother, professes her love for autumn, food, dogs, her children, mourns lost love, and longs for companionship.

Ella Hanshaw

In July 2018, I received an email from Ella Hanshaw's grandson-in-law Ethan Bullard. He was inquiring to see if the West Virginia Folklife Program (or my record label SPINSTER) would be interested in releasing an album of Ella's recordings. He wrote, "The recordings are original as well as traditional gospel numbers recorded by my partner's grandmother and friends in Clay County, WV back in the late '70s and early '80s. Some material was recorded on reel-to-reel using church equipment, other material was a bit more roughly recorded to cassette."

Ethan mailed me a CDR of Ella's original gospel music, recorded by the Hallelujah Hill Quartet (Ella; her husband, Tracy; and another couple), which performed out of the Trinity Missionary Baptist Church in Maysel, West Virginia. Their recordings are endearing and earnest, with four-part harmony and sparse accompaniment—usually Ella singing lead and playing rhythm on her flattop acoustic guitar and Tracy playing lead on electric. Although the topical content of the songs is religious and employs some standard gospel themes and phrases, the song format, instrumentation, vocal style, and guitar runs are those of conventional classic country. And it's abundantly clear that Ella was an exceptional talent, as both a musician and songwriter, delivering her religious message through catchy melodies sung in a sweet, clear twang. I was ready to work with Ella upon my first listen, but it was the secular country songs Ethan sent later that stunned me. Recorded into a tape recorder when Ella was a teenager and in her early twenties, they have a forlorn intimacy and quiet longing, seemingly recorded in a back bedroom during a free moment. In some of the recordings, there are the sounds of her children playing in the background.

Ella (Samples) Hanshaw was born in Procious, in Clay County, West Virginia, in 1934 into a family of farmers. Her father played the banjo, and both her parents sang. At about age twelve, Ella started playing a guitar borrowed from a classmate. After she became proficient, she and her parents would play and sing together in church. "I loved it. God just put it in me to want to sing!"[16] she told me, laughing. When they moved to Maysel, a neighbor gave Ella her own instrument. "I could hear a song and I could hear it maybe twice and I know it. I mean I could play it. I just had the music built in me I guess, because I picked it up by ear." Ella married Tracy when she was eighteen, and they moved up to northern Ohio for his job in the steel mills. The couple had five children, and Ella worked at home as a housewife and mother, leading the junior choir at church, and always writing and singing. In 1981, she and Tracy moved back to West Virginia from Ohio, and they formed the Hallelujah Hill Quartet, performing Ella's original gospel songs at churches across southern and central West Virginia.

Though Ella was raised Baptist, she became Pentecostal around age fifty-seven, encouraged by her daughters. She began experiencing holy visions around that same time. "He baptized me in that Holy Spirit, and I started speaking in the tongues. Honey, I had to go against my husband, I had to go against my pastor, I had to go against my friends, but I stood on God's word. I said I would not let God down. And I went through some pretty rough times too and it cost me a pacemaker!" she said, laughing. In Ella's visions, she battled demons with swords, threw lions into fiery pits, and visualized the Rapture. These visions often coincided with moments when Ella lacked agency—when she or a friend or family member were sick or tempted by sin. Though the experience of holy visions aligns with evangelical doctrine, it is evident that they also constituted an acceptable channel of empowerment, when few were available to her elsewhere. Even converting to Pentecostalism required her to "go against" her husband—something she was not able to do in other arenas. She said, "God uses me in a mighty way. I'm a prayer warrior and an intercessor and I take down the enemies."

Music always came easily to Ella. She learned to sing and play guitar and piano by ear and was extremely prolific, writing 200–300 songs in her lifetime. She generally "received" songs nearly whole—complete with melody and lyrics. To record them, she tried to first write down the lyrics, and then captured the melody on her recorder. She kept her song lyric pages and notebooks in attaché cases and boxes but seemed most concerned that her songs be "recorded" or "put to music," as she called it, meaning transcribed in musical notation. Though she said she remembered the melody to almost all of her songs and recorded many on cassette, she still considered having her songs notated on a staff to be the best way to document them. Perhaps she saw this as a more formal method of documentation, akin to what she was familiar with in hymnals at church. Presenting her writing in this format also allowed her songs to be shared and reanimated by others in worship.

Music was Ella's lifeline, the writing of which became available when she was sick or lonely or channeling God, the social aspect a point of relation with friends and family members, and performance in church an essential conduit for her faith. "Music is just—was built in me, I guess," she said, "and it really tore me up. Well, it didn't tear me up, but I just felt like I lost everything when I couldn't play the guitar and stuff no more—and sing. Because of the pacemaker and his [Tracy's] sickness and taking care of him constantly. And I just had to kind of give up my guitar playing for a while because I wasn't able . . . after that surgery. But I'm getting back." The renewed interest in Ella's music from her granddaughter and grandson-in-law, the friends they gave the CD of her music to, and me, had inspired Ella to continue writing and playing; her granddaughter Kelly told me that even on her deathbed, Ella played an invisible piano and mouthed lyrics. She was eventually able to tell me that these new songs were titled "Victory Mountain," "Return to Pentecost," and "Memories from the Past."[17] Her last song, "Victory Mountain," Kelly said, "truly is about West Virginia, which, of course, was her stand-in for heaven."[18]

When I met Ella and Tracy, they were living in Seville, Ohio, where they'd been for the past thirty-one years, after eight years back in West Virginia. I arranged to visit and interview Ella a few days before Thanksgiving 2018. Although she had just recovered from a bout of cancer and finished chemo treatments, she appeared spritely, with bright, welcoming eyes, and was earnest and sweet. Her husband, Tracy, who suffered severe hearing loss from work in the steel mill, sat in the living room watching a movie through headphones, while Ella and I talked at the dining room table.

Cora Lee Hairston

I met Cora Lee (Phillips) Hairston and her husband, Fred, at the Chief Logan State Park Museum in May 2016. They are both natives and nearly lifelong residents of Logan County, West Virginia, and Cora occasionally performs as Rosa Parks at the museum during Black History Month. That day Cora was dressed up, looking much younger than her seventy-three years in a lacy white tunic with a matching headscarf, and white earrings, bracelet, necklace, and rings (see plate 2.1). Later I learned that this was not unusual—she's always dressed impeccably, and once ran a clothing and hat store, where she says she was her own best customer. She was warm, vivacious, and talkative—clearly relishing the storytelling. Her husband Fred sat quietly, content to cede her the floor.

She began, "My name is Cora L. Hairston, my maiden name was Phillips and I was born in Sarah Ann up Crystal Block Hollow in 1942. Coal miner's daughter."[19] Cora grew up in a Black coal camp in Logan County. Both her parents were from North Carolina but moved the family up to West Virginia for her father's job in the mines. Her mother Louanna (aka "Baby Doll") was a housewife, worked as a domestic, and, as Cora said, "was the best cook in the world." Cora remembers her and her five siblings' childhood in the coal camp as joyous and communal. The children were not fully aware of their family's lack of financial resources. "It was a community of sharing, and so therefore I guess that's why no one ever went without, because if someone didn't have something and someone else did, then they shared it."

Music has always been a part of Cora's life. When she was a girl, a woman in her church formed an all-girl a cappella group, with Cora singing lead. As a high school senior, she was named "Best Female Vocalist" of Logan High School, which she attended two years after attending the segregated Black Aracoma High School in Logan County. Music was what initially connected her to her husband, Fred, a multi-instrumentalist who played in several bands in the area. "I could sing then and I sang all the time, it was just something that was in me. My husband and I had bands—singing groups, and I sang with him down through the years. I think we closed down every night club in Logan!"

Immediately after graduating high school, Cora moved to Chicago, living with her aunt and working as a secretary at Spiegel. There, she was offered an opportunity to travel as a professional singer and dancer with comedian Redd Foxx's Revue. She tells the story of what could have been a turning point in her life:

> We were at this particular club . . . and it was the Redd Foxx Revue. Any time a song came on the jukeboxes, I was always singing and so here we are, I'm singing along. . . . I was overheard and I was asked if I would sing on Redd Foxx's stage—are you kidding me? Not that particular night but it was going to be the following Saturday. Well, all my friends were all excited, they buy me this beautiful blue taffeta dress. . . . And after that Redd Foxx and one of his, I guess, assistants, came to my aunt's house to ask if I could travel with them. And my aunt was my guardian and in that day . . . you do as you're told, you follow instructions, you follow orders. I never had a desire to be a star or a singer. That was not in me . . . it just wasn't. I liked to sing but I never wanted to be a [star], per se, and so they were talking about me and I wasn't allowed to be in the room—I was in the kitchen, but I was listening. I was eavesdropping. My aunt was very soft spoken. . . . She was sitting there and she says, "Well, if one of her brothers goes with her, I might consider it. But I cannot allow her to go with you by herself." So that was the end of that.

Cora says she never regretted not going on tour with Redd Foxx. Shortly after, she moved back to Logan County and eventually married Fred. She got a job at Phico Manufacturing and later worked as a teacher's aide, nurse's aide, and file clerk, ultimately retiring as a radiology coordinator at Logan General Hospital. Through singing in bands with Fred, church singing, and writing, she still found a way to make music a part of her life. Cora eventually learned organ and piano by ear. Today, she serves as grand musician for Electra Prince Hall Masonic Lodge Eastern Stars, is the pianist for her church and church district, and performs gospel and her original songs at the annual local festival, Pickin' in the Park. She has written poems and over twenty songs—some religious, some personal, and some about world events. Though Cora performs occasionally, her most regular outlet is her daily rehearsal of her songs—what she calls her daily praise, singing and accompanying herself on piano. This personal performance constitutes her own spiritual practice, a regular devotional. She said, "To me they're beautiful. I mean, I get joy out of singing them. And I try to do them *every day,* some of them." Several times when I've called Cora, Fred has answered the phone, and told me Cora was in the middle of "doing her praise," and was wary of interrupting her.

Cora calls some of her pieces "inspired songs," like one she wrote for her sister when she was battling cancer, another for Michael Brown and her cousin Joan who lost her son, and one written for the mother of Trayvon Martin: "'Come on in now so that you can rest. / You've played and played, stayed and stayed now, / come on in the house little tired boy.' And this is mom calling her little boy in from play. / 'Come on in now, you've been out all day.'" These are offerings, intended to comfort and ease the suffering of family members and those she doesn't know but feels a kinship with. She finds subject matter in both family stories and national events, like the September 11 attacks or the election of the first African American president. Through the creative process, Cora develops conceptual personal relationships—whether with God or the mothers of slain Black boys.

Though navigating the logistics of recording and copyrighting seem to be a barrier for Cora, it isn't her greatest concern. "I've just never taken the time to have them copywritten [sic] and put in safety. But if I ever hear anybody singing, and I know it's my song, they're gonna have to deal with me! I have sang some of them out in public before." She has informally recorded her songs on her cassette recorder, and had her former neighbor Landau Eugene Murphy Junior, a local celebrity who won *America's Got Talent* in 2010, record two of her songs on his recording equipment. A local piano player recorded another of Cora's originals at his studio.

Cora has published two fictionalized accounts of her childhood, *Faces behind the Dust: The Story Told through the Eyes of a Coal Miner's Daughter (on the Black Side)* and *Hello World, Here Comes Claraby Rose: An Adolescent*

Black Girl Coming of Age.[20] She said, "My life reverts around my church work, my community work and my home and my family and my grandchildren . . . my music and writing and housework!"

Elaine Purkey

I first heard Elaine Purkey sing on the 2006 Smithsonian Folkways collection *Classic Labor Songs.*[21] Amid selections by Woody Guthrie, Florence Reece (who wrote "Which Side Are You On?"), and fellow West Virginian Hazel Dickens, Elaine's "One Day More" is an arresting rallying cry with a universal message to workers involved in any labor struggle. She wrote the song in 1992 to inspire the union steelworkers locked out of their jobs at the Ravenswood Aluminum plant.[22] In the liner notes of the album, she writes, "No matter how long the company or the corporations can stick around, we have enough strength, friendship, camaraderie about us and enough belief in what we're doing, we can be there one day more; whatever they do, we'll be there the day after."[23]

In October 2016, I traveled with mutual friend and activist Rick Wilson to meet Elaine at a family restaurant in her home county (see fig. 2.1). Rick and Elaine had become comrades during the 1989–90 strike against Pittston Coal Company, where Elaine's husband, Bethel, was a UMWA miner, and Rick prompted many of Elaine's first songs during that time. I found Elaine's presence to be as commanding as her songs, but she was also humble and joyful and plucky, punctuating our interview with laughter.

Elaine (Moore) Purkey was born on May 29, 1949, in Harts Creek in Lincoln County, West Virginia, on the same piece of property where she lived until she died. She was raised in a family of musicians and flatfoot dancers and attributed her electrifying voice to the a cappella singing she learned as a member of the Church of Christ. She recalled that as early as age five, she would stand on a rock in her grandfather's yard and sing "Frankie and Johnny" for family and friends. As a teenager she played in bands with her brother, and in early adulthood she was the lead singer of a local country band. In the 1980s, she began performing regularly on the *Wallace Horn Friendly Neighbor Show*, a live radio program out of Logan County that has been on the air since 1967; she eventually became the show's host and creative director. In 1996, she released a solo album, *Mountain Music, Mountain Struggle*, which includes her original labor songs, traditional folk songs, gospel, and country.[24] She was a featured performer at the Smithsonian's Labor Heritage Foundation and

FIGURE 2.1. Elaine Purkey at Skeeter's Restaurant in Harts, West Virginia, October 27, 2016. Photo by the author.

Folklife Festival three times. After the Pittston strike and Ravenswood lockout, Elaine worked as a community organizer with the West Virginia Organizing Project, and she continued to perform frequently for other labor and social justice events throughout the region. In the years before her death, she taught music to kids through the Big Ugly Community Center in her home county, and she and Bethel were also raising two great-grandchildren.

Inspired by the labor struggle she and her family were engaged in, Elaine used her music to build solidarity and group morale so others could continue to fight. Having witnessed firsthand the result of the long history of worker disenfranchisement and union busting in West Virginia, she was able to powerfully narrativize it in song. This is most evident in her most popular song, "One Day More," which borrows a slogan from the Pittston strike, "One Day Longer," but was written to give a "shot in the arm" to the steelworkers locked out of the Ravenswood Aluminum plant.

> One day more, one day more
> People let me tell you what we're fighting for
> We're fighting for our future don't you understand
> We don't need your pity we just need your helping hand
> To fight one day more, one day more
> If the company holds out 20 years, we'll hold out one day more.

Elaine said she wrote the song in about twelve minutes, and performed it at a rally for the workers, filmed by Barbara Kopple for her documentary, *Locked Out in America: Voices from Ravenswood*, as part of the PBS TV series, *We Do the Work*. Elaine recalled, "I had bronchitis, I could barely talk, and I don't know, something happened when I started doing that song—you'd never know I had anything wrong with me. And immediately afterward I could barely talk again. But I sang that song for like thirty minutes . . . they KNEW it was about them, and they climbed up on the tables." Elaine saw music as an effective tool for building worker solidarity. "Many people will listen to a message in a song when they won't listen to it in a speech. People can sing their message as they march or while standing in a group."[25]

Though Elaine envisioned a labor movement in which men and women are on equal footing, during the Pittston strike, negative, vulgar portrayals of women who picketed circulated even among the miners themselves. "There was a lot of women on the picket line. Pittston was really the turning point for that. They'd done it in a previous strike but they swore they'd never go back again because they were treated so badly," she said. She wrote her song "Picket Line Lady" as a rhetorical counternarrative, portraying the female picketers as she knew them—strong, moral women who were working alongside their husbands, in the service of the union and for the survival of their families. Her song embeds lyrics from "Amazing Grace" and the African American spiritual-turned-protest song, "We Shall Not Be Moved."

> Picket line lady, yellow ribbon in her hand
> Picket line lady, walkin' with her picket line man
> She's still a lady, no matter what you say
> Picket line lady, what will you do today?
> Picket line lady won't you stand and scream and yell
> She's right there on that line when they cart 'em off to jail
> She's right there at the courthouse when they take away the men
> Singing her union songs and a good old country hymn.

In Elaine's verse, while wives of union miners engage in the same work of resistance as their male counterparts, they are simultaneously singing. As in the classic labor song "Bread and Roses," which calls not only for the material means of survival but also the right to dignity and the beauty of life, the women Elaine knew on the picket line were, like herself, fighting for their families, while also engaged in aesthetic production through song: "Yes, it is bread we fight for, but we fight for roses, too." Though Elaine never walked the picket line herself (striking miners felt her presence was too risky, in that if she was in danger, it could compromise Bethel's ability to lead), she found her voice through creative work. Since she was a little girl singing on the rock in her grandfather's yard, Elaine always oriented her music toward performance, rarely for a mass public but rather for a specific audience of community, union, or family. Above all, she credited God as the primary influence and common thread across all of her music. Recalling her father, a fiddle and banjo player, she writes, "We both believe that if you don't share music, God will take it away from you."

The Tradition of Women's Songwriting and Record-Keeping in Appalachia

Shirley, Ella, Cora, and Elaine's dual identities as working-class women impose certain gender and class structures, while also affording certain opportunities. As Aaron Fox writes in *Real Country: Music and Language in Working-Class Culture*, his extensive ethnographic study of a rural country music community in Lockhart, Texas, "Working-class culture is concerned with the dignity and agency of the subject in direct proportion to the lack of dignity and agency entailed in working-class political and economic experience, and especially in alienated labor."[26] This is even more true for working-class women (and especially so for women of color) whose subjectivity is made invisible, creative agency is suppressed, and work is minimalized and eclipsed by the masculinization of blue collar labor and devaluing of social reproduction. Through songwriting, Shirley, Ella, Cora, and Elaine reclaim personal agency and dignity, the private nature of which enables them to at times transgress these structures of domination, but they do so within the bounds of the culturally acceptable practice of women's writing and diaristic traditions.

Writing—in the form of recording family stories, inscribing birth and death dates in a family Bible, sending letters, or annotating recipes in a cookbook—has historically been one of the few admissible creative outlets for women in the mountains.[27] In order to be considered socially acceptable, this work often had to be framed as the fulfillment of gendered responsibilities, such as accounting of domestic finances and genealogical record-keeping.[28] Folklorist Debora Kodish writes, "We have evidence from the 18th century to the present of the women's tradition of keeping enormous scrapbooks, or ballad books, filled with clippings and handwritten song texts to which they might refer for their own pleasure, to settle arguments, to entertain, or to provide words for other singers."[29] Keeping song lyric scrapbooks was part of this Anglo- and Irish American tradition too. In his piece on a woman manuscript songbook collector in New Brunswick, Neil Rosenberg argues that the practice of writing down song texts, often ignored by scholars more interested in oral transmission, has always been an integral part of oral song tradition, specifically women's ballad singing.[30] Though this writing practice indeed furthered the transmission of knowledge from generation to generation, women frequently used this outlet in subversive ways, recording alternate histories or developing a voice and identity outside of the prescribed, often submissive roles of mother and wife.

Vernacular poetry writing fits within that tradition as a convention historically accessible to working-class women. Shirley and Cora, who also write poetry, seemingly integrate their writing of verse into their songwriting practice. While poetic verse offers a different generic form than songs set to a melody, both women shared songs and poems with me, rarely distinguishing between the two forms. For Shirley, who did not perform in public, the final form of her songs and poems are as texts in her notebook, and to be read aloud to friends and family. In her notebooks, poems and songs appear side by side, and barring context she gave in conversation, are virtually indistinguishable from each other. While her songwriting remained a largely private practice, Shirley did, however, submit several poems to vernacular poetry contests, receiving recognition for her verse. Cora, who performs occasionally, reads her poems aloud as part of her musical performance.

"Troubles in a Bottle": Songwriting as Entextualization and Song Notebooks as Text-Artifact

Shirley, Ella, Cora, and Elaine's work involves both the practice of songwriting—the composing of melody and writing of lyrics—and the tangible, physical form that practice takes as a song text, or what Greg Urban and Michael Silverstein call the text-artifact, in the notebook.[31] Shirley had the strongest relationship to her notebooks, which constitute curated and organized material records of her own labor. She explained her early process and the trauma of being separated from the physical manifestation of her creative work:

A whole song would come to me, and then when I had a chance to have paper and pencil, I'd put them down. But then when daddy would go—it could be in the middle of the night or anything. . . . I don't know what made things like that happen. He'd just come in and he'd say, "We're gone, let's go." And I can remember one time that, it was that time he put that knife to my throat. . . . And I had a little box I'd been keeping my papers in, and I said, "Daddy, please let me take my music." And he said, "You can't do nothing," and we went and there it lay. I mean for years, I swear for years I wanted to go back and get . . . because it was kinda everything I had up until he came back. . . . I'd managed to keep it that long. But oh, all the previous years were gone when he did that. I tried so hard to remember them. But I just couldn't as the years went by. I just couldn't anymore.[32]

From early on, the practice of songwriting was a source of stability for Shirley, the culmination of the practice as text-artifact collected in a notebook being an important keepsake and record of her creative work and existence. The act of writing allowed her to create something tangible that she had some control over, and that she had hoped she could keep to weather the chaos of life with her father.

The practice of song and poetry composition is a means to "entextualize" a stretch of experience, that is, to extract discourse from its original context to produce the coherent and defined text of the text-artifact.[33] For Shirley, that act of entextualizing an experience and transforming it into a composed piece of writing as a song or poem was a coping mechanism—a productive catharsis to process trauma:

It was in the winter, and Daddy had gotten through just abusing me, and it was dark and there was a little shelf over in the corner and I looked over there and there were some old-timey medicine bottles and stuff, and I think I told you I wished I could put my troubles in that bottle and just seal it up. And that's when, from there that's the song. And that was a very bleak moment in my childhood. Very bleak. And it's burned in my brain, you know? But the song—the song doesn't really depress me or anything, but it was very meaningful."[34]

Throughout her life, the written page was Shirley's bottle, a receptacle for her inner emotional life and a way to externalize traumatic experience. She confided, "I don't know whether to call it tragedy or what, but [writing songs is] sometimes the only way if you have the inclination to write. . . . You just have to cope with it in that way." She wrote a song about that moment called "Troubles in a Bottle." Though the full lyrics are lost to her now, she remembered some of the verse, which she sang to me in a sentimental lilt:

> I have troubles I don't tell,
> but I guess it's just as well.
> I have no one who really cares for me.
> Sometimes my soul aches and my heart breaks
> but I keep it to myself.
> I keep my troubles in a bottle on the shelf.[35]

In the transient life of her childhood, Shirley had few things that endured; even her written pages were under threat. As a mother and in her working life as a dog groomer, caregiver, and flea market manager, many of the fruits of her labor were ephemeral. By keeping notebooks of her songs and poems that capture her experience, thoughts, and emotions, Shirley created both an entextualized bounded narrative and a text-object— a tangible artifact of her existence. In her study of women's scrapbooking practices in the 1990s and early 2000s, folklorist Danille Christensen writes, "Like handwritten receipt books and feminist zines, scrapbooks are tangible archives of everyday individual experience, concretizing the voices and activities that might otherwise get lost in the (unattended or intentionally dismissed) ebb and flow of daily life."[36] Song lyric notebooks or "ballad books," much like scrapbooks and recipe books, narrativize the ephemeral into a permanent record.

"Sometimes I Think You Write to Yourself": Writing as a "Public Private" Practice

In her article "I Write for Myself and Strangers: Private Diaries as Public Documents," scholar Lynn Bloom articulates the difference between "truly private" diaries and "public private" diaries. The former are written only for the author and generally take the form of barebones records and receipts, written with no concern for audience or authorial image. Because of this, they are not particularly scrutable to readers. In "public private" diaries, however, "the author creates and presents a central character, herself, as seen through a central consciousness, also herself," for a potential audience, whether close or distant.[37] Shirley Campbell's

notebooks of her songs and poems are similarly "public private" documents. She wrote for an imagined audience and was mindful of how
she constructed her character on the page. Though her songwriting was
always a personal diaristic practice and performance was never really her
end goal, she enjoyed sharing her writing with those interested and sub-
mitted poems to amateur poetry contests. When she lived in Oklahoma
City, she befriended a pianist who would perform Shirley's melodies at
her restaurant gig. "Nobody appreciated it but me sitting there listening, thinking, 'Yeah, that's mine. I did that.'"[38] Her standard byline, "By:
Shirley White Campbell," inscribed on the majority of her song and poem
pages, conveys that she did imagine a reader outside of herself. In Danille
Christensen's chapter "(Not) Going Public: Mediating Reception and
Managing Visibility in Contemporary Scrapbook Performance," she also
addresses this overlap of the public and private, citing linguistic anthropologist Susan Gal, who argues that the realms of public and private are
not a simple binary but a fractal, the two domains recursively entangled.[39]
While Shirley wrote in private, she imagined how her songs might be
reanimated by other musicians, or read by others in the future. Additionally, when she read her songs and poems aloud to me, recontextualizing
them within a narrative of her life, she was effectively performing for me
in a "public private" ethnographic interaction, as Christensen describes,
a "one on one encounter with [a] known interlocutor." Citing C. W. von
Sydow and Norm Cohen, Neil Rosenberg argues that "the manuscript
collection is a bridge between the private and public traditions."[40] The
existence of Shirley's songs as text-artifacts compiled in a keepsake notebook, from which they can be recontextualized and reanimated, is the
communicative vehicle for her "public private" practice.

In the free verse poem, "Dear Shirley," dated June 17, 1986, she reflexively engages the inherent contradiction of the "public private" binary
head on, admitting that she writes for an audience who may never read
her work.

Dear Shirley,
    Sometimes I think you write to
yourself.
    Half the stuff you write no one
else ever reads.
    Why, on earth, do you have to tell
yourself all the things you, obviously, already know?

They say, when the average citizen
cracks up that they often talk to themselves
and answer.
    Perhaps, when poets go over the edge
they write to themselves.
    Well, at least you haven't started
Answering any of my letters, yet.
        Sincerely,
        Shirley[41]

With wry self-referential and self-mocking humor (a characteristic common throughout her catalog), Shirley experiments with an epistolary form and questions her habit of transferring emotions and experiences that already exist in her mind and entextualizing them into a poem only she may read. And yet, she still wrote this piece, performing humility for a future audience outside of herself. This particular type of self-effacing narrator is a common country music trope, what Aaron Fox calls "the Fool in the Mirror," described as the splitting of the self into external presentation and internal representation. He theorizes that through "feeling," which can take the form of "gossip, narrative, and performative self presentation," the boundaries between the private self and public person become linked. Because the personal is socially scrutinized, one way to bring "person" and "self" into balance is to engage in self-scrutiny and self-characterization. When performed publicly, this self-scrutiny is a rhetorical device in which "the fool can be rescued from abjection by social engagement."[42] In this case, Shirley presents a textual performance of self-awareness and a socially appropriate performance of humility that can be deployed as a defense against how her "person" might be perceived by the reader.

"Oh to Be a Poet": Writing a New Identity

In her "Dear Shirley" poem, Shirley is making another important claim. In the text, she indirectly calls herself a poet, an identity she positions as more esteemed than "the average citizen," as writing to oneself is at least preferable to merely mumbling to oneself. "Poet" is an identity she asserts in numerous poems in her repertoire. In "Disgruntled Poet," dated January 30, 1972, she writes,

Prose and pot and poetry
Make an artist out of me.
I close my eyes and there I see
The things that live behind them.[43]

Writing helped Shirley access an interiority and simultaneously claim an identity. Throughout her life, roles were often bestowed, or even violently thrust, upon her; writing facilitated a time and space for her own subject-formation. In "Oh, to Be," dated August 27, 1971, she longingly contemplates other identities—a master weaver, the owner of a tropical island, a painter, a singer, a composer, an angel, a sculptor. In the last couplet, she ultimately settles on her own identity, "Oh, just to be a poet, / That I might master rhyme, / So I may write of all these things / Until the end of time."[44] In *Listening for a Life*, Patricia Sawin writes, "For women, furthermore, the contradictions of a patriarchal society and the multiplicity of inconsistent roles, expectations, and experiences through which we form our subjectivities provide conflicting input that promotes correspondingly conflicted self-constructions."[45] For Shirley, restricting her poetry and writing to a primarily "public private" audience may have been a way to ensure that her identity as a poet remained uncorrupted by other actors or societal pressures, a way of evading scrutiny of her personhood. In the face of personal abandonment, words were a steadfast companion, as she said, her "faithful partner."[46]

Like Shirley, Ella's roles in life were often relational and based on care-giving—mother, wife. But the label she identified with above all was not dependent on others; it is also the one in which she had the most agency: that of a singer. The first line of a one-page autobiography she had prepared prior to my visit reads, "I guess I've been a singer ever since I was big enough to know what a song was. I love singing." While that identity was not dependent on Ella's relationship to others like her children or husband, it was still embedded in her social ties. Whereas Shirley identified as a "poet," and was focused on the act of writing as the ultimate expression of her creativity, Ella was most interested in singing—performing her music at church or in an informal social context with friends or family members, another "public private" audience. Sawin writes, "Singing proved an acceptable form of artistic expression for a woman because it could be defined as a form of work in the service of one's family (lullabies) and one's religious community (offering solos in church)."[47] Both Ella's and Elaine's performance habits followed this pattern—Ella's in service to

God and Elaine's in service of the union and her family's survival (though she also credited God as her primary influence). For both of them, their music eventually facilitated a platform beyond traditional roles of wife and mother.

Elaine considered her role in the Pittston strike a turning point in her life and music. When I asked when she was born, she gave me two different dates—one for her literal birthday and one for the birth of her new identity:

> Well, I tell everybody, that my birthday, my actual natural birthday was May 29, 1949, but I really wasn't born until in the 1980s after I met Rick and got involved in all of this stuff because that's when my blood really started pumping. Always before that, people—I mean I was just mundane, I did all this singing and went to church, did all the things I was supposed to do, had babies and raised 'em and I cooked and I cleaned and took care of everything, and that was it! I was known by the company I kept, you know, nobody knew who I was. But that changed everything.[48]

Songwriting and performance of her original and classic labor songs were the vehicles through which Elaine found and cultivated a public identity as a leader and organizer, outside of relational identities formed solely through "the company she kept" in private domestic spaces. In her labor songwriting, she entextualized her experiences as a working-class mother and wife, and the performance of those songs allowed her to claim a new identity as a community organizer. She writes in her album liner notes, "My style comes from those early days of listening to mommy sing while she cooked, kept house and rocked babies." She continues, "My songs also express anger over what good people like my mom and dad had to endure so that the rich could get richer and the government could get more corrupt." Elaine's songwriting not only pairs domestic work and collective struggle but also inextricably twines them.

Though Elaine was known locally as a singer, she had never written a song until the Pittston strike. Ronni Gilbert of the Weavers had come to the UMWA's Camp Solidarity, where she learned of Elaine and demanded to meet her.

> So they called me and asked me if I'd come over there and do a couple of union songs. Well, I didn't know any union songs! I hadn't

done anything like that at all! And so I learned "Solidarity Forever" and . . . "Union Maid". . . . And so I was sittin' on the bed practicing one night and I was listening to the TV and I heard all this junk going on being said about the strike and people in the strike, and I thought, we shouldn't have to be doing this. We should not have to fight for our right to work and make a good wage! A good living! And that's when I wrote "America, Our Union'" and sang it over there. And got a standing ovation.[49]

Elaine and Rick said the song, written to the tune of "America, the Beautiful," became a "national anthem" of sorts for the movement. "America, America just open up your eyes / Their only greed is corporate greed, and ours is to survive."[50] The song takes the unity described in the original song and reimagines it as existing across a nationwide unionized workforce, crowning "the good with brotherhood from sea to shining sea." Elaine said she wrote the song out of necessity, needing an evocative message with a familiar melody that the miners could latch on to. Her involvement with the strike and growing political awareness during this time was a personal revelation within an uprising of her family's community. "Seemed like the skies had opened up and started puking right on top of me! And it was like everything was happening all at the same time!" she said.

The work of Shirley, Ella, Cora, and Elaine mediates between personal interiority and societal roles and responsibilities. Writing is the realm where each interprets and makes meaning of her world and experience, carves out a space for a personal creative pursuit and constructs a self-identity that is in conversation with but separate from her relational roles within the family, church and religion, union, or community. Their respective notebooks offer a rare space where they can set their own terms, outside of external obligation or judgment. Their writing is a reflexive process, a tool to examine their relationships with family and community, organize temporal experience, engage with memory, and produce creative work. Additionally, this artistic "primary practice," as anthropologist Gregory Bateson proposes, integrates inner life and disparate parts of selfhood into a connective whole.[51] For Shirley, Ella, Cora, and Elaine, songwriting is the arena where the duality of the subject, the relationship between "selfhood" (interiority and subjective experience) and "personhood" (externally constructed societal roles and responsibilities) is negotiated. It is the "dialectic interplay between externalized self-presentation and internalized self-representation."[52] As the next sections examine, these women employ conventions in popular country and gospel music and attribute their creative inspiration to God in order to express emotion based in lived experience and find artistic agency within socially acceptable genres and stylistic forms.

Country Music as Public Poetry

As a working-class genre that values songs which entextualize emotion and convey authentic lived experience, country music is a touchstone for much of the songwriting by Shirley, Ella, and Elaine. All three women have written and/or performed songs within the genre and cited country stars as major inspirations for their own work. As Aaron Fox writes, "Country is an articulate, public poetry, but it purports to reveal the inarticulate and pained interiority of subjective experience. Country serves up poetry when 'ordinary' speech fails."[53] Stylistically, the conventions of country songs are particularly suited to the negotiation and integration of notions of the "self" and the "person"; how a person is perceived by society versus her or his emotional and psychological interiority. Elaine's 1996 album features her originals alongside traditional gospel hymns and popular country songs she learned from Reba McIntyre, Connie Smith, and George Jones. She said she liked those artists in particular because they "felt and LIVED" their music—a quality she seeks in all music she wrote and performed. "I think the music that I did—and not just the songs that I wrote, the struggle songs that other people had written—but the traditional music of the mountains. It's soul music. It's people pouring out their heart and soul on a piece of paper and then putting music to it. And it's stories about people and about their feelings." These concepts of "feeling" and story, or meaning, are, as Fox argues, important markers of authenticity and value within country music as a social form. "'Feeling,'" he writes, "is a concept . . . that mediates between cognitive and embodied domains of cultural experience." Feeling and "the social and psychological process of 'relating'" unify the self and the collective through lyrical poetics and shared experience. Elaine's songs are built on these concepts, written with the intention of relating to the individual within the collective through an authentic emotional expression. This was the connection she sought with her audience:

> When my CD came out . . . one DJ said it [the radio success of the album] was because of the feeling that's in the CD. . . . This is from a place in Europe. He said people don't understand the words. But

they understand the feeling. And they call every night and request that song. And it was "America Our Union." The very first one that I wrote. And I wrote it because I felt it. And I tell everybody this story.

My husband was probably the best speech maker ever. He never used a note, he just spoke from his heart. And that's what made the difference. And he knew what he was speaking about because he was involved in it. I mean people have speech writers and all that stuff. Well, that's alright. But he knew what he was talking about. He didn't have the numbers that he needed, and I looked them up for him one time and put 'em on a piece of paper and he stuck them in his pocket and they stayed there. He made that speech without using those numbers and it was just as effective as if he'd had 'em. So, that's the way I'd like my music to be looked at and listened to.

Elaine valued the lived experience of working-class people over the institutional authority of professional speech writers, who may have fancy words but no experience of the hardship they describe. Her songs were her form of oration to her union brothers and sisters, intended to resonate with a familiar audience through personal experience, evoke an emotional response, and inspire subsequent action.

In her performances, Elaine integrated original, cover, and traditional gospel, labor, and country songs and she said that "Amazing Grace" and "How Great Thou Art" were the most requested songs when she sang at union or other community events. As a genre, gospel is historically deeply entwined with country music, sharing the importance of the evocation of "feeling" and "relating," to both the specific individual experience and the spiritual collective. Gospel music as a genre also provides a topical association and associated performance venue widely accessible and socially permissible to working-class women songwriters in Appalachia.

"God Always Gave Me a Pretty Song": Artistic Agency and Socially Acceptable Gendered Performance

By writing gospel music, performing in church, and attributing artistic talent and inspiration as gifts from God, these songwriters frame their work within a context where they can still assert artistic agency while simultaneously avoiding overt individual attention that they may feel is self-indulgent and socially unacceptable. Sawin witnessed this phenomenon in her work with Appalachian singer Bessie Eldreth, writing, "Church performance is necessarily hedged so that attention is deflected from the performer and toward the religious message and the spiritual uplift it is meant to inculcate."[54] Cora said, "I thank God every day for the gift of having the talent that I do have. I don't read music—can't play like anybody else, but I play like God wants me to. That's my way! And I just love it!" She considers her writing to also be a holy blessing. "Just this last week, I was given a poem. And when I say given, I always feel there's been a gift that's been passed down through me." In another interview she re-iterated, "They are not my songs. They were given to me. I was blessed with them."[55] Framing her music as a spiritual blessing serves a dual func-tion for Cora—it amplifies her faith while also facilitating a creative space that can be shared without risk of being perceived as being motivated by ego. Ella also asserted that her songs were given to her by God, and they often came to her when she was under the weather. "If I'd get sick or something, God always gave me a pretty song. Every time I got sick, I would come out of it by concentrating and writing a song." With her typical workload raising five children and all the cleaning, sewing, gar-dening, and cooking that entailed, resting during bouts of illness may have been one of the few occasions Ella had focused time to herself, offer-ing her a moment to reflect and channel her writing. She described her writing process:

> I'll be sitting and just thinking and just all of a sudden, they'll float through my mind. And I can write one in fifteen minutes. When-ever God gives it to me, I grab out my pencil. Usually there's one or two lines that I have to really work on. I have to go to the Bible you know, and find it or something. But he gives me them songs and within about fifteen minutes or less, I can write a song. And it's just been that way, and I don't know how many I've missed, honey, lying in bed at night, and oh, a pretty song will come, and I'll think, "Oh now in the morning I'll write that down as soon as I get up," but in the morning it's gone. If you don't grab it when it's there . . .

Cora also reports this sensation of being a spiritual conduit, receiving songs and poems as bursts of inspiration, sometimes when she's sleep-ing or riding a car, and she must rush to write them down before they evaporate. She said, "I never know when they're coming. I never sit down and say I'm gonna write me a song. I could be singing just an old hymn from a hymn book and finish that, and something will come that will flow and a song will come from that. So, however he gives them to me." In separating the act of writing from themselves as singular artists and attributing it to God instead, both Ella and Cora position their songwriting as an endeavor not for personal gain or recognition but in the service of a higher power. Though their spiritual experience is undoubtedly real, like the self-effacing narrator in the "Fool in the Mirror" trope, this is also a rhetorical technique that brings the self and the person into alignment, mitigating any possible perception that they might be overstepping societal rules that restrict the gendered "person" from displaying self-importance or arrogance.

Ella also attributed her spiritual visions to God, and often wrote them down in the same notebooks as her songs, at other times scribbling them on napkins or whatever she could find at the time. But she reported a marked difference in how she "received" the two forms. "I just received them [her songs], yeah. I would just start thinking of a pretty song, but no, when I see a vision, honey, it's just like I'm right there looking at it." While her visions were pure and direct transmissions, her songs required more effort from her. She said she needed to "think" of them, "concentrate" or "work them out." Some songs would remain unfinished, and she would return to their written pages later to continue working on them. "I had so much, so much good times writing the songs and working them out. Because you know, you can't just write them down. It takes so long to work them out." Though both her songs and visions are divinely inspired, her songs are her distinct creation and retain her authorial mark.

Shirley, Ella, and Cora all report experiencing a physical sensation when singing their original gospel songs and feel it to be an indication not only that their work is divinely inspired but also a direct message from God telling them the song should be shared. Singing transforms these songs from a written text of the internal self to an embodied experience and physical sensation, integrating self and person, body and mind. Ella described an instance where she was playing her song "Visions of Victory" and experienced physical feelings common to Pentecostal worship:

I got to play on it and when I get to a certain part of that, honey, my hands just [she demonstrates her hands shaking and laughs] and it's the same way with "Amazing Grace." I play that song and when I get down to that second verse—"the hour I first believed," my hands won't stay on that thing, and I played that and I thought, "Oh my." And then I started playing "Visions of Victory," and boy oh boy, my hands just didn't want to stay on those keys I was getting so blessed and I thought, "Well, I've got to bring that song out alive because I know that's what God was telling me. That one needs to be revived."

Shirley reported, "I do love to sing if nobody's around. I like to sing praise songs. That feeling will come over you and you just want to praise him. So I can really belt it then, by myself!" For her, gospel was subject to different rules and afforded more freedom than her more intimate poetry and songs inspired by past life events. "One of my favorite songs of all times that I've written is called 'Behold the Lamb' and I can't even say that title without—just my whole body goes in chills. And that's the one song I've ever written that I *wish* was performed. In churches or something, you know. Because it really has got a lot of spirit to it. I'm sure you understand that sometimes you feel like it was divine-inspired?" In Shirley's praise songs she was channeling a higher spirit outside of herself, more universal and less of her authorial hand. Perhaps this is why she wished they could be shared. Cora shared a similar sentiment, "I wrote a song that has a little 'Lean on Me' tingle to it. Now when I do that one, I am off in la-la land! I am high on praise then! And I get that joy out of me and God. All the time. I guess that's why I've never put them out there."[56] Both Shirley and Cora employ the gospel music they have composed as a form of devotion and prayer, experiencing personal satisfaction and religious connection through regular rehearsal of their songs.

As Patricia Sawin and Danille Christensen have found in their work with women ballad singers and scrapbookers, respectively, one common strategy women use to signal their creative talent while simultaneously performing socially required and gendered humility is through reported speech—quoting what others have said about their work rather than stating it directly.[57] When Ella talked about her creative ability, she credited God rather than any inherent personal trait, and presented any commendation of her musical skill by relaying what others in her community said rather than risk being perceived as boastful. She said, "But God just absolutely, he just blessed me with a talent to know how to play and sing. Like one of the guys at church, he was so amazed when I was playing the piano and singing and he says, 'My goodness!' He says the talent to play is talent but he says to be able to sing and play and keep on all them keys!" In doing so, Ella centered her fellow church member as the subject and decentered herself, even while speaking about her own musical skill.

By framing these praise songs as God's gift intended to be shared with others, Cora and Ella feel permitted to perform their work where they otherwise might be wary of drawing attention to themselves. While I believe that they truly have experienced the feeling that their writing has been given to them by God, this deflection may have also ensured their writing practice was acceptable within a working-class, patriarchal, and deeply religious culture where women's roles are often limited to private domestic spaces and relational family roles. Cora told me, "They're songs that I *need* to do something with because I feel that being a blessing to me, they may be a blessing to someone else." She worries that performing a solo concert outside of church or a local festival could be perceived as being self-aggrandizing. She said, "I have been thinking for the last several weeks about doing a concert with a litany of all of these originals and having a concert. I don't know how I would go about it and it's not for anything but just for them to be heard. But I want to not be seen as being braggadocious." Though Cora expresses this fear the most directly, she, Ella, and Elaine all find a socially acceptable context for their creativity and talent by couching their work within their framework of service to God or the union.

"How You Feel When You Get with Good Friends and You Play": Music and Participatory Performance

Earlier in her life, Ella had the opportunity to perform and professionalize her music. She told me about how she weighed those opportunities against her faith and family and social obligations. When she was younger, she fantasized about being a country star, had opportunities to play with several bands, and says she was offered a chance to play on the Midwestern Hayride. "I started to go and do one of them Jamborees and get started in music, but my kids just meant too much to me and Tracy was just absolutely too jealous, and I knew that it wouldn't last and I didn't try it." Ella knew any public, commercial success in music would mean sacrificing her family duty, and she wasn't willing to do that. She was also reluctant to play in bars and honky-tonks due to her religious beliefs. She described an incident where she auditioned for an all-women band in Brunswick, Ohio, and was offered the job of rhythm guitarist. But when she asked the bandleader if they would be playing in churches, the woman wavered, saying that while they wouldn't want to exclude them entirely, they would be focusing on bars and clubs. That night when Ella left practice, she nearly backed into a car parked behind her, and describes feeling God grab the wheel and steer her away from the other car.

I just started thanking God and I knew why he'd done it. Because I
had decided I was not gonna join that band and God protected me
and took care of me. So I called her [the bandleader] and told her
the next day that to find somebody else, that I wouldn't do it if they
wasn't gonna play in churches and stuff. So no, that's the reason—I
could have went and I probably could have made it big, because I
had a good voice. But my kids meant too much to me and then like
I say, my husband and I wasn't gonna tear up my family for nothing.

Resistant to the potential consequences of a professional music career as
a woman and mother, Ella preferred to keep her music a nonprofessional
pursuit, shared with family, friends, and local congregations. She said, "I
loved to play for the glory of it and the beauty in it, and how you feel when
you get with good friends and you play. But when you are doing it under
pressure, pretty soon they end up taking dope or something and then the
career ends and what's it all for?" In our interview, Ella was most ebul-
lient when she spoke of playing music with friends or her son Brooksy,
whom she'd play Ray Price duets with—her on guitar and Brooksy on
bass—when her husband was away. Recalling music parties when she was
younger, she related nostalgically, "We had friends that loved music and
we'd get together almost every weekend and then especially on holidays
or birthdays or something and we'd play until one or two in the morning, because we were young and we loved it." Outside of a social context,
church was the main performance venue accessible to her, without the
risks of a touring musician's life, and offered a platform where she could
still perform while maintaining her duties to home, family, and faith.

Ella's preference for musical notation as the finished form of her songs
also aligned with her desire that her music be shared, not necessarily by
her as a performer, but more importantly in worship by others. She said,
"I have written so many songs that I just can't imagine, and if I had them,
if I had somebody to help me put some of them to music [transcribe them
to a musical staff] I would sure do it, because I think I've got some that's
really touching to people." She also valued the recordings she made and
felt that the reason people respond to her recorded songs on the CD produced by her granddaughter and grandson-in-law was because they were
blessed by God. "I said those songs were anointed by God and I know he's
watching over them and that's why they're being circulated. That's why
you seen them and liked them, you know? And we've never charged for
one. I had all them made and I've given them to friends, I've given them to

church family and I've never charged anybody for one because I just want them to be blessed." Ella's creative motivation existed outside of commercial structures, in part because community social spaces, the domestic sphere, and church were the performance venues most accessible to her, but she also chose to circumvent channels that could have brought her financial gain.

Of the four women songwriters profiled here, Elaine's music has had the highest public profile. But family and community were always Elaine's highest priority. Like Ella, Elaine knew that a full career in music was not possible with her family responsibilities, but she found a way to balance both. Comparing herself to trailblazing bluegrass musician, labor songwriter, and West Virginia native Hazel Dickens, Elaine said, "Of course, she became a legend, but I got married and had a family, which kept me from going where I could have furthered my music."[58] Elaine and her husband were also raising grandchildren and great-grandchildren, which limited her ability to travel for music. But she still used her music locally, teaching songwriting and traditional mountain songs to children at the Big Ugly Community Center in her rural home county, instructing them on how to use their individual voices to share emotion and personal experience. The liberating, empowering aspect of writing as both a way to communicate with other people and a tool for personal growth was something Elaine both found for herself through her own songwriting and advocated for others.

> I don't know who this is gonna go out to, but if there's anybody listening to this or reading this and you've got any idea that you can do anything—write a story about what you're going through, tell it, write it in a poem, just put it on paper and try to put music to it or put it on paper and try to get somebody else to put music to it. Just get it out there! Just get it out there and let people know what you're thinking. And you'll be surprised how much it will free you up and help you out. Because it did me. It made a monster out of me.

While Cora is interested in recording her original songs and is proud to receive them as gifts from God, she primarily performs in church and as the leader of a gospel music worship on the culminating Sunday of a local festival, Aunt Jennie Wilson's Pickin' in the Park. She said, "I'm blessed every year to be asked by [Aunt Jennie Wilson's] grandson to come and participate, you know? So I get the pleasure of doing it on Sunday because I do all gospel and it's a great honor because they allow me to pray over the food, and I'm like alright now! Just let me preach a little bit here!"[59] Cora expresses appreciation for the gift God gives her by using the songs as a form of holy praise, in both her private home space and with members of her congregation and local community.

The obscuring of self may be read as primarily a gendered practice, crucial for women working within a patriarchal culture, but it also aligns with vernacular approaches to music in working-class communities, where music is shared not in performative contexts but rather in participatory communal settings—a picking party on a neighbor's porch or a congregational gospel sing, where the focus is not on the adulation of a singular artist but rather on group participation in a social activity. In his book *Music as Social Life*, ethnomusicologist Tom Turino argues that participatory musical practice—as opposed to a presentational musical form where performers play for a listening audience—is focused inward to the community of participants, devalues individual virtuosity, and presents music less as a commodity than as a social process. Though Turino applies this model to music events, like square dances or old-time jams, it is applicable to how Shirley, Ella, Cora, and Elaine approach music as a resource or experience to be shared in social contexts, even though their songwriting is an individual and personal pursuit.[60] They are uninterested in becoming virtuosic stars but rather hope to engage with others socially through collective musical experience. This value of music as a participatory form could explain why Cora feels comfortable "tooting her own horn" when it comes to the books she's written but deflects authorship of her songs, describing herself instead as a channel for the music she "receives." In various ways for all four women, music is a collective practice to be shared in social contexts—in church, at union events, family gatherings, or in a notebook—with a "public private audience." Music is the arena where the self and person are negotiated and performed within communal contexts.

Shirley Campbell, Ella Hanshaw, Cora Hairston, and Elaine Purkey all engage in their songwriting practice within an Appalachian tradition of women's writing, using rhetorical strategies and framing devices to ensure that their work is socially acceptable in the context of their gender and social standing. They also write and perform outside of a commercial music industry, even a local one. But they are working within a working-class culture that is imbued with participatory music. Commercial country, soul, and gospel—particularly of the 1960s and 1970s—are their textual and musical reference points: Bill Withers (himself from a southern West Virginia working-class background), Loretta Lynn, Merle Haggard, and Mahalia Jackson, among others. In their communities, music is most often engaged in in participatory, community-based contexts—whether hymns in church, a jam in a private home, or part of a union rally. The songs of Shirley, Ella, Cora, and Elaine draw on and are of that culture, in conversation with commercial music and church hymns, and based on a participatory relationship with music making, within a social context of dangerous and arduous manual labor (by themselves or their husbands), the threat of poverty, shifting gender relations, and hierarchies of gender, race, and class. Aaron Fox writes, "Working-class culture is in large part shaped in response to the commodification of human agency in industrialized capitalist society—that is to say, in response to 'class' in all its sociological and lived complexity."[61] Though restricted in some ways by their gender, Shirley, Ella, Cora, and Elaine have found opportunities to engage in creative work while simultaneously rejecting the commodification of it. As a personal endeavor contextualized within their respective local communities of family, church, and union, Shirley's, Ella's, Cora's, and Elaine's writing resists being exported or commercialized, in the midst of a place from which resources—including cultural ones—have long been exported without benefit to those who live there.

To be sure, certain limitations and a lack of agency are imposed on the creative opportunities of working-class women like Shirley, Ella, Cora, and Elaine, but that is not the whole story. I read their work as a resistance to a structure of extraction and patriarchal confinements. These four women have been immersed to varying degrees in a "public private" practice based on a participatory approach to music that has allowed them to retain ownership and control over their own work by restricting access to their notebooks in "public private" conversations where they could determine how their work is contextualized, and by limiting their performances to church, union, and other community-based venues. This creative production as a mediation between the "self" and the "person" has enabled them to craft new identities—those of poet, singer, musician, organizer, or prayer warrior—and envision roles for themselves that appear acceptable within, but simultaneously resist, patriarchal and class domination. Their songwriting, whether a gift from God, a gift to their community, or a gift to their own self-worth, functions to offer praise, celebrate joy, create a working future, or provide personal catharsis. With their notebooks, pens, words, songs, and performance, they stake territory, singing sometimes loudly to an audience, sometimes quietly to themselves, "I exist; we exist."

THERE GOES MY BIG EVERYTHING

When Shirley Campbell writes of food, it is often the regionally specific fare she ate growing up or among the Reed's and Campbell's Appalachian migrant community, as in her parody of the country song "There Goes My Everything," which Jack Greene made a hit in 1966.

(To the tune of " There Goes My Everything)

There Goes My Big Everything

I hear footsteps slowly, stomping,
As they shake across a weakened, wooden floor.
And a voice is rasping, loudly:
Deadbeat, this will be good-by forevermore.

Chorus :
There goes my biscuits and gravy.
There goes my fat-back and greens.
There goes my blackberry cobbler.
There goes my big everything.

As my fingers turn the cookbook pages,
I remember when I used to eat at four.
Now, the flapjacks that once held me through the morning
Have just floated up and out the kitchen door.

2nd Chorus:
There goes my chicken and dumplings.
There goes my cornbread and beans.
There goes my apple-pan-dowdy.
There goes my big everything.
There goes my strawberry shortcake.
There goes my big everything

Opptional Fade Out:
I guess it's Big Mac's again tonight,
Or, maybe the Colnel.
I sure could go for some homefries.

By: Shirley White Campbell

FIGURE 2.2. "There Goes My Big Everything," written by Shirley White Campbell, date unknown.

LITTLE BLACK BOOK

"Little Black Book" is one of Ella Hanshaw's secular country songs, composed when she was in her early twenties.

I know I'm not listed in your little black book
But I'm always in your kitchen when it's time to cook
I'm not the one in your dreams every night
Thought I'm bathing your babies to kiss them goodnight.

    Chorus:
I hold my head up like the proud girl I am
Holding to my dreams like some heartbroken clown
Praying each night your love will return
But like Cinderella I wonder how long.

If I had the money you spend on your flings
I could pass it around and buy me new things
Then Cinderella could go to her ball
And find her Prince Charming and bring him back home.

    Chorus

Yes, like Cinderella, I wonder how long.

THE DREAM

In Cora Hairston's poem "The Dream," she twines the personal with the universal, imagining how her enslaved great-great-grandmother might react to Barack Obama's presidency.

I had a dream one night of a day
I thought I'd never live ta see
A man that is President a da United States
With color, just like me.
Da dream was so real an' exciting ta me
For as a slave, I was not free
How in da world could dis be, huh!
I saw myself in my dress a blue
As da parade in yo' honor was passing through.
Oh my God, can dis be real?
Us colored folks getting a thrill,
From toil an' soil, sweat an' tears
Hard, hard labor down through da years?
Oh Lawd, don't let me wake
An' find dat dis was all fake,
Dis kind a joke, I just can't take!
A fool a me my dream would make.
Well, thank God I did awake
To find out it was not a fake.
You see it was my great-great-grandmother's dream
She had talked about when she was a teen
She had told my grandmother as a child
Just wait, you'll see it in a lil' while.
To my mother the dream was passed,
And on to me the dream came true at last, at last.

WAYFARIN' WORKER (EXCERPT)

Elaine Purkey imagines a working-class uprising originating with a West Virginia miner who withdraws his labor as union brothers and sisters follow suit. Her songs present a vision of working-class solidarity that comprises both men and women, and is multiracial, national, and in some cases international. In her song "Wayfarin' Worker," set to the melody of "Wayfaring Stranger," she aligns the fate of an Appalachian coal miner suffering from black lung with that of a woman vineyard worker in California poisoned by pesticides and a Cuban migrant who is seeking work and about to be deported. In the last verse, they speak together as one.

I'm the working class of every nation
All over this world, struggle is the same
They take our lives and give us nothing.
They all get rich and we're to blame.
It's time to stand and band together
Workers of this world should all unite
No one could stop so great an army
No more rich man's laws, no more government lies.

CHAPTER 3

Up Here You Use What You've Got

Foodways and the Elasticity of
Tradition in the Swiss Community
of Helvetia, West Virginia

IT'S A CHILLY FRIDAY MORNING in February 2016 and I'm standing over a cast-iron pot of hot oil in Eleanor Betler's farmhouse kitchen, just outside Helvetia, West Virginia. Simon and Garfunkel's familiar refrain, "They've all—come—to look for A-merrr-ica!" rings out over the oil sizzles, and the bright kitchen smells of grease and sugar. I hold a long-stemmed tool that resembles a branding iron with an eight-petaled floral design on the end. It looks like a miniature stained-glass window without the glass. Eleanor takes my picture with my camera, her terrier Jazzy bouncing around at my feet. Sharon Rollins and Linda "Bunch" Smith peer over my shoulder as I dip the iron first into the hot oil, then into a bowl of batter, and again into the grease. A few seconds later, the batter releases from the iron as a fully formed rosette, delicate and crispy, with a rounded top and a hollow shell on the bottom. "There you go!" Sharon exclaims. "Keep the iron hot, dip the grease off of it, and don't cover it up," says Eleanor. "Those are the three main rules of this game!"

Eleanor Betler, now eighty-one, is energetic and spritely, with short-cropped white hair and eyes that crinkle when she smiles. She was born in 1940 and raised in Cleveland, Ohio, but her mother's family settled in Helvetia in 1872, and Eleanor spent the summers of her childhood there at her grandparents' home. "I never wanted to go back to the city. Although [Cleveland] was lovely at the time and a nice place to be, I was a Helvetia girl, all my life."

Helvetia, population fifty-nine, is a Swiss community nestled along the Buckhannon River in a high mountain valley of Randolph County, West Virginia. The remote village was settled in 1869 by a group of Swiss and German families who first immigrated to Brooklyn, New York, during the Civil War. In Brooklyn, these families belonged to a Swiss and German mutual aid society called the Gruetli Verein, and together sought a place where they could live freely and practice their respective crafts and occupations. One of their members had done some surveying in West Virginia and spoke of the large tracts of land, beautiful mountains, streams full of fish, and plentiful forests of game. The group eventually found affordable acreage for sale in the area and established a village, calling it Helvetia, the Latin name for Switzerland.

To call the presence of a Swiss community in a remote area of the Mountain State unlikely would be to deny the history and impact of the waves of immigration and relocation to Central Appalachia by diverse ethnic and cultural groups. In fact, there were several Swiss settlements scattered across the region in the late nineteenth century.[1] But what makes Helvetia unusual is not only the celebration of this shared heritage and physical preservation of the colorful alpine village with its Cheese Haus, Honey Haus, gingerbread-adorned Hütte Swiss Restaurant, and two dance halls, but also something less tangible. There is a creative enchantment about the place, gleaned from the whimsical hand-painted signs peppered throughout the village, the camaraderie of the Helvetia Star Band (now in its fifth generation), and the friendly competition on display in the canned goods, embroidery, and prize tomato entries at the annual agricultural fair.[2] The intimacy of this network, whose families have been neighbors, friends, and colleagues for generations, yields its own form of magic.

When Eleanor married her husband, Bud, in 1961, she got her "dream come true," and they moved to the old Helvetia hilltop farm where they kept hogs, beef cattle, sheep, a dairy cow, and maintained a small apple orchard.[3] She's lived there ever since. Though Bud passed away in 2010, Eleanor remains in the comfortable farmhouse where they raised their children. A black-and-white photo of a young Eleanor cutting cinnamon bread hangs next to a tile trivet that reads "Eleanor's Kitchen." She serves as the community's historian, managing the Helvetia History Project and Archives housed in a log cabin schoolhouse adjacent to the public library on the historic square. Eleanor, Sharon, and Bunch are all members of the Helvetia Farm Women's Club, which leads community service projects and hosts fundraisers like the annual ramp supper. Today they are gathered in Eleanor's kitchen to make rosettes and *hozablatz*, or "knee patches," a crispy rectangular fried dough "thin enough to be able to read a newspaper through," to serve to locals and guests at tomorrow's square dance (plate 3.1).

I'm here to document that process for the West Virginia Folklife Program and the Southern Foodways Alliance Oral History Program—the first of my fieldwork trips in over a year-long project documenting the foodways and seasonal celebrations of the community. Though I've been visiting Helvetia since 2011, interviewed Eleanor over the phone the year prior in 2015, and recognize Sharon from her volunteer work at the Hütte, this is my first time meeting the three women in person.

The Saturday square dance the women are cooking for is not just one of the regular monthly dances held in the Helvetia Community Hall but also part of the community's pre-Lenten holiday, *Fasnacht* (translating as "Fast night")—an amalgam of the traditional Swiss Fasnacht and Sechelauten, a rite of spring. Helvetia's take on the event is, like most things in Helvetia, a homespun affair, where locals and visitors don homemade papier-mâché masks and process in a lampion parade between the two town dance halls (participants carry small paper lanterns a distance of about two blocks). They also compete for miniature handmade felt Swiss flags in a mask contest, enjoy homemade fried pastries; square dance, schottische, and waltz under an effigy of Old Man Winter (see plate 3.2); and at the stroke of midnight, cut the old man from the rafters and burn him on the bonfire outside to jeers and a triumphant a capella rendition of John Denver's "Country Roads."[4]

In Helvetia's early days, Fasnacht was an insular local event in which residents would go "begging" at each other's homes, indulging in the foods and activities they'd refrain from during Lent.[5] "The reason we make these deep-fat-fried treats is because it's Fat Tuesday, before the Lenten fast," Eleanor tells me. "They would eat rich foods for the last time for forty days. People don't do that so much anymore in general, but here [in Helvetia] it was a general thing. They didn't dance during Lent and they had a big celebration before Ash Wednesday. And then it was

shut off until Easter Sunday." In the 150-plus years since the town's founding, the Swiss traditions practiced by Helvetians have evolved in various
ways. During the World Wars when societal anti-German sentiments ran
high, the community decided it would be best to downplay their Swiss-
German heritage, wanting instead to express the pride they felt as American citizens.[6] Around the time of the town's centennial in the late 1960s,
Helvetia native and town matriarch Eleanor Mailloux (1917–2011) and her
friend Delores Baggerly began an initiative to reinvigorate the community's Swiss traditions, establishing the Hütte Swiss Restaurant, producing
a community cookbook, and turning Fasnacht from a private event to a
more public celebration.

Today, Fasnacht doesn't feel so much like a last hurrah before a period
of austerity as it does a bright spot in the dead of winter, intended both
to reinforce locals' cultural identity and to lure tourists to the secluded
town, providing a much-needed economic boost during the sparse winter months (see chapter 8 on how Fasnacht has recently attracted new
attendees through the video game *Fallout 76*). Nevertheless, the tradition
of eating fried rosettes, hozablatz, and yeast-raised donuts has remained
part of the Fasnacht celebration. Members of the Farm Women's Club
serve the treats on a side table during the dance as attendees jockey to get
to them; they disappear quickly.

Sitting open on Eleanor Betler's table is a well-worn copy of *Oppis Guet's
Vo Helvetia* (*Something Good from Helvetia*), a cookbook of community recipes collected by Mailloux for the Helvetia centennial in 1969, the year
after Fasnacht was revived as a public holiday.[7] The book is a dog-eared
standby in all Helvetia home kitchens and is still printed by the town's
Alpenrose Garden Club and sold at the Kultur Haus (which serves as the
village general store, post office, and Fasnacht mask museum). In addition
to Swiss German recipes like horseradish *klossli* (dumplings), *stollen* (fruit
and raisin bread), and *bölleflade* (onion pie) and instructions for making
homemade dandelion, potato-raisin, and elderberry wines (Helvetians
are known to be prodigious wine makers), the collection also includes
medicinal remedies, "household hints" and cures, such as directions for
a plantain liniment, "How to Wash Black Stockings," and "In Case You're
Struck by Lightening [*sic*]."[8] Many of the recipes assume access to equipment and ingredients of farm life: a wood-burning stove, long kitchen
tables, tallow, cracklins, and "the 5th or 6th milking from a fresh cow."[9]
In addition to its function as a cookbook, *Oppis Guet's Vo Helvetia* is also
something of a collective sensory memoir. Woven through the recipes are

accounts of music and sausage-making parties, fresh bread and a "hunk of country butter" left in a neighbor's mailbox, and a walk through "the green meadow alive with violets and into the Hemlock wood where the thrushes sang."

As texts written as instructions to be enacted at some future date, recipes are the vehicle through which the memories in *Oppis Guet's Vo Helvetia* become tangible in the present. The recipe for rosettes is listed just under a recipe for "Old Fashioned Fruit Cake," both originating from the kitchen of Alma Burky. "The Rosette iron we use came from Switzerland with the Burkies [*sic*] a century ago. It is well aged!!!" reads the typed headnote. Underneath the recipe, Eleanor has written an addendum in her looped cursive, "My Grandma, Anne McNeal told me her secret to crispiness is adding about a Tablespoon of bourbon." To the ingredient list of cream, eggs, and flour, she's added "1 T. whisky." While the necessary ingredients are minimal, the process requires some practice, not to mention the special rosette iron. As is often the case with community cookbooks whose intended audience is the home cooks of the community itself, the instructions are sparse: "Beat cream, eggs and flour together until light. Heat fat very hot for deep frying. Rosette iron should be in the fat heating at the same time. Dip hot Rosette iron into batter, almost to the top edge of iron. Put immediately into hot fat and remove iron as soon as Rosette slips off. Brown on both sides (this is easier than it sounds— and is great fun). Put on paper and sprinkle with sugar." There's no specification of type of fat or sugar, nor timing or temperature (Eleanor keeps her oil at 385 degrees Fahrenheit and has a staple indicating that temperature on her thermometer so she remembers). Though to an outsider the recipe's terseness could feel like frustrating omissions, this assumption of knowledge, communicated through the text, is a way of ensuring that rosettes are not parsed from their local story, oral history, and personal relationships. In Helvetia, rosette-making is a process best learned in person rather than from a book. Eleanor remembers her aunt and mother making rosettes for Easter and when she visited in the summer, but when Eleanor moved to Helvetia after she got married, she relearned how to make them from her family members. "Fasnacht needed them, so I went down to my grandmother and her older daughter to renew my knowledge. And I just like doing it. . . . I need to teach Jerianne so she can do [it] for the next generation."

The lack of specificity in the recipe inspires conversation, even for those in the know. As Bunch stacks the cooled rosettes and prepares to dust them with sugar, she asks Eleanor what type to use. "Some of the people use regular and some use powdered sugar," Eleanor replies. I chime in, "I remember last year when I interviewed you, you said, 'Well, you use what you've got!'" "That's right!" Eleanor says, and the women agree, completing each other's sentences. "Up here you use what you've got, because . . ." "Or what your neighbor has!" "You have to improvise once in a while." "You can't get to the grocery store very often." They decide to sprinkle powdered sugar on the rosettes, noting that if they don't like them this time, they'll try something different next year. They're casual about the process, negotiating the various steps each time they gather to make them. But Eleanor, who grew up with the fried confections and learned the process from her family matriarchs, is deferred to as the authority. When the Betlers were raising and butchering hogs on the farm, Eleanor fried her rosettes in lard—they had plenty on hand. But now that she doesn't keep pigs, lard is expensive to purchase, and she only buys it to make soap. She made the switch to frying rosettes in vegetable oil not just for economy but also for health reasons. "Not that deep-fat-fried is healthy. Whatsoever," she wryly explains. In the evolution of her rosette-making process, Eleanor enacts folklorist Henry Glassie's definition of tradition as "the creation of the future out of the past."[10] While ingredients, techniques, styles, and tools change according to time and context, the tradition persists, with Eleanor as its creative agent.

With a pint of medium cream, six eggs, two cups of flour, and, if you're smart, a tablespoon of whiskey, the recipe yields a deceptively large quantity of rosettes. When I asked the women how much it makes, Sharon responded, "A bucketful! It's the way we measure here." "That's the Swiss way of measuring," Eleanor jested. Indeed, she, Sharon, and Bunch stacked them in a large bucket—the high sides protect the delicate fritters and make it easy to transport them (see fig. 3.1). The recipe yield indicates that in Helvetia, rosettes are intended for a large gathering—a special occasion that will feed many. Aside from Fasnacht, Eleanor sometimes makes them for Easter, but only when she has company. "It's too much for just me," she says. She's also made double batches for Helvetian weddings. Rosettes are a social food—a treat you never eat alone—and, as the recipe denotes, their creation is part of their communal nature. While Fasnacht has evolved from a private holiday to a celebration shared with tourists, the fried treats made by the women of the community are a subtle yet potent symbol of tradition and ritual. They are an edible link to Helvetian heritage, whether the consumer is from Helvetia or away. When you

FIGURE 3.1. A bucketful of rosettes made by Eleanor Betler, Sharon Rollins, and "Bunch" Smith, February 5, 2016. Photo by the author.

take a bite of a delicate, handmade rosette, you partake in the place and, consciously or not, experience a sensory manifestation of its domestic history. Eleanor put it more practically: "Food is a very important part of any Helvetia event, because when you come at least an hour from any large town, you want food! It's what really brings people here."

Helvetians have an extremely local identity. They're Helvetians first, West Virginians and Appalachians second. Eleanor Betler told me, "We are not a typical Appalachian culture, but we are part of its history and a living history at that." In Helvetia, food is a carrier of that localized identity. The Hütte Swiss Restaurant, which sits like a golden welcome beacon on the town's main intersection and confluence of the Left and Right Forks of the Buckhannon River, is a community institution and the public face of the town (see plate 3.3). Open daily since the late 1960s and now owned by a collective of Mailloux's descendants, its menu offers a range of Swiss dishes from *rosti* (fried potatoes) to *sauerbraten* (sour beef) to homemade sauerkraut. Many of the recipes came from those Mailloux collected from local residents and are prepared with influences from other Southern Appalachian traditions and flavors that Mailloux brought home from her travels abroad. Helvetia Cheese was commonly made at home by Helvetia's first residents and then was made and sold by several local farm women, including the Balli sisters.[11] In the 1970s, Eleanor Mailloux's daughter Heidi Arnett produced it out of the Cheese Haus. Now the restaurant buys a similar baby Swiss from an Amish farm in Ohio. (Some Helvetia residents occasionally still make the cheese at home, though the fresh milk the recipe calls for is no longer easy to find. Though Helvetia was once known for its Swiss herds, today it is home to only one dairy cow.)

In its fifty years of operation, the Hütte has played a crucial role in the preservation and continuation of the community's foodways traditions, shared narrative, and cohesion. As then-college student Morgan Rice, who waitresses at the restaurant and whose father is a co-owner, told me in 2016, "With the Hütte, it wouldn't be the same if people came to Helvetia or if I come home from college and I don't smell the sausage cooking or I don't smell the chicken cooking because that just gives it the Swiss feel." Locals treat the restaurant like their communal dining room, stopping by the kitchen to serve themselves a cup of coffee in the morning, placing their orders from memory (no need for the menu), and gathering around one of the Hütte's woodstoves for a glass of homemade wine and an impromptu music session when there's a power outage. The restaurant is also an ad hoc living community museum. The walls are filled with old black and white photographs taken by early Helvetia photographers Gottfried and Walter Aegerter, vintage farm tools, cloth-bound books, and other antiques bought by Mailloux and Baggerly when some families sold off their farms.[12] Written alongside the fare on the Hütte menu is an inscription conveying that the communally curated physical space of the restaurant is just as important as the food: "The Hütte is not just another restaurant; rather, it is an emotional happening. . . . Walking into the little dining room is like stepping into the warm inviting kitchen of some loved one out of the past." As the menu notes, all of the Hütte's furnishings and decorations were bequeathed by former Helvetia residents—there is "Grandma" Fischer's old cupboard, Mrs. Karlen's stove, and John Martis's cherry brandy jug. The Hütte is meaningful as a physical space because it preserves items from many of the local residents, living and deceased. Betty Biggs, a Helvetia native, noted that her mother's and sister's embroidery work still hangs in the restaurant, and some of her own hand-carved chairs serve as guest seats. But the Hütte is also an "emotional happening" because of the role it plays in the community, transcending the function of a typical restaurant. "Kids will be out playing," Biggs said, "and they'll get all hot and thirsty and go to the door and they'll say, 'Can I have a piece of bread?' or 'Can I have a can of pop?' and of course, they just give it to them, you know? And the local fishermen will be out fishing and if they don't happen to have any fish eggs with them, they'll stop [at the Hütte] and say, "Oh, give me some bait," and they'll give them some cheese or corn. And you know if you run out of something you can run to the Hütte and borrow it if they have it."[13]

IN MY WORK, which regularly takes me into communities not my own, I'm accustomed to being humbled, finding ease in unfamiliarity. I ask questions—whether intentionally or inadvertently—whose answers must sometimes seem self-evident to insiders. But a seemingly simple inquiry can be the key that unlocks an interview, an opportunity for us to reach a common understanding and deeply consider a seemingly basic element of a cultural practice or identity, something an insider might take for granted or has never fully explained before. New understandings arise out of our conversations, just as they do in the making of a recipe. In both, there's a list of steps to follow, but the improvisation required in a conversation or a cooking process is what makes the final product. Both are creative remakings of the world. Sometimes, as with Bunch, Sharon, and Eleanor, that remaking happens between individuals within the same community, but there's also a value in dialogues between those of different backgrounds. In the negotiation of understanding, revelations emerge that allow us to conceptualize or understand our own identity, culture, or work in a new way. Like the process of making rosettes and the dialogic evolution of tradition constantly negotiated by communities, collaborative ethnographic interviews and fieldwork are informal conversations, discussed and moderated at each step. There's a prescribed structure, but the interpretation is a product of the specific individuals involved, unique every time.

In Helvetia, my fieldwork has consisted of multiple visits, starting in 2014 and spread across several years, with focused work specifically related to foodways traditions and seasonal celebrations for a little over one year in 2016. I recorded interviews with foodways practitioners—Hütte cooks and servers, home cooks and bakers like Eleanor Betler, Ramp Supper volunteers, foragers, ramp diggers, cheese makers, and wine makers. For a *Bitter Southerner* piece on my experience of Helvetia's seasonal celebrations, I asked local filmmakers Clara Lehmann (Eleanor Mailloux's granddaughter) and Jonathan Lacocque to produce a short film focusing

on the daily life of Helvetia—capturing those moments only a local is
privy to. It was an ideal complement to my narrative written from the
perspective of a visitor documenting the town during its public events.
Ultimately Clara and Jonathan chose to forgo payment for the production
of the video; they offered it to me, and together we decided to donate it to
the Helvetia Farm Women's Club as a small token of thanks and reciproc-
ity for all their work hosting and volunteering at the events I wrote about.

I've also spent a lot of time in Helvetia without an audio recorder or
camera, just observing and participating—helping cut ham for the ramp
dinner, judging the float contest during the Community Fair parade, playing fiddle with Vernon Burky in the Star Band Hall, allowing Eleanor to
document me as I first dipped the rosette iron into the fat, then batter,
then fat. Some of the most valuable work was informal—those conversations over glasses of homemade wine or a Hütte rosti that unconsciously
fostered trust and friendship. I also did archival research on my own, the
results of which I brought back to the community as information and
questions, the reactions and answers to which deepened my understanding, and, so it seems, informed how my consultants contextualize their
own traditions.

When I first wrote about rosettes for National Public Radio, some
readers commented that rosettes are not in fact Swiss but Scandinavian.
Eleanor said, "The rosettes, I don't even know if that's a Swiss thing. Well,
it has to be because everybody, every family has a big rosette iron that
they brought from Switzerland, so it must have been very important." I
figured that they could have both Swiss and Scandinavian roots, considering the history of Western European and Scandinavian migration and
travel. When I looked up *rosettes* in the *Oxford Companion to Sugar and
Sweets*, though, I found out that the migratory patterns and origins of
rosettes may be wider than I imagined. Adam Balic writes, "The fritters
are known as *rosetbakkelser* (rosettes) in Norway, *struvor* in Sweden, and
dok jok in Thailand [which have black and white sesame seeds in the batter, along with tapioca and rice flour]. Turkey has *demir tatlisi* (iron pud-
ding), Tunisia *chebbak el-janna* (windows of paradise), and Kerala *achap-
pam*. Afghani fritters are called *kulcha-e-panjerei* (window biscuits); in
Indonesia they are known as *kembang goyang* (swaying flowers)."[14] Other
analogs include Colombian *solteritas con crema* and Iranian *nan-e pan-
jerehi*, which are made with cardamom and rosewater. Sri Lankan *kokis*
or *koekjes* call for rice flour, coconut milk, and turmeric and are fried in
coconut oil. When I asked Eleanor if she knew of these rosette equivalents

in other cultures, she said she wasn't surprised—growing up in Cleveland in a Slavic neighborhood, she often identified similarities between her family's Irish and Swiss heritage, the traditions of her Slavic neighbors, and those of other immigrant communities in the city. Mirroring the symbol of the rosette pattern with eight lines radiating out from a single center, connected by a common circle, rosettes connect Helvetia to cultural communities across the globe.

In her essay, "Moulds for Shaping and Decorating Food in Turkey," food historian Priscilla Mary Isin notes that fritters shaped with long-stemmed patterned irons date back at least five centuries; they are first mentioned in print in 1570 by the Italian Renaissance chef Bartolomeo Scappi. Many varieties of fried pastries, whether made with an iron or not, can be traced to the Middle Ages, when open-fire cooking was more common and accessible than oven baking. I imagine this may be why they were popular in the log cabin kitchens of early Helvetia too. A singular point of origin for rosettes and their kin has not been pinpointed, but Isin posits that they may have originated in the Islamic world, possibly rural Turkey, and spread from there. In some cases, fritters came to areas through colonization, as was the case with Sri Lankan *koekjes*, which Dutch colonists brought to the country in the mid-seventeenth to late eighteenth centuries. The resemblance between cattle branding irons and rosette irons may not be coincidental; in the city of Van and its surrounding areas in western Turkey, each family had a distinctive fritter iron pattern, comparable to livestock branding symbols indicating ownership by a particular family. These custom irons were fashioned by local blacksmiths to the specifications of each family. Adam Balic notes that in Europe the irons were sometimes made in the form of coats of arms, and in England they were called "stock fritters" or "fritters of arms."[15]

While Eleanor Betler doesn't recall any familial proprietary rosette irons in Helvetia, coat of arms symbols are signature elements in Helvetia's visual culture. The exterior of the community hall that houses the monthly square dances, as well as Fasnacht, the Ramp Supper, the Community Fair, and other local events, is adorned with wooden hand-painted coats of arms that symbolize the Swiss cantons of each original family. Helvetia also has a signature crest, created by Eleanor Mailloux. The Swiss cross appears in the upper left corner on a red background, with a heart and flower on the opposite side, painted in green and yellow. Clara Lehmann and Jonathan Lacocque's Helvetia- and Chicago-based film production company is named Coat of Arms Post, an allusion to the symbol's significance in Lehmann's hometown. The company sells its coat of arms–themed card decks at the Kultur Haus.

When I visited Helvetia for the Maple Syrup Festival in nearby Pickens in the spring of 2017, I stopped by the Helvetia Archives and Museum table, where Eleanor Betler was sitting with fellow historians Anna May Chandler and Cheryl Mail. I told them about the Turkish fritter irons and their distinctive family patterns. "It's like our porch railings!" Anna excitedly replied, explaining that when the first families built their homes in Helvetia, each had a particular baluster pattern on its porch railing, indicating whose home it was. She pulled up over a dozen photos on the archive computer, each depicting a family's unique baluster design.[16] The Burkys' feature a heart cut out of the center of each baluster; the Koerners' are designed in a wide hourglass; and what's thought to be the Kerlen/Kuenzler families' are shaped like an angel's harp, mirrored on the top and bottom. Even relative newcomers, like Dave Whipp, who moved to Helvetia after retirement, have adopted the tradition—his balcony balusters form two faces in profile, creating a wine glass between them. (Dave is an avid home winemaker.)

In the early immigrant community of Helvetia, material culture was important—a value that persists today as evinced by the fine embroidery, furs, and other crafts exhibited at the annual Community Fair, the wool yarn and blankets produced by the Helvetia Shepherd's Association, and the Fasnacht masks, displayed and preserved in the Kultur Haus. Living in a rural place where a trip to the store is an hour drive or more, objects are all the more valuable. Helvetia's original families could only bring their most important possessions with them from Switzerland, so it's notable that rosette irons were among them. Today, rosette irons are found on display at the Hütte and in the homes of the McNeals (Eleanor's grandmother's family), the Burkys, the Detweilers, and the Betlers, among others. Most irons have an eight-petaled pattern, though others are shaped like stars and scalloped circles and squares. Eleanor's favorite iron came from Amish country in Ohio. It has a nonstick coating and is somewhat smaller than the one her mother got her from Pier 1 in Cleveland or her family's steel heirloom iron, so it is better suited to making a large quantity for the Fasnacht crowd (see fig. 3.2).

I also told Clara that Turkish rosette irons are patterned as family crests. Though she, like Eleanor, doesn't believe this was ever the case in Helvetia, she liked the idea, and asked a local blacksmith if he would make customized rosette irons—including a commemorative iron—to

FIGURE 3.2. One of Eleanor Betler's rosette irons, February 5, 2016. Photo by the author.

sell at the 2017 Helvetia Community Fair. While Henry Glassie asserts that tradition is the "creation of the future out of the past," I'd phrase it another way for this context—that tradition puts the past and the future in conversation. Traditions are elastic. They mutate and evolve as they encounter and enter into dialogue with influences inside and out, global and local: the grandmother who adds whiskey to the printed recipe; the friends who decide to try powdered sugar instead of granulated this year; the home cook who swaps her lard for vegetable oil and an heirloom tool for a smaller, more practical version to feed a crowd; the midwesterner folklorist who learns to make rosettes from the home cook, finds her own iron online, and introduces the treat to her friends; the granddaughter who learns about a Turkish tradition from said folklorist and adapts it for her West Virginia Swiss community. And what better symbol for this than a rosette iron—a physical embodiment of that past and future negotiation? Metal forged centuries ago will make fresh rosettes tomorrow.

CHAPTER 4

Something Deeply Rooted

The Invisible Landscape of
Breece D'J Pancake's Milton, West Virginia

"I PURPOSELY FORGET where Breece's grave is so I have to find it each time," my friend Rick Wilson tells me as we climb the hill of the Milton Cemetery one crisp October morning in 2019. In the moment, I don't understand why or how he could forget, and wonder if maybe he hasn't been here as much as he says he has. The cemetery, bounded by a chain link fence and overlooking a trailer park on one side, a row of two-story houses on the other, is small and unremarkable. It would be hard to misplace a grave here. I walk ahead and find it—or perhaps he lets me find it—at the crest of the hill on the left side, toward the back—a large rectangular tombstone spelling out PANCAKE. On the ground is an unassuming plaque, next to his mother's and father's. It reads,

BREECE D'J PANCAKE
JUNE 29 1952   APRIL 8 1979

Later, I read in a *Washington Post* article that came out the year after Breece's book was published that he had mixed the mortar for his father's gravestone himself.[1] After I take a few photos, I feel a bit awkward; reverent in the morning chill, unsure what to say. We walk away from the grave, not speaking until we're a few yards away. Rick makes me take a picture of a road sign on the cemetery's main road. He points it out from the back so I have to turn to see it. It says, "DEAD END."

BREECE PANCAKE was born in South Charleston, West Virginia, in 1952, and raised in Milton, West Virginia, then a town of about 1,500 near the Ohio and Kentucky borders. His father, Clarence, worked at the Union Carbide plant, and his mother, Helen, was a homemaker, and later a librarian. As Breece's two sisters were ten and twelve years older, he spent much of his childhood effectively as an only child, enjoying hunting, fishing, and fossil collecting. Classmates knew him as a loner, with few friends his own age—he considered his father his best friend. He began writing in elementary school and from early on was fascinated with local folklore, legends, and traditional practices he'd learned about from Milton elders and transients passing through, often incorporating their ghost stories, tales of local hangings, and ballad forms into his writing. In 1970, he entered college at West Virginia Wesleyan in Buckhannon but transferred to Marshall University in Huntington to be closer to his father, who had been diagnosed with multiple sclerosis. Upon graduating with a degree in English education, Breece had hoped to teach high school English in West Virginia but could not find a job in the state. Instead, he landed one at Fork Union Military Academy in Virginia and a year later transferred to a job at Staunton Military Academy (where one of his favorite musicians, Phil Ochs, had been a student).

Shortly after, on September 8, 1975, his father died. Then just three weeks later, his good friend and former Fork Union coworker Matthew Heard was violently killed in a car accident. These two tragedies dealt an extreme emotional blow to Breece. In a documentary about his life, Breece's mother, Helen, remarked that he had hoped Matthew would be a pillar of support during Breece's bereavement and said Matthew's death "liked to kill that boy." In 1976, Breece was awarded a fellowship to the University of Virginia's creative writing master of fine arts program. There he was known as a dedicated teacher and prodigious, diligent writer. Inspired by fellow West Virginia authors Chuck Kinder and Tom Kromer, who revealed and storied the lives of those on the margins, Breece developed a lucid, sparse, and rhythmic style, infused with sense of place—almost hauntingly so.[2] His characters can read like archetypal ghosts destined to stalk the specific places that formed them; like geologic features they belong uniquely to the circumstances of their time and location as the world moves around them.

In 1977, Breece sold a story, "Trilobites," to the *Atlantic Monthly*; it was published in the December issue that year and caught the attention of *New Yorker* fiction editor Daniel Menaker. On Palm Sunday 1979, at the age of twenty-six, Breece died from a self-inflicted gunshot. His lone collection of short stories, *The Stories of Breece D'J Pancake*, was published in 1983, containing twelve stories and a foreword by his teacher and friend, writer James Alan McPherson.[3]

RICK HAS BEEN telling me about his Breece Pancake tour of Milton—Pancake's hometown and the basis for the fictional Rock Camp, where many of the stories in his collection are set—since we first bonded over radical politics and transcendental literature five years ago, during a fieldwork trip to interview labor songwriter Elaine Purkey in Lincoln County (see chapter 2). We talked about the elements of folklore in Pancake's writing—not merely the local stories and ghost tales but the whole array of folkways he had absorbed from people in his hometown—the vernacular language and verbal art shared on porch stoops and hunting camps, the occupational culture of farmers and miners, truckers and riverboat men, the superstitions related to weather and livestock and babies cursed by the evil their mothers encountered while pregnant, and the foodways of sorghum cane boils, fish roe, and jars of moonshine.[4] This tour, Rick tells me, explores the sites—old train depots and diners, hills and holler neighborhoods, bank steps and covered bridges—as well as the more atmospheric settings that inspired many of Breece's stories, mixed with several locations from his life and death. It is a mapping and narrativization of place and memory held by a few individuals here, namely Rick and his friend Robert Jackson, a childhood buddy of Breece's. Their recounting of stories and retracing of steps has become their own folklore as vernacular stories transmitted through the oral tradition. Their honed narratives appear in other books and films about Breece on which they've advised and circulate among the handful of people they've taken on the tour.

Breece's stories are stunning and devastating—certainly worthy of focused study—but in this context I'm interested primarily in how Rick and Robert employ Breece's life and his writing, which drew heavily from local tales and fading ways of life in his hometown to evoke a sense of place that twines experience, narrative, and landscape. We can think of this sense of place vis-à-vis Henry Glassie's conception of tradition as "the creation of the future out of the past," alongside geographer Edward Relph's assertion that places are "the present expressions of past experiences and events."[5] Scholar Kent Ryden refers to this particular pairing of folklore and story within a specific location as "the invisible landscape," writing, "Folk narrative is a vital and powerful means by which knowledge of the invisible landscape is communicated, expressed, and maintained. In fact, the sense of place—the sense of dwelling in the invisible landscape—is in large part a creation of folklore and is expressed most eloquently as folklore."[6]

Rick, like Breece, is a native son of Milton and also a writer, though Rick would balk at my equating them. His work has mainly taken the form of nonfiction essays published on his blog and newspaper op-eds on social justice issues. He didn't know Breece well—they had met a few times; Breece was closer to his older brother's age—but Rick had watched with admiration and a little jealousy from back home in Milton when Breece's stories were published by the *Atlantic*. At the time of Breece's suicide, Rick was working at the public library with Breece's mother, Helen; she as a librarian, he as a custodian. Over the next several years, they became close, and he witnessed her bereavement, which she eased through her determined efforts to get Breece's short story collection published. She told Rick, "The day they put him in the ground, I swore I'd see his book published."[7] In 1983, it finally was. It has never been out of print since.

I first read the collection about two years before I'd moved to West Virginia. A friend and former teacher at a literature program in the woods of New England lent me a copy, knowing of my interest in working-class rural American fiction with a strong voice and sense of place (we had both taught and loved the work of Maine writer Carolyn Chute). But over time and without a geographic contextual foothold in which I could situate Breece's stories, they had become garbled, bleeding together in my mind. Before the day we'd picked for the tour, or as Rick called it in an email, "Breece Day," he'd instructed me to read the book again, and bring it with me on the tour. This reading was different. Maybe it's because I was now living just miles from Breece's hometown, within the "Chemical Valley," that I was now able to focus on the intricate craft of the storytelling, the raw tone that seems so effortless. Breece's stories feel like they were wrought from a single piece of wood, whittled and carved into being, with all the elements there from the start—an exercise in removal rather than construction.

BREECE'S GRAVE IS NOT in fact the first location on the tour. Rick reserves that for the site of Breece's childhood home, just yards from the Interstate 64, whose construction began when Breece was five and finished when he was eight. His family's home was torn down, and now a Wendy's sits on the site. Without much to see there, other than travelers filling up on a coffee pit stop and locals getting their morning biscuits, we just whip around the parking lot, not getting out of the truck.

After visiting the grave, we drive through a neighborhood headed toward downtown. Rick points out Breece's elementary school, which is still the public school in Milton. I imagine most kids in Milton don't go to school knowing a writer of some renown once walked the same halls, ate in their cafeteria, and searched for fossils on the playground. We park at the public library, where Rick worked with Helen, and walk past a salon and auto body shop en route to Main Street. Our next stop is the café described in Breece's most famous story, "Trilobites" (Rick says Helen pronounced it "trill-o-bites"), where the main character, Colly, sits, eyeing Tinker Reilly's little sister, and dreaming about Ginny, Colly's girlfriend, who left him behind for college in Florida. His angst manifests in his disgust for the café's cups hanging on pegs, covered in dust and the "crisp skeletons of flies" on the windowsill.[8] Breece describes a typical small town soda fountain scene, the type of place you imagine today when the *New York Times* sets its latest rural poverty porn piece at a diner in a flyover state. But now it is a Mexican restaurant, East Tenampa, or it was, a Milton resident told me, until it was allegedly raided by Immigration and Customs Enforcement and shut down in 2017. The sign still hangs outside. I peer in the storefront windows under the red awning and see that most of the furniture has been moved out, but a few tables and pieces of kitchen equipment are scattered in the middle of the tile floor. I can imagine crisp fly skeletons, roasted by the sun through the large window panes.

We continue down the street to the old Milton Bank Building on the corner. It's no longer a bank, and all but boarded up, with a "No Trespassing" sign hanging on the door. Rick stops and takes a seat on the broad cement steps, telling me that this is where he used to smoke cigarettes as a teen, performing toughness (see plate 4.1).[9] In a letter to the author of Breece's biography, Helen wrote of her husband, "Bud was drafted on a low order number regardless of two baby daughters, while young single men loafed on the Old Bank steps."[10] They were a gathering place for "generations of Milton ne'er-do-wells," and one of Breece's favorite hangouts, where he would sit and listen to old-timers' yarns.[11] Breece uses the popular loitering spot in his story, "The Honored Dead," as the place where the narrator, William Haywood, sits, waiting "for the sun to come up over the hills; wait like I waited for the bus to the draft physical." Rick, who, like Breece was a Wobbly for a stint, says that the name William Haywood refers to the cofounder of the Industrial Workers of the World; later in the story the narrator recalls his grandfather telling him of his last strike in the mines and refers to the "One Big Union." Rick believes that for that story and "A Room Forever," set in Huntington, West Virginia, Breece drew upon literature published by the Appalachian Movement Press, an independent leftist print shop based in Huntington from 1969 to 1979.[12]

As we sit on the steps, I start to realize that even my second reading of the collection did not adequately prepare me for the detail of this tour. I hadn't read closely enough. I do not remember the Old Bank steps, didn't catch the William Haywood reference. To locate these stories here in Milton, Rick is effectively laying the text over the town like a map, animating what Kent Ryden notes is "the way in which history piles up on the land, of the way terrain absorbs and recalls history, of the way narrative is an unstated component of any map and thus of any landscape."[13] Rick has an insider's knowledge, of Milton, yes, but also of Breece's Rock Camp stories he's so carefully studied. The "history" piling up on the land is not a general textbook history of Milton but a vernacular history, filtered through Rick's lived experience and his understanding of Breece's life and writing.

Poet April Bernard writes about the delusion pilgrimages to writers' homes operate under—as if one could fully comprehend a writer's psyche by merely visiting his or her former place of residence. "Here's what I hate about Writers' Houses: The basic mistakes. That art can be understood by examining the chewed pencils of a writer. That visiting such a house can substitute for reading the work. That writers can be sanctified. That private life, even of the dead, is ours to plunder."[14] I understand what she means. It's the same annoyance I feel when biopics of artists insist on painstakingly reconstructing on-screen the exact words of the artist's song or poem, as if inspiration always and only is the result of direct, literal experience.[15] But that's not what is going on here. Aside from not centering on the sites of Breece's life (his house no longer being there to visit, anyway), Rick's tour is rather a personal and intertextual recounting of the vernacular history of each place—what they are now, what they were then, and how they've changed since. The locations we're visiting inform a reading of the stories, and, conversely, the stories illuminate these places too. The tour is not a literal or direct reconstruction but a process of discovery, a dialogue between place, text, and people. I understand now why Rick wants to find the grave anew each time. In a letter to a young playwright who was interested in developing a one-man show based on "Trilobites," Helen tells him, "As for your visiting Milton—it isn't

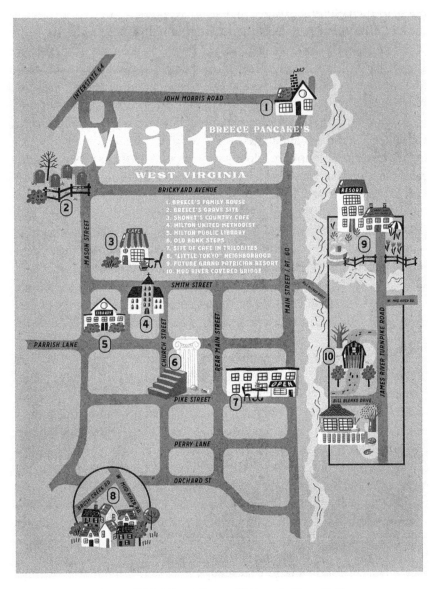

FIGURE 4.1. Map of Rick Wilson's Breece D'J Pancake Tour of Milton.
Illustration by Dan Davis.

the town Breece grew up in, Ninety % of the people are gone we knew."[16]
The fact that in the forty years since Breece wrote the Rock Camp stories,
the places and context have drastically changed doesn't subtract from
this exercise but rather enhances it. Breece's stories are deeply engaged in
the passing of time on multiple, simultaneous scales—a human lifetime,

generations, a geologic era. Reading them now, here, feels like a fitting engagement with those timelines.

After I make Rick pose for a picture on the steps, we walk back to the library and go inside. A locked glass display case in the genealogy room is the only traceable evidence in town, aside from Breece's grave, of his origins here. On the shelves are copies of the various editions of his short story collection, the biography by Thomas Douglass, and framed photographs of Breece, captioned in an expert calligraphy and detailed, if quirky, intimacy: "This was made just before his father came down with M.S. / Breece was telling his father a story totally unaware this was snapped. Christmas 1970." "Captain Breece D'J Pancake Teaching at Fork Union Military Acd. Fork Union, Va. 1974–1975. They made him shave his beard and he only wore glasses a short time." "Breece D'J Pancake in Telluride, Colo., Aug. 1978—When In The Dry was published by *Atlantic Monthly*, he was well pleased." I feel like I should linger here longer, but that's all there is—the archival collections of Breece's papers are held at West Virginia University and the University of Virginia. Rick takes me to the main reading room and shows me a picture of Helen, whom he worked with there every Tuesday and every other Saturday. "She was a storyteller—not exactly a gossip but a collector of and elaborator on local stories," he says. "You could see where Breece got it from."

We get back in the truck and drive by a few more story locations: the bridge in "The Honored Dead" where "Beck the Sport" fished with dynamite, ultimately blowing up himself and his 1951 Chevy in the process; the pool hall (now an Apostolic church) in "Salvation of Me," where Rick ate lunch in junior high school; and the riverbank along the old high school sports fields (now a pre-K playground) where the covered bridge used to be. When the narrator of "The Honored Dead" gets kicked off the high school track team for draft dodging, he sits under the bridge, waiting for practice to be over. "Every car passing over sprinkled a little dust between the boards, sifted it into my hair. I watched the narrow river roll by, its waters slow but muddy like pictures I had seen of rivers on the TV news."[17] I don't recall any of this from my second reading, and the covered bridge isn't there anymore; it's been rebuilt as "The Disneyland version," as Rick calls it, in the city's new Pumpkin Park. On the old site, the road just ends in the river, marked by a barricade, so a car can't accidentally roll right into the water. We drive along the bridge in "The Salvation of Me," where there was "enough hump that hitting it at 45 would send us airborne every time and make the buggy rock like a chair until we could get new shocks on it."[18] Rick remembers doing this as a teenager, in pursuit of a cheap thrill, but the thrill is gone—they smoothed out the road several years ago.

More and more, we seem to be not merely retracing the inspiration for the settings of these stories but mentally rebuilding them in their entirety—the childhood home, the pool hall, the covered bridge. Despite, or maybe because of this impossibility, I find myself become even more invested in this challenge, the process of uncovering and recovering this town that even then Breece described as forgotten, a holdover from a time more prosperous and hopeful. What's happening, I think, is that Milton is becoming more of a "place," to me. Where it was once another town I passed by on the interstate, now it is vivified through an interpretation of Breece's text, the vernacular narrative shared by Rick, and my own sensory experience, all rooted to a specific location; an invisible landscape, as Kent Ryden calls it, now annotates the physical landscape of this place. He explains, "For those who have developed a sense of place, then, it is as though there is an unseen layer of usage, memory, and significance—an invisible landscape . . . of imaginative landmarks—superimposed upon the geographical surface and the two-dimensional map."[19]

WE STOP ALONG the railroad tracks, where the foundation of an old building sits, overgrown with grass and saplings and covered in rotting wood pallets and other rubble. Though the building is no longer there, I recognize this from "Trilobites," as the boarded-up old depot where Colly and Ginny break in, Ginny cutting her arm on a broken window pane. The depot was abandoned in the 1970s, after the hold the C&O Railroad had on Milton was eclipsed by other industries, oil and gas among them.[20] When I go back to read the story again, I find mention of the gas wells, "pumps to suck the ancient gases," in the "field sown with timothy" across the tracks.

"Breece saw the loss of industrialization coming right before it hit," Rick says as we get back in the car. In the Rock Camp stories, "Trilobites" in particular, time seems to move on a metaphysical scale, slowly, in millennial increments. The story begins, "I open the truck's door, step onto the brick side street. I look at Company Hill again, all sort of worn down and round. A long time ago it was real craggy and stood like an island in the Teays River. It took over a million years to make that smooth little hill, and I've looked all over it for trilobites. I think how it has always been there and always will be, at least for as long as it matters."[21] Colly searches for a fossil of a trilobite, one of the earliest known marine arthropods, but finds a gastropod instead. The age of the land and its slow movement

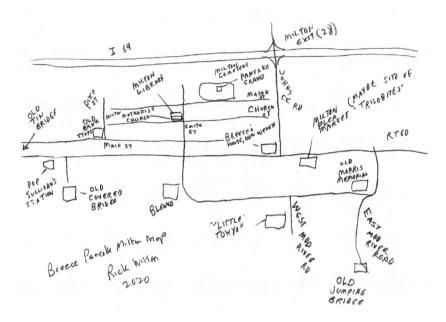

FIGURE 4.2. Rick Wilson's sketch of his Breece D'J Pancake Tour of Milton, July 30, 2020.

are ever-present in his awareness of place. He sees things—bison, ancient suns, old rivers, pterodactyls—that were once but are no longer. That reading and imagining of place, in place, is what's required too on this tour—a stratified vision, with Breece's life, layered over by what he knew of the land and this town's history, stacked over his fiction, laid on top of what Rick has learned from reading and talk and Breece's biography, presented now here to me, as we physically retrace each step. In Colly's desperation and discontentment, that protracted approach to time is a comfort, a conduit for disassociation from the minutiae of his daily reality. The last line reads, "I feel my fear moving away in rings through time for a million years."

Back in the truck, we head out to "Little Tokyo Hollow," which appears in "Salvation of Me." Rick tells me "it has a bit of a reputation in the story" and warns me not to take pictures there. "You might get Stranger with a Camera-ed," he says.[22] In this foothills neighborhood, peppered with trailers and small single-story homes, Rick feels like an outsider too but mostly doesn't want people to feel observed and uncomfortable. A three-legged dog follows our truck for a few blocks as we drive toward Colly's anchor point, Company Hill, rising up over the holler.[23]

We take the long way around back to town, driving past the Union Baptist Church, mentioned in "The Honored Dead," where Union soldiers were garrisoned during the Civil War. Along a left-hand bend in the road we pass the construction site of the future Grand Patrician Resort, owned by Jeff Hoops, whose coal company, Blackjewel LLC, filed bankruptcy in 2019 and stiffed employees out of their last two paychecks, spurring miners in Harlan County, Kentucky, to block the final shipment of Blackjewel coal from leaving town by train.[24] Currently the Grand Patrician looks more like an old army barracks than the Greenbrier competitor Hoops aspires to; the austere stone building seems fitting for a Pancake story, but the ostentatious multicolumned classic revival luxury hotel does not. It's hard to imagine it will ever be real.

RICK STOPS in a parking lot so I can snap a photo of the Rock Camp Road sign, while he calls Robert Jackson to tell him we're ready to meet for lunch. Robert, Rick tells me, was the inspiration for the character Chester in "The Salvation of Me," which he says is the only funny story in the whole Pancake collection. He's right, but even so, the comedy is brutally dark. Shonet's, Milton's greasy spoon, smells like fried apples, not from the actual fried apples they serve but from artificial potpourri, overwhelming the air. Despite the strip mall setting, the place is cozy and packed to the gills with primitives. Robert has instructed us to snag a booth in the back where we can speak freely, so my recorder and mic don't draw unnecessary attention. He comes in in a flurry, clutching a Xeroxed copy of "The Salvation of Me." He's flamboyant and warm, irreverent and hilarious, leading off with a childhood story about going fossil hunting with Breece and shitting his pants because they were too far away from a bathroom. He and Breece, both being towheads and about the same age, were often confused for each other in school and at the United Methodist Church they both attended, but they ultimately led very different lives. Robert went to New York to pursue his acting dreams, but when his wife became pregnant, they moved back to Milton, where Robert worked as a banker.

Over our "Poorman's Specials" of fried potatoes and beans and cornbread, Robert recounts the first time he read Breece's stories:

> Well, it was January, and it was a bleak midwinter and Helen gave me a copy of the book and so I persevered. It was very, very depressing. And because I knew those people that he wrote of, those people who had no hope of ever having anything better than what he described. And I couldn't think of anything that would help them.

Anyway, it was hard to get through, but . . . then you know, about two-thirds of the way through the book is this story called, "The Salvation of Me." And it starts out . . . [paraphrasing] "but Chester wasn't any ordinary shithouse mouse, he got out while the gettin' was good," and it talks somewhere in the story about, he could sing and dance and had gone I think to "Chicago that toddlin' town." And it was obviously me! [laughs] And anyway, as I read on, you know, Chester isn't a very nice person. And I thought, "Oh!" So when I saw Helen at some point in the bank, I said, "Helen, am I Chester?" and she said, "Yeeesss" [imitating her in a long drawl]. And I said, "Did Breece really hate me?" "Oh no, Robert, Breece loved you. That was the fiction."

I always thought Breece—maybe he didn't resent me, but I don't think he had a great deal of respect for the person that I was. I was, as I said, more social, I enjoyed being with people, I also enjoyed being by myself. But you know, I could rally with the troops, and I don't think he could. And that might have been sometimes hard on him, since we had been so much of the same ilk as children, then to see me be able to do some things socially that he did not want to do.[25]

Robert is both sympathetic and matter-of-fact—the years since Breece's death have left clarity where there was once raw emotion. He shares that both he and Breece had alcoholic fathers, and wonders how that may have impacted Breece's home life and upbringing. We talk about my job and Robert and Rick catch up, updating each other on their wives and families and work. Rick teases Robert for leading with a story about soiled drawers, so Robert offers another example of his and Breece's paralleled, then divergent paths:

I can remember once we were in high school on a Sunday afternoon; I was in my bedroom looking out the window at the hills. And at this point the interstate had been cut through the middle of our hills. And I could see Breece on the other side of the interstate climbing the hill to the woods. And he had a walking stick cut from, you know, just wood—not anything that had been fashioned into a walking stick. It was a tree branch. And a red bandana tied around his head, his forehead, and sort of like a sweatband, and just an army fatigue jacket of some sort. . . . That's before it was cool to be walking around in army fatigues and camouflage, and I just looked at him up there and I thought, "You are definitely marching to a different drummer." Because nobody was climbing the hillsides period, in their teen spells, and much less with a walking stick and a red bandana looking like something out of a history book from the 1800s. But this was the world he was living in, and that's where he enjoyed seeing himself as he crossed the great frontier [laughs].[26]

We finish up lunch and Robert says he wants to take us to his church, where he and Breece were both members of the Methodist Youth Fellowship, Breece begrudgingly so. We park outside and walk into the sanctuary, now empty, quiet, and unlit, except for the sunlight streaming onto the curved pews and red carpet through the lancet stained glass windows. Robert becomes contemplative, telling us that the last time he saw Breece, shortly before he died, was in that sanctuary (see plate 4.2).

It was a particular Sunday, and I was in the choir loft and he was seated in one of the old oak pews (this church was built in 1912). And he was under the huge stained glass window that lends a golden light to this sanctuary, and he was . . . he was always robust. And he wasn't heavy, but he was full, he had a full face, and you know, he wasn't muscled or defined, but he wasn't pudgy, but he was . . . just normal looking. And I was struck by, not having seen him in ten years, how emaciated and how gaunt his face had become. And of course, he was losing his hair and it was very golden still, and particularly in this golden light and his beard—he was in his late twenties at that point. Maybe twenty-seven?[27] And I remember looking at him, and just thinking he looked almost . . . I can't think of the word—ethereal? You know how when you're in a light streaming in, and the person sort of becomes diffused in the light? And I was struck by how much he had changed since the robust young boy I knew who was seventeen years old. And here he was ten years older and he did not look healthy, and he did not look happy. He looked haunted. And I didn't know why, but I could recognize the difference, yes.[28]

Outside the red brick church, I take a picture of the two old friends, Robert dapper in sunglasses, blue jeans, and a button-down green gingham shirt, Rick in his red wildcat strike tee, khakis, and running shoes. Before we part ways, Robert gives me a burned DVD of a documentary about Breece, produced by a West Virginia public television station in 1989.[29] A few days later, I watch it at home and see a younger Robert, recounting the same stories he told me, using the same turns of phrase: Breece in a red bandana and army jacket setting out for the hills, the "bleak midwinter" during which he first read the collection. Breece's mother tells a story I'd heard from Rick, about how shortly before his death, Breece said he'd had a dream where he was hunting with his cousin, and every time they'd shoot a rabbit or deer, it would pop back up and run away again. She wonders, stifling a sob, if Breece in his delusion may have thought the same thing would happen to him after he shot himself. These are the same stories that appear in Thomas Douglass's biography, and the issue of *Appalachian Heritage* dedicated to Breece.[30] The anecdotes told by the handful of people left in Milton who knew him are surprisingly few and have become honed and codified through their retelling.

In a letter to his parents shortly after Breece started grad school at the University of Virginia, he writes, "I'm going back to West Virginia when this is over. There's something ancient and deeply rooted in my soul. I like to think that I've left my ghost up one of those hollows and I'll never be able to leave for good until I find it—and I don't want to look for it because I might find it and have to leave."[31] Rick and Robert say that Helen always held out hope that Breece would come back to Milton. Though Breece expressed this desire too, they believed it would never have actually been viable for him. "She wanted him to come back and write in the house where he grew up, with his old typewriter bangin' around, writing his stories," Robert says. "And it was just a pipe dream. That was nothing that he could come back to." In the WPBY documentary, West Virginia writer Denise Giardina says, "In a way Breece never left West Virginia"; his writing is evidence that his mind was always here. In the pages of the "Trilobites" manuscript, Breece left a piece of notebook paper where he listed Milton locations he referenced in the story. Douglass writes, "He felt compelled to leave a trail, maybe for the same reasons he had written and rewritten his last will when he was in Charlottesville and jotted notes on the back of things he owned, instructing his mother or someone to 'dispose' or to 'keep.'"[32]

Helen did this too, I assume after Breece's death. In a five-notebook-page document titled "The Stories of Breece D'J Pancake—Locations + Life," she details the places and experiential details that inspired each story. For "Trilobites," she notes, "Teays River bed, a prehistoric river once flowing from Kanawha through the valleys of Putnam and Cabell Co's into the Guyandotte and Ohio Rivers. . . . The farm is where Breece first saw cane growing. Ginny was a former girlfriend of course creatively changed." Some of these locations are depicted in the documentary—the Old Bank steps, the Rock Camp Road sign, Company Hill, the C&O Railroad tracks. When I go back to read the collection a third time, I realize that the graveyard that Breece describes in "The Honored Dead" is the one where here's now buried—a transmutation from nonfiction to fiction turned material again. At the risk of this sounding cliché, there does seem to be a specter of him left in Milton, one traceable when you've overlaid text on the place, read of his walks along the hillsides, and retraced his pen strokes. It's always a faint outline, diffuse in the light.

CHAPTER 5

The Daughters of Mother Jones

Lessons of Care Work and Labor Struggle in the Expressive Culture of the West Virginia Teachers' Strike

AFTER CUTS TO their state-sponsored health insurance were implemented in May 2017, West Virginia teachers began organizing online. Through what became the "West Virginia Public Employees" Facebook group, teachers and other school workers shared their frustrations over rising insurance premiums and mandatory participation in an invasive fitness tracker app, enforced with monetary penalties. After teacher actions at the governor's State of the State address and a union rally on Martin Luther King Day 2018, the Facebook group grew to over 21,000 members and activity spiked. On February 22, 2018, with support from their unions, West Virginia public school teachers and school service employees, most of them women, walked out of their classrooms in what would become a nine-day statewide strike, fighting for a 5 percent raise and affordable health-care coverage. On February 28, after union leadership accepted the governor's deal of a 5 percent raise but no fix to health insurance, the rank and file rejected the deal, and the strike went wildcat. On March 7, union leaders, the rank and file, and the governor finally reached an agreement, which would give teachers a 5 percent raise, freeze insurance premiums, and create a task force to propose a permanent fix to state health insurance.

What the teachers' statements, speeches, and protest signs indicated, though, was that the strike was not just a protest for personal compensation but a struggle for better social conditions for the future of their communities. This became abundantly clear in 2019, when they again went out on strike for two days, ultimately shutting down the "Omnibus bill," which would give them another raise but would siphon money away from public education, allocating public money for private charter schools.

I was on site at the capitol seven of the nine days of the 2018 teachers' strike, interviewing teachers, students, and other community members present, and documenting the expressive culture of the strike, as it was forming, through shared language, homemade signs, clothing, songs, chants, and food. I also collected strike-related memes shared on social media. Much of this expressive culture was ephemeral, necessitating documentation in the moment, as the events of the strike were unfolding. In the summer of 2018, I worked with writer and historian Elizabeth Catte and writer and West Virginia teacher Jessica Salfia to coedit a book, *55 Strong: Inside the West Virginia Teachers' Strike*, which includes personal accounts by West Virginia teachers on their strike experiences, an essay by Catte, transcripts of some of my vox pop interviews conducted at the capitol during the strike, and a selection of photos I took of teachers' strike signs and attire.[1] We felt it was important to publish a multivocal record of the strike, in teachers' own words, immediately, before the strike narrative could be altered and appropriated by politicians and other entities. In 2019, I conducted longer follow-up interviews with several teachers to discuss organizing, the strike's expressive culture, and the teachers' ongoing struggle for their original demands.

At the time of writing, the fight continues, as during a summer 2019 special session, the West Virginia legislature passed a new version of the Omnibus bill opening up the state to charter schools. Meanwhile, insurance issues remain unresolved.

JESSICA SALFIA, forty, is a public high school teacher in Martinsburg, West Virginia. She is a mother of three children and her husband, Mark, is the principal at her school. Salfia teaches advanced placement language and composition and creative writing classes, is an advisor of the school Diversity Club and literary and art magazine, coordinates the homecoming parade, and serves on three countywide school committees. She's also coached the track and volleyball teams. She describes the reality of her day-to-day work:

> My administrators expect instruction to occur bell to bell. Our school and my performance are evaluated by my students' performance on a test I don't get to see. I have to prepare students for college, for jobs, for scholarships. I teach them to write literary analysis and resumes. To be empathetic, critical, smart, fair and professional . . . And now in this day and age, I must prepare my students for the potential threat of an active shooter. . . . We are expected to take a bullet for the students in our classroom while preparing them to be the future leaders of West Virginia. But we won't be able to afford the medical bills if we survive.[2]

Teachers are directly enmeshed in, even held responsible for, anywhere from twenty to over a hundred (depending on grade level and class size) young lives each year—directing their education, of course—but also picking them up when they skin their knee on the playground, waiting for their bus at the end of the day, making sure they eat lunch, mediating their disagreements, talking them through issues at home, writing their college letters of recommendation, bearing the emotional weight of their needs and worries and joy. Teachers also regularly spend personal money so their students can have school supplies and their classrooms can be properly equipped. The everyday life of a teacher is to be engaged in care work that constitutes part of the social reproduction of the everyday life of others. Some of this care work is remunerated, but some is not, exceeding teachers' job descriptions to ensure their students have what they need to survive and excel. In states like West Virginia, where state spending per student fell $1,000 between 2011 and 2017, austerity measures, including budget cuts for public education, and a push for privatization that shifts education to corporate entities like charter schools constitute a public disinvestment from the common good.[3] Austerity policies dismantle social services across the board, which strains the unpaid domestic care work of parents and families, and intensifies the care work asked of teachers, demanding more of their unremunerated time and personal money to provide for their students. This makes it more and more impossible for teachers to do their jobs (not to mention the unpaid care work for their own families), which are essential in sustaining the everyday life of their communities.[4]

Scholar and activist Silvia Federici conceptualizes everyday life as the origin point of social change, "a fundamental condition of all history."[5] When West Virginia public school teachers and school personnel across the state went out on strike for nine days in the winter of 2018 in a fight for affordable health care through the state-sponsored WV Public Employees Insurance Agency (PEIA) and a 5 percent salary increase, it was a collective acknowledgment that their work—essential to the function of everyday life—had become so jeopardized that they must disrupt everyday life in order to sustain its very operation, now and into the future. Striking teachers were explicit about this in their reasons for the work stoppage. One president of a local chapter of the American Federation of Teachers union told me, "You know, it's hard to believe for a lot of people, but the truth is, this is not about the money and the PEIA for the teachers we already have, this is more about taking care of the children in the future."[6] A high school student who joined the teacher protest at the capitol expressed a similar reason for her solidarity, "I just feel like we should always support our teachers because they're making our future."[7] When West Virginia teachers went out on strike again the following year, ultimately shutting down the Omnibus bill penned by the conservative American Legislative Exchange Council that would privatize public education by diverting public money to charter schools and penalize teachers for striking, while also granting them their 5 percent raise, they demonstrated their willingness to prioritize their students over their own livable wage by rejecting this blatant attempt to buy their compliance. West Virginia teachers made clear that public schools are not just a workplace but a life-making place; their protest was about not only current work conditions but also the ability to reproduce the life conditions of their communities. Teachers leveraged their essential role in the sustaining of everyday life to become the origin point for social change. Workplace struggle became social struggle.[8]

West Virginia teachers and school service employees sparked a wave of public teacher strikes across the country, and the flexing of collective power they had built in successfully shutting down the Omnibus bill in the two-day 2019 strike shows how West Virginia teachers have created a new everyday reality. During the first days of the 2018 strike, public schools claimed to be closed due to a "snow emergency." Writer and West Virginia native Aaron Bady reflects on the aptness of that metaphor for what happened in both 2018 and 2019. Of the two-day 2019 strike he writes, "This year, they didn't know if last year was a fluke. Now they know it isn't, that the emergency has become a ritual, and that a new reality has emerged. When the storm came, it was anticipated, managed and came to an end."[9] Though, as Bady points out, the strike was, unlike weather, created by workers, striking, like winter storms, became normalized. It was an unusual event perhaps, but not out of the ordinary.

Folklorists, too, employ the concept of everyday life as the social base of creative expression, often defining folklife as "the art of everyday life." Folklorists are interested in the creative works that are twined with the process of life-making social reproduction—lullabies sung to lull babies to sleep, hand-stitched quilts that adorn beds and provide warmth, songs of enslaved people that encoded instructions for freedom, rituals for planting crops, jokes that reinforce latent community values, the preparation of a favorite family meal—and the role of those expressions in the social lives of communities. As West Virginia teachers organized and assembled in the lead-up to, during, and after their strikes, they developed their own expressive culture, forming in real time along with the new reality they were creating, which had both an aesthetic and a social function to communicate the value of their work to legislators and the public. The new conditions of labor struggle facilitated new traditions and expressions that reinforced the group identity of the teachers and enabled them to resist austerity, privatization, and conditions they felt would compromise the viability of their own everyday lives and the everyday lives of their communities. To witness the teacher strike as it evolved was to witness the social function of expressive culture and its ability to create a new reality in resistance to dominant power structures.[10]

In the lead-up to and during the nine-day strike in 2018, West Virginia teachers maintained a strong physical presence at both the state capitol and in "picket lines" outside their schools.[11] Inside the capitol building, teachers filled the Senate and House galleries and the hallway between the two chambers, where they led chants, sang songs, and held homemade signs. Most teachers wore red, a color that has long been associated with labor solidarity and struggle, and was adopted by the #RedforEd movement, which started in Arizona in the spring of 2018 and quickly spread across the nation.[12] They also occupied the space outside the building, congregating on the capitol steps and along the roadside, prompting cars to honk in solidarity (see plate 5.1). There, several rallies were held, featuring speakers such as United Mine Workers of America (UMWA) president Cecil Roberts, American Federation of Teachers president Randi Weingarten, and National Education Association president Lily Eskelsen Garcia, with members of the public joining in to show solidarity or bear witness.

Reporters focused their attention on this space as well, with NBC News broadcasting live from the capitol steps during the rally on the evening of February 27, 2018, where the union presidents announced a deal with Governor Jim Justice. (The deal was subsequently rejected by union rank and file, initiating a wildcat strike.) Local chefs set up food tables, serving free meals to teachers so they did not have to leave the capitol grounds. Donated boxes of pizza and coffee cartons lined the capitol steps. This occupation of state-sanctioned space disrupted the everyday work of the legislature, temporarily creating a dialogic, communally constructed social space of resistance on the capitol grounds. The noise created from the teachers' chanting and conversation was loud, audible in both House and Senate chambers. With the building reaching capacity, long lines to enter the capitol circled the grounds, and capitol police regularly stopped granting visitors entry early in the day, whether they were there for the teachers' strike or not. The official legislative space became the vernacular. For those two weeks, the news and social media feeds (mine anyway) were flooded with images of passionate teachers in red shirts holding creative homemade signs, fists in the air. Normally confined to the interior of a classroom, teachers turned their work of social reproduction out, making its value visible—loud, with numbers, and a directive. Hundreds, sometimes thousands showed up each day, some driving up to five hours each morning just to add another body to the crowd. Many I spoke with at the capitol specifically addressed the importance of being there. Jay O'Neal, a teacher from Charleston's Stonewall Jackson Middle School (renamed West Side Middle School in July 2020), said, "I'm here, physically occupying space and just showing them, hey, we haven't forgotten and we're gonna be here as long as it takes."[13] When I asked a middle school student why she decided to show her support at the capitol, she replied pithily, "Every person counts that comes."[14]

Members of the UMWA were present and visible at the capitol most days, expressing their solidarity for their "union brothers and sisters," many sporting camo shirts with the phrase "We are everywhere" printed in yellow text on the back.[15] Teachers viewed the UMWA members' presence as an opportunity for cross-generational transmission of knowledge, benefiting from union miners' long experience with labor struggle. One elementary school teacher told me, "It was really thrilling to see those guys come out! . . . It's very cool to have the people that do know how to have the demonstrations, to fund the demonstrations—like [UMWA member] was talking about a strike fund if it would go that long—I mean these are the folks that know how to do it, and we need people to teach us how to be effective."[16] Normally a space where laws are crafted by a select few, mostly white men over age fifty-five, the capitol grounds became a place of intergenerational discourse.[17] For the two weeks of the strike, West Virginia teachers enacted a vision of their legislature as a more communal public entity, imagining conditions where policy that determines the work and life conditions of a group of workers and their social reproduction of their communities might actually be crafted with the voices of the workers and community members themselves.

Though much of the internal organizing of the strike was done through a private Facebook group and closed meetings, the public face of the strike at the capitol and on the local "picket lines" was a space where expressive culture was being created and evolved in a visible, public forum. Protesting teachers developed chants, shouted in the capitol and outside its walls. The simple "55 United" and "55 Strong" chants (also used as a hashtag in digital spaces) referred to the Mountain State's fifty-five counties and the statewide school system solidarity. "Fed up, fired up" and county-by-county roll calls also rang out in the halls of the capitol. "Move Mitch, Get Out the Way," a spoof of Ludacris's "Move Bitch Get Out da Way," and "Mitch Better Have My Money," inspired by Rihanna's "Bitch Better Have My Money," called out Senate president Mitch Carmichael, whose opposition to the teachers' demands and comments many viewed as disrespectful made him a primary target.[18] In 2019, the chant "Public Schools Yes, Charter Schools No" became the direct message voiced by the crowd. Favorite songs played at rallies included Tom Petty's "I Won't Back Down" and Twisted Sister's "We're Not Gonna Take It." As is the case after most public events in West Virginia, "Country Roads" concluded most gatherings, though during the strike it took on a particularly emotional component, evoking solidarity and a commitment to the teachers' home state, with those present holding hands and singing along, swaying, in a sea of red T-shirts. It also may have had additional resonance for teachers from border counties, who recognized, as evidenced in some signs and memes, the lure to teach in neighboring states, where they might earn significantly higher salaries and better benefits.

Inside the capitol, chants were often led by Cabell County teacher Perry Casto, dressed as Uncle Sam. Casto writes, "My sole intention was that by wearing the Uncle Sam costume, I could help unite our efforts by being a symbol of justice and solidarity."[19] Similar to Elaine Purkey's use of the "America the Beautiful" melody for her labor song "America Our

Union" (see chapter 2), Casto's daily embodiment of the most iconic personification of government effectively mocked the state's governmental institutions of authority and their ability to implement just wages, and transfer that power to the teachers, accrediting them as more capable arbiters of justice and solidarity. Casto describes how he instigated these chants, encouraging his colleagues to externalize their frustration, "You see, there really isn't a playbook by which to encourage people to participate in public dissent. You could feel an air of internal rage churning. . . . I knew that for our cause to be successful, there needed to be one or multiple 'cheerleaders' or 'chant leaders' to help sustain a high and consistent level of outrage we all possessed."[20]

Casto's costume, the songs, chants, and signs that called out Mitch Carmichael and other politicians, and the sheer decibel levels of the teachers' chants within the capitol formed a sort of "rough music," a loose daily ritual deriding public officials for their betrayal of the teachers' values and demands. In his book *Customs in Common* on the traditional popular culture of eighteenth-century England's working class, E. P. Thompson describes rough music, a variant of what the French call "charivari," as "the term which has been generally used in England since the end of the seventeenth century to denote a rude cacophony with or without more elaborate ritual, which usually directed mockery or hostility against individuals who offended against certain community norms."[21] In eighteenth-century England, rough music was invoked by communities both to affirm emic social conventions, generally "domestic" norms of proper marital relations, as well as to shame public officials, law enforcement, or property owners for perceived infractions—a vernacular enforcement of populist justice. Groups might stage a mock trial or street drama, burn an effigy, or gather outside their chosen victim's home, beating pots and pans, clanging bells, shouting, and generally making discordant noise. Crowds would also sing original mocking songs, set to popular melodies.[22] Though not all of the teachers' protests fit this description, and it's debatable whether the "rough music" was effective in actually shaming Mitch Carmichael (though he did eventually lose his Senate seat), the more satirical and directed chants and signs (some bearing mocking images of Carmichael, Justice, and other politicians) had similar goals and motivations as the rough music E. P. Thompson describes—to regulate the values the teachers wanted to communicate, publicly convey community judgment, and productively channel anger.[23] Folklorist Violet Alford notes that on historical occasions in England and

Europe where rough music was employed in domestic scenarios, communities generally employed the form to reprimand perceived betrayals of the reproduction of the community—a worker who refuses to work, a marriage or individual that will not produce children. Though not quite so literal, striking teachers used similar methods of public noise and ridicule to disrupt what they saw as impediments to their ability to engage in their work of social reproduction through the education of West Virginia's youth.[24]

During the strike, food served not only as nourishment for teachers and students out of school but as a form of solidarity, care, and resistance created out of the literal sustenance of everyday life. When teachers across the state were merely threatening to strike, Republican legislators attempted to weaponize teachers' caregiving against them, warning that if teachers closed the schools, many children would not eat. But teachers had already organized to collect donations and pack lunches to ensure no student would go hungry. In a slide show Jessica Salfia compiled to accompany her paper "Food as Solidarity in the West Virginia Teacher Strike" at the 2018 Appalachian Food Summit, she included images of teachers in red shirts amid piles of chips, fruit cups, and loaves of bread, packing lunches into paper bags. During the strike, teachers shouted on "picket lines" by day, and packed lunches for students by night. Salfia said, "The packing of the lunches was first an act of love but also an act of strategy because it sent a clear message to both the public and the legislators that this was not about leaving our students behind."[25] In doing so, teachers made visible to the public the care work that they engage in daily—both paid and unpaid. Though some legislators attempted to leverage teachers' care work (which constitutes the majority of their salaried jobs) against them, teachers defended themselves by demonstrating how that care work—here in the form of collecting donated food and packing lunches for students when school was not in session—*always* exceeds their job description and salaried work, benefiting the common good inside and outside school walls. In some communities, teachers collected so many food donations that they were able to donate surplus items to the local food pantry.

Community members also expressed their solidarity through food by having pizzas and sandwiches delivered to the capitol or local "picket lines," leaving gift cards for teachers at local restaurants, and baking #55Strong cupcakes and cookies to raise spirits. One care package prepared by students and their parents included homemade pepperoni rolls with the note, "Pepperoni Rolls and teachers are the heart of West Virginia."[26] Teacher unions from across the country called in food orders so teachers could maintain their presence on the capitol floor. The recognition of the care work that teachers provide generated other expressions of care, locally and across the country. Salfia said, "I think I cried every day over food. I have never seen support in the form of food in such a way."[27]

As I have noted, most teachers who came to the capitol and stood on the "picket lines" outside their schools wore red as a symbol of solidarity, resistance, and labor struggle. Some groups designed their own T-shirts. Boone County, in the southern coalfields, made "BOONE COUNTY UNION THUG" shirts, an homage to the area's history of labor struggle. Other screen-printed shirts read, "55 UNITED" and "WEST VIRGINIA UNITED" across a map of the state. Charleston-based company Kin Ship Goods sold T-shirts that read, "Don't be a worm, support teachers," with an image of a worm eating its way through an outline of the state. A percentage of proceeds from the shirt went to a school supply fund. Most evocative in terms of wardrobe were the red bandanas teachers wore around their necks, a reference to the Mine Wars of 1912–22, when miners in southern West Virginia went out on strike in a fight against the coal companies for union recognition, and subsequently better pay and more control over their life and work conditions. Neither willing nor able to purchase goods from the company store, all miners were already in possession of red bandanas, and they wore them around their necks to signify their union membership and to prevent friendly fire. In West Virginia, this is widely considered to be the origin of the term *redneck*, which many in the state claim as a point of pride and as a reminder of working-class struggle.[28] Though friendly fire was not a concern during the teachers' strike, the red shirts and bandanas were similarly a way teachers identified themselves when at the capitol and out in their respective communities.

The most formidable creative expressions of the strike were the homemade signs carried by teachers (and some students and community members) on the "picket lines." The two teachers' unions, the American Federation of Teachers (AFT) and the West Virginia Education Association (WVEA), did not create any official strike signage. But armed with their bulletin board production experience and unique skill in crafting a message so that even bored and angsty middle schoolers, let alone state legislators, might pay attention—teachers, as it turns out, can make one hell of a protest sign. As West Virginia University professors Rosemary Hathaway, Audra Slocum, and Malayna Bernstein write in their article "Striking Signs: The Diverse Discourse of the 2018 West Virginia Teachers' Strike,"

"As a group, the signs were evidence of the creativity and brainpower of West Virginia's teachers—a visible lesson plan aimed at educating legislators, the public, and the media about their cause, about what teachers' jobs actually entail, and what the true value of public education is, both in the present and for the state's future."[29]

Each day I was at the capitol, I documented these homemade creations of poster board, magic markers, paint, and collage. Some even had lights. With inspiration from Slocum, Hathaway, and Bernstein, and from Hathaway's paper, "If You Can Read This, Thank a Media-Savvy Teacher: Signs from the 2018 West Virginia Teachers' Strike," presented at the 2018 American Folklore Society annual meeting, I created a taxonomy of the signs and memes I documented and collected, organizing into type by style, the work their messages were doing, and their intended audience. I identified nine categories, with some subsets: Personal Testimony; Profession-Specific; Teaching as Preferable to Striking; Union Solidarity; Pop Culture References; West Virginia/Appalachian History and Identity; Solution-Based; and Future Warnings. Some signs and memes fit into several categories. The succinct, often witty statements paired with images conveyed direct messages of teachers' values and identity. As the strike continued, teachers created new signs each day that referenced other signs and forms of the strike's expressive culture, including chants, songs, apparel, and memes used in protest, as well as the oppositional comments by the governor and state legislators. The individually created pronouncements began to show evidence that a shared, intertextual culture was forming within this heteroglossic network, one with a common language, mission, and sense of its role in society at large—both within West Virginia and throughout the country as other teachers' unions were watching for inspiration and instruction. This shared culture reinforced and amplified, as vernacular expression often does, the group identity of the striking teachers. Their new in-jokes and common language and experiences further strengthened their bonds and organizing power.

Personal Testimony

Signs of personal testimony were self-referential, confessional, and serious, addressing real medical issues and economic struggles to communicate how individual teachers' survival and that of their families depends on the decisions of the legislators. One such sign read, "Masters Degree + 45 and Can <u>Barely</u> Afford to Stay Alive," the text circling a drawing of an insulin bottle, with the subhead, "FACT: No Fitness App will <u>cure</u> Type I

Diabetes!," a reference to the state health insurer's plans to force members to use a fitness app that would track their activity and other health data. Another read, "Local State Worker for 23 Plus Years Could Qualify for Food Stamps." These signs expressed the material conditions and motivations for striking in an appeal to critics and politicians, to stress that the work stoppage was not frivolous but an imperative for everyday survival.

Profession-Specific

Profession-specific signs alluded to the work of teaching and the multiple, specific skills that teachers have. Many positioned legislators as the students, with messages like "You Were Taught Better," or compared the legislators to passing youth fads (which are also forms of modern children's folklore), like the sign that read, "WE OUTLASTED [drawing of spinning water bottles and fidget spinners] AND WE WILL OUTLAST YOU!" (see fig. 5.1). A popular meme shared after the Senate approved the wrong version of the bill featured a photo of Mitch Carmichael with his head in his hands, and the text "HOLY SHIT WE SHOULD HAVE HAD A TEACHER PROOF READ THE BILL." Humor was used to mock legislators, turning the insults they directed at teachers back on them. In a sense, most of the teachers' signs, regardless of message, could be seen as profession-specific, in that they publicly displayed the teachers' creativity, wit, knowledge, and pedagogical skill. Some profession-specific signs were in fact subject-specific, citing math problems, science topics, music, and young adult literature, referencing the teachers' subject areas and the diversity of skills within the network. Rosemary Hathaway says that this allowed teachers from across the state who teach the same subject to find each other at rallies at the capitol, an echo of the signifying power of the union miners' red bandanas. Those teachers exchanged contact information and formed subject-specific organizing groups on Facebook. In this way, the teachers' expressive culture prompted real action and strengthened the group's identity and collective power.

Teaching as Preferable to Striking

Signs bearing messages such as "We'd Rather TEACH Than Strike" or "Fix PEIA so I can get back to teaching!" were undoubtedly honest statements but were also direct responses to critics—politicians and community members—who told teachers to return to their classrooms, some suggesting they were lazy or overly demanding. These messages com-

FIGURE 5.1. West Virginia striking teacher's sign referencing fidget spinners, February 27, 2018. Photo by the author.

municated that teaching and striking for better work and life conditions were interdependent: We'd rather teach, but in order to do so, we MUST strike. Striking was an imperative so that the teachers' work of social reproduction could continue. Several young students held similar signs in solidarity, such as one that read, "I'd rather be in SCHOOL."

Union Solidarity

Signs expressing solidarity from other unions or that referred to teachers' own position as "union bosses" or "union thugs" demonstrated the union and labor values still present in the state, in spite of ongoing union-busting efforts and West Virginia's being a "right-to-work" state.[30] Members of other unions who were present on the capitol steps were largely representatives of unions of industrial, building, and trade occupations, such as the UMWA and the Laborers' International Union of North America. Most of them were men. Their expression of solidarity with and knowledge transmission to striking teachers and school service employees can be read as a symbolic passing of the baton, marking the shift in the paid labor force that has taken place in Appalachia and increasingly, the world, over the past decade, from men to women, and from industrial work to care work. While need for care work jobs has increased, anthropologist David Graeber reports that "productivity in this caring sector has actually decreased across the developed world (largely due to the weight of bureaucratization imposed by the burgeoning numbers of administrators). This decline has put the squeeze on wages: it's hardly a coincidence that in developed economies across the world, the most dramatic strikes and labor struggles since the 2008 crash have involved teachers, nurses, junior doctors, university workers, nursing home workers, or cleaners." With recent austerity measures, it has become increasingly difficult for these workers to perform the most basic function of their job—provide care.[31] Austerity has stymied the reproduction of everyday life, both for those who engage in care work as part of their paid jobs and for the private unpaid care work undertaken by families.

Pop Culture References

Some of the most creative, clever, and funny signs used pop cultural references to appeal to a wide public audience. Signs referencing *Star Wars*, *Harry Potter*, *Mean Girls*, the Incredible Hulk, or *The Simpsons*' Mr. Burns related the specific struggle of the teachers to other more universally known narratives of struggle against power structures and authority (see fig. 5.2). As Hathaway mentioned in her American Folklore Society paper on the signs, some took the format of digital memes, like one that used the "Most Interesting Man in the World" format (a meme inspired by a prevalent Dos Equis beer commercial), reading "I don't always protest, But when I do, it's for fair wages, decent insurance, and highly qualified teachers." These pop cultural references were particularly effective, as they served as touchstones for a mass audience but could be vernacularized on hand-painted signs and memes and applied to the specific context of teachers' occupational culture and the particular struggle of the strike.

West Virginia/Appalachian History and Identity

This category of signs indicates a deep engagement with a West Virginia and/or Appalachian identity, labor in particular. One adapted West Virginia bluegrass musician and labor songwriter Hazel Dickens's lyrics:

FIGURE 5.2. Striking West Virginia teachers protesting at the state capitol hold signs referencing *Star Wars*, February 26, 2018. Photo by the author.

"WE WON'T BE BOUGHT / WE WON'T BE SOLD / TO BE TREATED RIGHT / AND FIX PEIA / WELL THAT'S / OUR GOAL" (see fig. 5.3).[32] Others read, "Mother Jones' Proxy" or "We are the daughters of Mother Jones." Both Dickens and Jones were beacons for this new women-led movement. A digital graphic shared after the strike went wildcat depicted a hissing black cat over a red map of West Virginia, with the words "'DO IT LIKE BLAIR MOUNTAIN, STRIKE WITH WEST VIRGINIA!" This was a reference to the Battle of Blair Mountain, the largest labor uprising in U.S. history and culminating event of the West Virginia Mine Wars, where in August 1921, an estimated 7,000–20,000 miners who were marching to rescue jailed union miners were met by state and coal company–sponsored militia forces.[33] Teachers felt that they were embodying that history and could now understand it experientially. Brandon Wolford, a Mingo County teacher, writes of how his experience in the teachers' strike illuminated the state's past labor struggle: "It is also fair to say that I soon learned the true meaning behind the labor movements in Appalachia— it is not strictly about the contracts, wages, or benefits; it is something much deeper. Those people had fought for the dignity they so rightfully deserved, and together they stood in unity as brothers and sisters."[34]

FIGURE 5.3. Striking West Virginia teacher holds a sign referencing Hazel Dickens lyrics, March 2, 2018. Photo by the author.

Many of the teacher essays in *55 Strong* position their strike within a legacy of labor history and recall relatives who were part of the Mine Wars, the Pittston strike, the Ravenswood lockout, or the 1990 teachers' strike.[35]

Some of the signs referencing West Virginia and Appalachian identity were alluding to out-migration. West Virginia is currently experiencing the highest rate of population decline per capita, and out-migration tied to the boom and bust of the coal industry has long been responsible for significant fluctuations in the Mountain State's population, with high rates of out-migration in the 1920s, 1950s, and the past decade. Out-migration too became a talking point for teachers, as they pointed out that many could travel just a few miles across the border to jobs in Virginia, Maryland, or Pennsylvania and almost double their salaries. Signs read, "WEST VIRGINIA EXPORTS: COAL / NATURAL GAS / TEACHERS"; "Country Roads / Leading Teachers Out of West Virginia"; and "LAST TEACHER OUT OF THE STATE TURN OFF THE LIGHTS" (see plate 5.2).

Solution-Based and Future Warnings

Solution-based signs were oriented to an audience of the public and the legislators, offering solutions that could in fact fund PEIA, meet the teachers' demands, and end the strike. Various signs expressed support for a soda tax, a severance tax on oil and gas, and HB4491, the bill for legal cannabis production that proponents said could bring the state billions of dollars of revenue.³⁶

Warning signs were directed at legislators, cautioning that teachers would "Remember in November" during the state elections, and vote out politicians who did not support the strike.³⁷ Another called on national public opinion, "THE NATION'S [ILLUSTRATED EYES] ARE ON YOU! IT'S TIME TO FIX THIS MESS." One with the text "The redneck dumb bunny made a rare appearance at the WV Capitol carrying a November 6th ballot. / The dumb bunnies really do vote!" and a drawing of a ballot-carrying bunny with a red bandana around its neck referenced comments Governor Justice had made, calling the teachers "dumb bunnies" and referring to one as "the town redneck."

As the teachers' strike wave spread to other states, including Oklahoma, Arizona, and Kentucky, teachers there chanted and made signs that warned, "Don't Make Us Go West Virginia on You."³⁸ The state's name had become synonymous with its teachers' unyielding struggle for both work and the conditions of everyday life.

THE DIGITAL SPACES of the strike worked in conversation with the physical spaces, facilitating internal communication as well as broadening the strike's reach to a statewide, national, and international audience. Much of the initial organizing happened through a private Facebook group, "West Virginia Teachers UNITED" (renamed "West Virginia Public Employees UNITED" by November 2017), started by Jay O'Neal in May 2017 to address PEIA hikes and facilitate cross-union solidarity and organizing. When one member asked, "Just curious if there are any talks of striking," activity in the group surged. Later that month O'Neal, Emily Comer, and a group of other teachers unfurled a banner with the message, "Public Employee Healthcare, Not Corporate Welfare: Fund PEIA" at Governor Justice's State of the State address, and posted a video to the group. This, and a WVEA MLK Day rally for education inspired even more group activity, as teachers shared their frustrations after meetings with legislators. These physical actions inspired more participation in the digital forum—by February 2018 the group boasted over 21,000 members.³⁹ In the lead-up to and during the strike, teachers and public employees used the Facebook group to livestream protests, share information, and make collective decisions. Jessica Salfia describes going to bed on February 27, unsatisfied with the deal accepted by union leadership. When she woke up the next morning and logged on to Facebook to see a livestream of fellow teachers back protesting at the capitol during the supposed "cool-ing off day," she knew the strike was not over. Unofficial livestreams like this enabled the teachers to open the space of the capitol to more par-ticipants and witnesses. Salfia's home county was one of the last to go wildcat, and the teachers in her school watched the school closure map as they organized over Facebook Messenger:

> They're not going to close.
>
> We have to form lines at the entrances and block the cars.
>
> We have to make them cross our line.
>
> Who can meet me at the bus garage at 3:00? We have to have lines at the bus garage to stop the busses from being able to run.
>
> Why do we have to block the entrances?
>
> Because that's a real strike. You shut it down and make them cross your line or they go home. You stop school from happening.[40]

Salfia and her colleagues were prepared to go wildcat without the support of their school system, though eventually the Berkeley County superin-tendent closed schools, maintaining the 55 Strong statewide solidarity. But through internal digital organizing, the teachers of Spring Mills High School in Martinsburg prepared to put their bodies on the line. Teachers and public employees also used public digital forums to communicate their message and narrative of events to a wider public audience and inspire local, national, and international solidarity; West Virginia teach-ers regularly received and shared "solidarity photos" from and for other teachers, unions, and groups around the globe. In claiming private and public digital spaces for the strike, teachers bolstered collective power and group identity, garnered public support, and strengthened their actions in physical spaces.

Memes were created and shared in both public forums and private teacher-only Facebook groups. Many used popular meme formats, such as "The Distracted Boyfriend" in one instance, to convey that West Virginia teachers were eyeing higher-paying jobs in the border states of Virginia, Pennsylvania, and Maryland. Memes reflected the content and themes of the signs, most falling in the categories of Profession-Specific and West Virginia/Appalachian Identity, but generally employing a more pointed humor and sarcasm, adhering to vernacular meme standards. Memes calling on insider knowledge of West Virginia vernacular culture—particularly West Virginia hot dogs, pepperoni rolls, and WVU's football rivalry with the University of Pittsburgh—conveyed a place-based digital folklore. A pair of memes each featured a photo of Mitch Carmichael, with text overlaid. One read, "Mitch Carmichael / Orders ketchup on Yann dogs," referencing the belovedly ornery Fairmont hot dog stand, Yann's, where locals know that the proprietor may eject you for asking for ketchup (or coleslaw, being located above West Virginia's "slaw line"; see chapter 6). The other read, "MITCH CARMICHAEL / HATES PEPPERONI ROLLS / & LOVES PITT." At one point during the strike, someone edited Carmichael's Wikipedia page to read, "Mitch apparently hates all teachers and public employees of West Virginia. Rumor has it, he hates pepperoni rolls, too. Possible Pitt fan."

Much like historical iterations of "rough music" which often effectively manifested as a collectively enforced purging of individuals who did not obey a community's rules and conventions, these subversively humorous memes used imagined transgressions of West Virginia vernacular culture to position Carmichael not only as an outsider but also as an enemy. As Thompson writes, the power of rough music is that it makes visible privately held opinions and frames them as a collective rebuke. "What had before been gossip or hostile glances becomes common, overt, stripped of the disguises which, however flimsy and artificial, are part of the currency of everyday intercourse."[41] Rough music leverages vernacular authority (in this case that of West Virginia's public school teachers) and lobs it at official authority (West Virginia's legislators). While traditional rough music was a ritualized performance event contained within the community itself, digital rough music has the additional potential of reaching a wider public audience—amplifying the public shaming function of the form while reinforcing internally held community values.

In the lead-up to, during, and following the 2018 and 2019 teachers' strikes, West Virginia teachers realized that their pedagogical power need not be confined within the walls of their schools. Spring Mills High School teacher Karla Hilliard (no relation) describes a realization she had after convening her AP English class at a local Panera Bread during the 2018 strike:

> The West Virginia teacher strike reminded me of what it means to be a teacher. It reminded me of what my friend Jay Nickerson

says of teaching—that it "is a human endeavor." And it reminded
me of what Parker Palmer says in *The Courage to Teach*, that "my
ability to connect with my students, and to connect with the subject, depends less on the methods I use than on the degree . . . I am
willing to make [myself] available and vulnerable in the service of
learning.". . . For days I'd watched my colleagues and teachers across
the state give our students an education, and that education was
different in both kind and degree. Students stood on picket lines,
wrote editorials, called lawmakers, organized rallies, and learned,
first hand, the power of a collective voice.[42]

Hilliard remembered that teaching can in fact happen anywhere, whether
in a classroom or not. But it wasn't only students who received an experiential education through the strike. Teachers took a broad local, state,
national, and international public as their students. The steps and halls
of the capitol, the "picket lines" outside their schools, local businesses,
newspaper op-eds, and online spaces became their classrooms where they
could educate the public about their experiences, their demands for a livable wage and affordable health care for all public employees, and vision
for an investment in West Virginia's public education. The takeover of
state-sanctioned space, occupied by signs and speeches and chants and
songs and thousands of bodies in red shirts and bandanas—mirrored by
their digital manifestations—was in fact a mobile classroom, its walls
turned out. The expressive culture of the strike made visible to the teachers and their many students the collective power that teachers built outside of classrooms and official structures.

    In 2018 West Virginia teachers received their 5 percent raise, but as
of this writing, PEIA has still not been permanently fixed. In the summer of 2019, despite teacher protests and polls indicating that 88 percent
of West Virginians oppose charter schools, the West Virginia legislature
passed a version of the Omnibus bill that opens up the state to charter
schools. Though it also issues public school workers a pay raise, the bill
was strongly opposed by the teachers' unions and the rank and file members because of the extent of other changes, including charter schools,
that they viewed as being detrimental to public education in the state.[43]
Despite the unresolved issues, teachers leveraged their care work—so crucial to the social reproduction of everyday life—to usher in a new everyday reality. They showed that they are able to organize efficiently and
effectively, during the school year or not, in the cold of winter, online

and in physical spaces. They will take the lessons of the strike, both taught and learned, back to the classroom, embedding their own experiences in the long legacy of working-class labor struggle in West Virginia. Young West Virginians will grow up knowing this history. Teachers have demonstrated the social power of the "art of everyday life," through what became their "symbolic vocabulary," a toolbox for collective labor struggle that drew heavily on the expressive forms of music, verbal art, visual art, foodways, attire, and digital folklore.[44] Their role as creators of everyday life is embedded in the messages of these forms; through their struggle emerged a new aesthetic culture of social reproduction. That struggle is a protest of work and life conditions, because as care workers they are so inherently entwined with the social conditions of their communities. As Kelli Douglas, a teacher at Charleston's Overbrook Elementary, told me, "We are with the children of the future for predominantly most of their lives. We care for them, we give them food, we give them shelter, we give them love, and West Virginia has been looking down on us for some reason for trying to care for their children. And I don't think it's fair for us. We deserve more respect, we deserve more fair treatment, and we deserve the love that we give to kids every single day."[45]

CHAPTER 6

Friends of Coleslaw

On the West Virginia Hot Dog

CHILI, SLAW (USUALLY), mustard, and onions: Since moving to West Virginia, I've learned to answer with that refrain—the prescriptive version of "with everything"—when asked how I want my hot dog dressed. My travels for fieldwork interviews with vernacular artists and tradition bearers often include stops at hot dog joints—lunch counters, ice cream stands, and country stores that are sometimes the only meal option in a rural area. I would round a corner on some winding mountain road and there would be another low-roofed cinder-block building with a neon or hand-painted sign, claiming to have the best hot dogs in town. I struck up a conversation with the bartender at my favorite local dive and she told me that she and her sister live next to each other and like to meet in their yards and eat hot dogs; her sister makes the slaw, and she makes the chili (though lately she's been "cheating" and buying Custard Stand chili from Kroger). West Virginia is a place that loves its hot dogs so much, it even boasts a "hot dog" pastry—a split-bun éclair, drizzled with chocolate "mustard," ensuring that even dessert can include a dog.[1] Those experiences and the passionate declarations of loyalty I'd witnessed—to particular hot dog joints and subregional varieties—suggested that there was more to hot dogs in the Mountain State than just that four-ingredient list. As I explored more, though, through interviews with hot dog purveyors, writers, cooks, and fans; historical research; and fieldwork at hot dog joints across the state (which of course included taste testing), I discovered that the hot dog is not only a beloved West Virginia tradition but also a cultural mirror, revealing issues of race, gender, class, labor, the built environment, and how the triviality barrier impacts the historical record and cultural preservation.

My first encounter with the West Virginia hot dog occurred at Bob's Hot Dogs (RIP) outside of Elkins, during a trip there for an old-time music festival when I was still living in Washington, D.C. Bob's admittedly did not have the best example of a standard West Virginia hot dog, but with its hand-painted wooden cutouts of oversized mustard-slathered wieners and extensive menu, it was an effective ambassador. A few years later when I moved to Charleston, I discovered the West Virginia Hot Dog Blog, founded in 2006 by a West Virginia native whose nom de guerre is "Stanton." The blog, which has established him as a de facto expert on West Virginia dogs, is a compendium of reviews of hot dog joints across the state, written mostly by him, and occasionally other "weenie wonks," delivered in his doctrinaire, sports radio talk show style. He says chili, slaw, mustard, and onions are "as God intends hot dogs to be prepared" and takes offense at an unsteamed bun and the mere suggestion of ketchup.

As far as broader hot dog style territories go, I grew up smack in the middle of Detroit's chili-slathered Coney dogs and the vegetable-heavy Chicago dogs, which are said to be "dragged through a garden." Both styles are particular about the type of sausage—Vienna Beef for Chicago dogs and an all-beef frankfurter with natural casing for Coneys. What most consider to be a standard West Virginia dog, however, focuses less on the dog itself and more on the interplay of spicy, hot chili and cool, sweet coleslaw, topped with yellow mustard and diced onions (see plate 6.1). Likewise, there are no specifications for the cooking of the wiener—steamed, grilled, or boiled are all acceptable. The bun is traditionally steamed, making the whole affair a gooey mess—albeit one you can still hold in your hand. It is an exercise in balance. "We have a language barrier with Chicago hot dog fans, who don't understand it's not about what type or brand of weenie we use," Stanton said.[2] In West Virginia, a hot dog is about the whole package—weenie, toppings, and bun.

The Hot Dog Blog's Facebook page is often the forum for heated debate over specific terminology and the merits of a good West Virginia dog. Its 7,000-plus readers post West Virginia hot dog–specific memes and original art. Over the blog's fifteen years, Stanton has reviewed and ranked over 300 hot dog joints, but he has also elucidated a taxonomy of hot dog styles (the utilitarian, the genteel, and the artisan), and, most important, developed a Slaw Mapping Project—a vernacular digital humanities initiative in its own right.

West Virginians recognize the "Slaw Line" as a kind of Mason-Dixon of condiments that runs through the top fourth of the state. Above the line, slaw is not always available, usually not offered, and in the two northernmost counties of the Northern Panhandle, "not offered at any known hot dog joint." Stanton has mapped this county by county so it appears as a gradient of dwindling slaw as you travel north. In the north-central counties like Harrison, Marion, and Monongalia, pepperoni rolls—another handheld food which originated in that area among Italian miners' families—reign supreme. There, where slaw is often unavailable, chili is referred to as "sauce" (this is also true in most western counties that border the Ohio River). It's thin and extremely spicy, compared to the meat-heavy sauces in other areas, and it doubles as a pepperoni roll topping.

There are a few anomalies. At Fairmont's beloved Yann's in Marion County, customers would reportedly get thrown out by former proprietor Russell Yann (who drew comparisons to *Seinfeld*'s "Soup Nazi") if they asked for slaw.[3] Don't even think about ketchup. The dogs are smaller—a full lunch generally includes three, as opposed to the two-dog standard—and the sauce is extremely spicy, necessitating a bottle of chocolate milk and a bag of Mister Bee's potato chips. At Woody's, the other Fairmont classic hot dog joint, slaw is available but does not come standard in a "with everything" order. At Chum's, a walk-up stand in Marmet outside of Charleston, the slaw is made with yellow mustard rather than mayonnaise and is much sweeter than its creamy cousin, meriting a spicier chili. The yellow slaw is thought to have originated in the 1930s at the Marmet restaurant Blackie's, which was later renamed the Canary Cottage. In the 1970s, the Dairy Post continued the yellow slaw hot dog tradition in Marmet until it closed in the early 2000s. When Chum's opened in 2008, the former Dairy Post co-owner Lou Kinder offered owner Frances Armentrout the use of her slaw recipe, which is still in use today.[4]

The phenomenon of the West Virginia hot dog joint—whether serving chili or sauce, slaw or none—is most prevalent in historically industrial areas in the state—particularly the southern and northern coalfields, and the Ohio River cities of Parkersburg and Huntington. This is grounded in the historical roots of the food in the Mountain State, as the hot dog's arrival and prevalence were linked to industry and immigration, as I'll explain. Like pepperoni rolls, which originated in the north-central part of the state but now are embraced statewide, West Virginia hot dogs have also gained popularity in other areas. Because new hot dog joints are constantly opening and closing, the total number of them in the state is difficult to tally, but based on my count, there are at least 350 in West Virginia (and that's playing it safe). Nearly each one claims to serve the "Best Hot Dogs in Town." In a small state, with fewer than 2 million people scattered across 24,000-odd mountainous square miles, that's a surfeit of hot dogs.

"One of the Greatest Places on Earth for 'Hot Dog' Eaters": Immigration, Class, Labor, and the Fairmont Hot Dog Stand Wars of 1922

There's no single conclusive story about the hot dog's journey to and popularization in West Virginia specifically, but we can piece together its history in the state through family accounts and historical records. The earliest mention I could find of hot dogs in a West Virginia newspaper was in the September 8, 1897, edition of the *Wheeling Daily Intelligencer*, in the article, "Notes of the Fair," which refers to a "wiener-wurst vendor."[5] Generally, hot dogs became popular in the United States during a period of urbanization, the popularization of mass culture, and European migration in the late nineteenth and early twentieth century, and West Virginia hot dogs are no exception.[6] The food appeared to boom in the state in the late 1910s and early 1920s and, like Michigan Coney dogs, were largely brought by Greek (and possibly Italian) immigrants, who set up hot dog stands and wagons in Charleston, Clarksburg, Fairmont, Parkersburg, and Wheeling. A 1916 article in Clarksburg's *Daily Telegram* tells of "hot dog man" Gus Lopez, likely an Italian immigrant, who "revolutionized the local sandwich business" and fulfilled what the paper claims was a long-standing demand for hot dogs in the city.[7] His business, which sold "wiener-worst tucked between a bun and coated with chili sauce, mustard, diced onions and the like," was apparently successful; its initial sales of 1,200–1,300 hot dogs per day had doubled by the time of the article's publication.

In the early 1920s, the Fairmont newspaper referred to the capital city of Charleston as "one of the greatest places on earth for 'hot dog' eaters." In 1920, the *Charleston Daily Mail* reported that an astonishing 22,000 hot dogs on average—about one for every two residents—were sold each day out of the city's four dog stands (at least three of the four were owned by Greeks). A follow-up article expressed the bounty more visually: "If all the hot dogs consumed in a year in Charleston were strung together, the string could extend to Huntington and back and still have enough left to run down to St. Albans on one side of the road and back on the other. Or if strung in another direction they would run to Morgantown."[8] Lest you retrospectively worry over the cholesterol level of Jazz Age Charlestonians, rest assured that hot dogs at that time were four inches long as opposed to today's six-inch standard weenies.

In the summer of 1922, a veritable hot dog stand war erupted between city officials and hot dog stand owners in the city of Fairmont, spurred by city officials' racist and classist resentment of the largely immigrant proprietors and their customers—mainly factory workers and high school students. This occurred during an era of rapid expansion for the city, with new industrialization leading to a doubling of Fairmont's population between 1910 and 1930.[9] Many of the new residents were European immigrants and African American migrants who came to work in the city's glass factories and coal mines. As described in chapter 1 on the Scotts Run community, immigrants and migrants from diverse backgrounds were explicitly recruited by coal companies and factories, not just for cheap labor but also as an antiunionization strategy, as the companies believed that the workers' dislocation paired with their cultural and linguistic barriers would inhibit them from organizing. In the summer of 1922, the coal industry was in decline, and union miners in the Fairmont field, the majority of whom were foreigners, were striking.[10] Fairmont city officials' disapproval of the proliferation of hot dog stands, most of which were operated by working-class immigrants, was ostensibly a reaction to widespread economic concerns and anxieties about the city's changing demographics.

Articles in the local papers from 1922 are rife with antiforeign sentiments and fear that Black and foreign workers would form radical coalitions, with numerous calls for Americanization of "the foreign element," demanding "closer adherence to the traditions of this country."[11] On May 23, city officials refused to grant a license to an "itinerant hot-dog stand," citing complaints from residents of "a swell residential section." A member of the Board of Affairs who rejected the application commented, "I think Fairmonters should have enough civic pride to realize that such things as hot dog wagons are not wanted here. They lower the standards of the city. They are dangerous to the safety of our citizens. The wagons are unsightly and also disreputable-looking. And they are so unnecessary."[12] For the next several months, over a half dozen articles about hot dog stands appeared in the local newspaper. Some of them mocked the "city fathers'" obsession with squelching the growth of the establishments in the city. "Wonder if, well, if many things more important to the public welfare than picking on the hot dog wagons can not hold the supreme interest of the authorities," writes an editor in response to the Board's May 23 decision.[13] One businessman who was accused of opening a hot dog stand was incensed at the mere suggestion. "'My place of business is not going to be a hot-dog stand,' declared E. C. Stemple of Stemple's newsstands. . . . 'I have seen it referred to as a hot-dog stand and it made me hot under the collar.'"[14] With their foreign and working-class associations, hot dog stands at the time were considered by white city elites to be base, aligned with other disreputable establishments such as dives and beer joints.

From the beginning, the popularity of hot dogs in West Virginia has been linked to the industrial labor that boomed in the late nineteenth and early twentieth century, just as hot dogs were spreading west from New York. As early as 1916, hot dogs were noted to be "in special demand in factory and university towns."[15] Andrew James "A. J." Valos (b. 1894), a native of Sagkas, Greece, worked as an indentured servant in the hot dog business in New York before moving to Parkersburg, West Virginia, where he opened his Broadway Sandwich Shop in 1939. Valos's descendants attribute much of the success of the shop to its prime location across the street from the Mountain State Steel Foundries. Valos served lunches to workers from the foundry, the nearby Ames Baldwin Shovel and Tool Company, and to students at the school across the street.[16] Though Valos passed away in 1950, his shop is still in operation today and remains in the family.[17] Much as in the origin stories of pepperoni rolls, coal miners, steel workers, and other laborers needed a quick meal they could eat between or during shifts, and hot dogs proved a cheap and filling option. On the other side of the counter, inexpensive ingredients, population influx, and demand from laborers presented an opportunity for enterprising hot dog vendors.

In the early twentieth century, most hot dogs in West Virginia consisted of chili, mustard, and onions—there was no slaw no matter how far north or south you were. It's a little unclear when slaw was added and became a standard topping on dogs in most areas of the state. The first mention of a full West Virginia dog with slaw I could find was in January 1949. It curiously appears in an article detailing the techniques incarcerated people at the Raleigh County jail were using to smuggle in saw blades. "Hot dogs are another good method. Break the blades in half. Slit open the wiener, insert the blade, flip the wiener upside down so the slit won't show, insert it in a bun, apply mustard, chili sauce, and slaw. Jailers are on to this one too. It's messy, but they poke around in the mustard, slaw and onions."[18] Judging by the article's nonchalant tone, these ingredients were already widely known to be normal hot dog toppings, but in the imaginary of this article, incarcerated people might have developed a particular inclination for slaw because the additional topping heaped upon the wiener could better conceal a weapon! Slaw only gained popularity (below the slaw line) as a topping from there, soon served along with its spicier counterparts at church sales, school cafeterias, local drive-ins, family picnics, and state park concession stands.

Below the Slaw Line: A Southern West Virginia Hot Dog Tour

To dive into crucial comparative participant-observation research on the West Virginia hot dog phenomenon, I enlisted my friend, illustrator, fellow folklorist, and hot dog aficionado Emily Wallace. In the summer of 2016, we embarked on a 286-mile hot dog tour through the southern coalfields with stops at drive-ins, convenience stores, and an ice cream stand (see plate 6.2). She showed up at my Charleston apartment wearing a hot-dog T-shirt and a pickle pin, and had prepped for our journey by illustrating a shared Google map with hot dog doodles (they still pop up on my phone, whenever I near one of the dog stops).

We arrived at a small country store at dusk, giddy for our first hot dog. The hand-painted sign outside Buddy B's in Sissonville, West Virginia, advertised fresh produce, pinto beans, and cornbread, and "Best in Town Hot Dogs" (see plate 6.3). Inside, bulk seeds, bags of peanuts, and jars of penny candy lined the red gingham–papered walls, and a cash register and food counter stood on either side of the door. We gawked like tourists at the hot dog clock and hand-lettered hot dog sign, outlined by the triple-underlined text, TRY OUR HOT DOGS THEY ARE GO-O-O-O-D, and surreptitiously took pictures as the cashier-cum-cook prepared our dogs. "Watch out, she's the meanest thing here," a man said to us, as he walked past, lugging a twenty-pound tube of ground beef from the self-serve meat case over his shoulder. Recognizing the jest was intended for her, the cook countered, "Get outta here, trouble," rehearsing familiar banter. She wordlessly slid our dogs through a side pickup window, and we retreated, tray and a bag of peanuts in hand, to the diner booth outside. Lifting our dogs in the air as coleslaw and chili dribbled onto the waxed paper below, we toasted to the kickoff of our trip.

The morning after our Buddy B's dinner, we drove along the winding road just outside Charleston back to Sissonville to be first on the scene at Skeenies, eagerly peering in the windows to the unlit kitchen before it opened at 10 a.m. Opening for business in 1953, the yellow and white roadside stand with its vintage hand-painted sign that looms over the building, and its superior dog, inspired both local loyalty and expat longing. Mrs. Skeen (as she was reverently known), in her nineties, ran the place with her son Joshua. As Emily wondered out loud if they had any signature waxed hot dog bags she could take home as souvenirs, Joshua "Andy" Skeen, who lived next door with his mother, walked over to greet us. "Just one hot dog?" he asked, amused by our order. (We had decided to pace ourselves.) I wondered if the dog-happy ball-capped boy on the sign might be Joshua himself at a younger age (see fig. 6.1).

Just a stone's throw from Skeenies is the site of the former Stopette Drive-In, arguably the originator of the slaw dog in the Mountain State. Stanton says that the Stopette was advertising slaw dogs in the local newspaper by the 1920s, referencing a 1922 ad that proclaimed, "Everybody's talking about Stopette's hot dog with slaw." Cabbage was cheap and plentiful then—a common home garden crop—and the addition of coleslaw, variants of which are found in the foodways of numerous West Virginia immigrant communities, was a way to make a hot dog more filling. While other states like North Carolina and Georgia also pair chili and slaw on dogs, those slaw dog traditions don't always include the obligatory mustard, onions, and steamed bun of their West Virginia counterparts. Stanton believes laborers from West Virginia brought the practice with them when they moved south for work. He cites a humor piece in a 1951 *Charlotte (N.C.) Observer* newspaper that joked how the only good thing all the West Virginia hillbillies brought with them was slaw on their hot

FIGURE 6.1. Sign advertising Skeenies Hot Dogs, Sissonville, West Virginia, June 10, 2016. Photo by the author.

dogs.[19] A major flood in 1961 destroyed the Stopette, but its legacy remains as slaw continues to top dogs across most of the state.

After Skeenies, Emily and I made our way about an hour south to the 1,800-person town of Logan, which boasts two hot dog–slinging drive-ins. Parkway, with its red-capped carhop sign, is located near the home of folk legend and banjo player "Aunt Jennie" Wilson, adjacent to Chief Logan State Park. Morrison's Drive-In sits alongside the Guyandotte River, just south of town. CHICKEN IN THE FINGERS HERE IN THE BOX TO GO reads the inscrutable message on the faded red-and-white sign of the business, which first opened in January 1947.[20] We ordered one dog at each, in exchange for a couple of crumpled dollars from my pocket. The meagerness of our order got us strange looks from our waitresses. Maybe they thought we were stingy, but more likely just odd. It didn't help when I pulled out my trusty red Swiss Army knife to slice our dogs in half. Buddy B's, Skeenies, Parkway, and Morrison's all offer a classic example of the West Virginia dog—what Stanton classifies as "utilitarian": cheap, no-frills, with little heed paid to presentation. They were served wrapped in plastic cellophane or wax paper, which mushes the ingredients together and ensures that each bite contains that perfect synergy of slow-cooked chili and fresh slaw.

Around back at Morrison's, leather-clad bikers convened at the picnic tables, while families in minivans and couples in trucks circled the perimeter—a Saturday at noon, the place was hopping. Our server brought our lone dog out on a metal tray and hooked it over our car window. Though she asked for no clarification on our order of "one hot dog," generally a sign it would arrive with the standard four ingredients, it surprisingly came slawless. Emily, determined not to be deprived of her cabbage, jumped out of the car to ask the waitress for a slaw side.

After that third dog we grew weary, even a little queasy. Emily blamed the curvy mountain roads. I blamed the June heat. But the promise of J's Grocery in Kegley, which one of the Hot Dog Blog's "weenie wonks" called "the fulfillment of some hot dog shaman's ancient prophecy," beckoned. We made a call to the convenience store, nearly a hundred miles away. It was our second dial there that day. "Is Marie *still* making dogs?" I asked, seeking encouragement. Her husband, who answered again, confirmed that indeed she was, but asked, puzzled, and maybe somewhat annoyed, "Who *is* this?" We pressed onward.

Driving south through the mountains past rolling rivers, mine sites, and grandiose yet abandoned company stores, we stopped in the small town of Oceana to stretch our legs, check out an antique store, and buy snap beans from a roadside stand. Walking through town, a group gathering donations for a local political candidate flagged us over and asked if we wanted free hot dogs. We replied with a polite "no, thank you."

Late that afternoon, we pulled into J's Grocery in Kegley, an unincorporated community some twenty miles from the Virginia state line. Kegley is in fact so small that J's is listed on the town's Wikipedia page as one of only two businesses. Inside the convenience store, which also serves as the village post office, gas station, and alterations shop, Marie Burrell stood at the food counter, chatting and stacking a hot ham 'n' cheese. From counter stool perches, we ogled the menu hanging above: Homemade buttermilk biscuits, hand-pattied hamburgers, and pizza. Though tempted to mission creep, we gave Marie our standard one hot dog order. She side-eyed us and asked, smiling, "Are you two the ones that called earlier?"

Our cover blown, we told her and her husband, Junior, who both live in the house next door, that we'd made the trip specifically to see her. Though at that point J's had been in business for thirty years, with the Burrells owning it for thirteen, they had struggled recently to get local support, and were increasingly dependent on travelers. "No one spends money on food around here, just on pills. It's been bad for West Virginia's economy," said Marie. Mercer County, where Kegley sits, has been hit hard by the opioid epidemic, and the Burrells said they felt the impact on their food business. In addition to their store and gas station, Marie also started working as a seamstress and artist, designing her own logo and offering garment alterations out of the store.

Marie presented the paper-wrapped hot dog in front of us, steaming hot in a freshly grilled eggy "English style" bun, brushed with butter. Topped with homemade chili, thick-cut onions, and gobs of mustard, it achieved the ideal synergy present in the best West Virginia dogs. She said she serves both these and regular buns, and makes her slaw to order, customized to the consistency preferences of the customer. While steamed regular buns are standard fare, the grilled and buttered New England bun balanced the texture of the toppings and maintained structural integrity. The dog was unassuming but distinctive, well worth the drive. Emily and I promised we'd be back for biscuits sometime soon.

We turned north toward home, making a few more stops along the way. In Hinton, Kirk's and Dairy Queen sit side by side along the New River. Both offer fantastic views of Bushes Island with birds fishing along the riverbank, and both serve hot dogs with homemade chili; they each have their respective followings.[21] At Tom's Carry Out in Oak Hill, the brown paper bag our dog was served in advertised for a candidate for county commission. King Tut in Beckley, our last stop, is an eight-stalled, two-car-deep drive-in with a giant vintage neon sign, and an extensive menu that, along with hot dogs, includes a pan-fried liver dinner, a meatloaf sandwich, and homemade pies (see fig. 6.2). Hot dogs, with toasted New England or, as they say, English buns, and chili and slaw made from scratch, are their best seller, though. "We sell those like gangbusters," said owner Dave McKay. There we placed our standard order for one hot dog. It was good, but we were full. We belly-ached back toward Charleston, ready for salad, our snap beans, and a beer to wash it all down.

Curb Girls, Waitresses, and Fast Food Women

At King Tut, and every other hot dog joint we visited aside from Skeenies, we were served exclusively by women. Though we weren't always able to see inside kitchens, most places, like Morrison's Drive-In, seemed to be all-women workplaces, from curb girls to cooks to managers. Dave McKay says that most of his employees are women who have held a long tenure in the position. When I interviewed him, he told me that a King Tut curb girl with forty years of experience had just passed away, and his day shift manager Diana Hamilton celebrated her forty-year work anniversary in the fall of 2019. "The curb girls there, Kathy—she's relatively new, maybe twenty years of service [laughs] and then the rest of them have less than that. . . . I've got guys in here, but they're all new."[22] In King Tut's early days, the position was specifically advertised to women. The drive-in's job postings from 1949 through the 1960s sought curb girls, grill girls, and "female help" (by the mid-1970s the gendered modifier was dropped and ads simply sought a "person").[23] As high-paying industrial blue-collar jobs like coal mining, logging, and construction were not readily available to them, one of the few sectors working-class women had access to in their communities was the food service industry, mainly in low-wage and part-time jobs without benefits. Though longevity in a position seems to be more prevalent in locally owned drive-ins and restaurants, as with King Tut and Morrison's, jobs in fast food chain restaurants are notoriously precarious, as the nature of the work and structure of the business makes workers expendable, fulfilling the human end of mostly automated systems. As the coal industry steadily declined, women's participation in the workforce increased; generally speaking, when men lost their jobs, women went to work.[24] These traditionally gendered industries have been historically linked in the region, as filmmaker Anne Lewis's 1991 film *Fast Food Women* reveals. A manager at Druther's fast food restaurant in Whitesburg, Kentucky, who appears in the film says, "95% of the applications I take in are female. . . . Most applications I'm getting now is women whose husbands are laid off. They're having to go out in the workforce because there's no other income coming in." He reports that men, particularly married men or those with children, won't take these jobs, but with the current "coal situation" he's seen a spike in applications from women, for whom there are few other employment options. Angie Hogg, a worker at Pizza Hut, asks the camera, "Where else are you going to get a job in Whitesburg? I guess the guy driving around in a Mercedes could tell me that, couldn't he?" Unsurprisingly, employment in the food service industry is especially high in places where a high percentage of residents live in poverty. Between 2000 and 2010, the increase in employment in the food service industry was significantly higher in "distressed counties" in Appalachia, while jobs in mining, agriculture, and timber industries declined more than in statistically better-faring counties.[25]

Hot dogs and the businesses that sell them are important aspects of

West Virginia's cultural heritage and social life, but they are ultimately part of a precarious economy, relying on nonunion low-wage labor done mostly by women who are left with few options for employment elsewhere. The service industry is particularly susceptible to the economic, social, and environmental drag in a state with a declining population and growing unemployment. When Emily and I met Joshua Skeen in 2016, he told us that profit margins aren't what they used to be. His mother made more money when Skeenies charged ten cents per dog in 1953 (equivalent to about $1 in today's money).[26] In 2016, when fully loaded dogs cost $1.90, the profit margins were lower. Just days after our road trip in late June 2016, devastating floods swept through the state. Clendenin's Dairy Queen, a beloved hot dog spot, was destroyed. Near Buddy B's and Skeenies in Sissonville, high waters swept through roads, farmers' fields, and family camps, rendering them unsalvageable. On July 1, 2016, J's Grocery in Kegley announced that it would no longer be peddling food. "Working people used to come through on the train, but the coal mines here shut down and they haven't run the rail since October," Marie said. "It just got so slow—we started having to throw things out," Marie said. "We painstakingly made that decision to stop." The Burrells hope they'll be able to bring back food service in the future once the train returns and things pick up again. In May 2018, the West Virginia Hot Dog Blog Facebook page reported that Joshua Skeen had passed away and Skeenies had permanently closed.

Hot Dog Heritage, the Surround, and the Triviality Barrier

The very structures of things—institutions, communities, employment, the landscape—have changed rapidly in West Virginia. For example, McDowell County—home to the seventy-five-year-old Sterling Drive-In— whose population reached 100,000 in 1950, now has under 20,000 residents.[27] Mountaintop-removal mining has leveled and laid bare what were once forested peaks. Community graveyards and forested commons have been destroyed by strip mines and gas companies. In 2006, a Walmart opened in Kimball, quickly became the biggest employer in the county, then left just ten years later. But somehow these drive-ins in the coalfields have stuck around. They are a nostalgic relic to some—Diana Hamilton says King Tut is a frequent stopping place for vintage car collectors on their way to an antique car show. But mostly they provide a sense of stability, their owners sometimes going to extreme measures to preserve

FIGURE 6.2. Neon sign at King Tut Drive-In in Beckley, West Virginia, June 11, 2016. Photo by the author.

that consistency. Dave McKay says it costs him a "dang fortune" to keep King Tut's vintage neon sign blazing. And when suppliers have changed, he's retrofitted the recipes to keep the menu and its offerings the same as they ever were, with some recipes dating back to the 1930s-era books his grandmother kept.

Like pimento cheese sandwiches in North Carolina, slug burgers in Mississippi, and West Virginia's own pepperoni rolls, hot dogs are fast and filling.[28] Priced at a buck or three, they're cheap and convenient, pervasive and dependable. Local joints try to hang on, often fulfilling a need in

food-insecure areas. "The type of customer that comes here is not necessarily somebody who's got time or the money to go sit in the sit-down
restaurant," said McKay. "So we also keep the prices absolutely as low as
we can. I don't take a lot of money out of this place. I don't need to. So if
we can keep the prices down we will, and it serves a segment of the society that needs it, too. Besides the fact it's good food."[29] Because hot dog
establishments are a central and sometimes the only gathering place in
town, they function as multipurpose community centers. From a first job
to a first date, hot dog joints are often the sites of life milestones, the place
you go to celebrate, meet up with your friends, or just grab a quick meal.
As West Virginia writer V. C. McCabe put it, her hometown hot dog stand
was a "building of memories." The double meaning of "building" as both
a noun that describes a physical structure, and a gerund that represents
the layering of meaning was, I think, intentional.

Some cultural traditions can be so embedded they are barely perceptible from the inside. They are part of the cultural "surround," which
folklorist Dorothy Noyes says comprises the "spatiotemporal, material,
linguistic, and gestural frameworks of social interaction."[30] Some might
call it "sense of place." Hot dogs in West Virginia are one of those cultural
forms and practices that are so deeply ingrained in social life that they can
be easy to take for granted, only missed once they're no longer available.
Stanton calls them a "symphony of taste that quite possibly is the reason
that many transplanted West Virginians can never really be happy living
anywhere else."[31] There are in fact many comments on his blog from West
Virginia expats who report that West Virginia dogs are the one thing they
miss from home. Elements of "the surround" characteristically provide
comfort, a return to the sense of place, of the familiar. As Noyes puts it,
"The folklore of the surround inures us gently to the real, making it an old
robe in which we can relax."[32] Hot dogs are indeed an aesthetic expression
significant in the cultural life of the state—a storied and regional form
and foodways practice with ties to immigrant history and gendered labor.
The hot dog joints that pepper the West Virginia landscape constitute
an important element of the built environment, examples of vernacular
architecture in concrete and neon. The steamed bun and frank with its
perfect synergy of toppings is one of the everyday ordinary things that
give West Virginia its West Virginia–ness.

But the cultural forms and practices that constitute the surround have
a tendency to fade into the background, become invisible from an emic
perspective, and be viewed as insignificant, unworthy of attention. Hot

dogs in particular are subject to an additional triviality barrier because they are small, seemingly unserious or juvenile, and frankly, fun.[33] And like all foodways, they're ephemeral, gone upon consumption. Additionally, West Virginia hot dogs are a hybridized form—part mass culture and part vernacular, the factory-produced bun and weenie paired with from-scratch slaw and chili. While many favorite family recipes are ritually prepared for holidays and passed down through generations, hot dogs are more likely to be bought at local drive-ins and restaurants. For these reasons, cultural forms like hot dogs often fall through the cracks of the documentation and preservation efforts of folklorists and cultural workers who concern themselves with sustaining community-based practices and expressions. The people who make the beloved hot dogs, mostly women earning below a livable wage, are not recognized by James Beard Awards or the National Heritage Fellowships (the National Endowment for the Arts has in fact never awarded the nation's highest honor in the folk and traditional arts to a foodways practitioner). Hot dog joints do not qualify for cultural heritage grants.[34]

Historical archeologist James Deetz writes of the triviality barrier in the context of museums, considering that the types of historical objects most likely to be preserved in such institutions and documented for the archival record are not necessarily those that are part of the everyday cultural surround. "The question of the factors that favor survival of certain objects and the disappearance of others is important here. . . . If we were to rely on museum collections, we might get an impression of a much richer level of material wealth than truly was the case. This is because most museums save the unusual and the valuable object, and individuals now and in the past consign commonplace objects to the dump."[35] Though hot dogs and the drive-ins that sell them may be a pervasive aspect of West Virginia place, culture, and social life, and have been for almost the entire life of the state, how will that be represented in the historical record? More important, how can we support the home cooks, recipe holders, and "buildings of memories" now?

As always, we can look to the work of these practitioners, tradition bearers, and local communities themselves for ideas. As communities recover from twinned environmental and economic calamities, hot dogs find their way into new circumstances in the surround. After the 2016 flood that killed twenty-three people and destroyed over 1,500 homes and businesses in West Virginia, Chum's set up a temporary stand in Clendenin, one of the hardest-hit areas.[36] They gave away free dogs to the flood victims and volunteers helping with recovery efforts. Stewart's Hot Dogs in Huntington and Kenova became drop-off sites for flood victim supplies. Hot dogs are embedded in the social life of the state—whether the event is celebratory or tragic or somewhere in between. Ubiquitous, almost imperceptibly so, they are the source of stories, strong opinions, nostalgic longing, family meals, and social spaces. While a hot dog can't restore what West Virginia has lost, it can offer sustenance—nutritional and communal, affirming the strong ties that bind specific dog preferences and make hot dog joints important social spaces. Folklorists and cultural workers working in local communities around the country can help by paying attention to the cultural surround and examining what is considered valuable, ensuring that other forms that may be considered insignificant and are aligned with the working class, women, immigrants, and other marginalized groups do not succumb to the triviality barrier. We might consider how we support the practitioners of these forms and traditions—the carriers of the recipes and the social spaces that emerge around them. This phenomenon, of course, extends beyond hot dogs, but here in West Virginia, they offer a delicious, historical, and culturally embedded example of such a form, where people share a common refrain of chili, slaw, mustard, and onions.

CHAPTER 7

Will the Squared Circle Be Unbroken?

Independent Pro Wrestling as a West Virginia Tradition

In memory of Shirley Love (1933–2020)

IT'S SATURDAY NIGHT in Madison, West Virginia, the county seat of Boone County, population 3,076. A crowd of a few hundred mills about the Madison Civic Center, grabbing cups of pop and slices of pizza from the concession tables and finding their seats under the stark fluorescent gym lights. The families and groups of middle-aged men in T-shirts, jeans, and ball caps could be fans at a local high school basketball game, but tonight the basketball hoops are pulled up toward the ceiling, out of reach. Advertisements for local businesses line the wall: personal injury lawyers, a motorcycle club, a black lung clinic. In the center of the floor is a square ring enclosed by three red, white, and blue rubber ropes, with metal folding chairs surrounding it. At 7 p.m. sharp, an announcer's sing-song voice echoes across the gym, "Ladies and Gentlemen, it's time for All Star Wrestling's Thirteenth Anniversary, live from the Civic Center in beautiful Madison, West Virginia." The crowd stands for a recording of the national anthem, heads turning toward a small American flag hanging on a curtain divider. The old man behind me makes a cymbal sound with his cheeks after every musical phrase, his "chhhh!" buzzing in my ear.

We take our seats and, with little fanfare, launch into the first match of the card—a special memorial battle royale between local independent wrestlers, regional legends from Smoky Mountain Wrestling and Oak Hill, West Virginia's Saturday Nite Wrestlin', along with a few World Wrestling Entertainment (WWE) Hall of Famers. Altogether about two dozen wrestlers pile into the ring, jostling for space and an opportunity to take shots at whoever gets shoved their way. Bedlam ensues. A Fidel Castro look-alike, the Cuban Assassin #2, enlists his tag team partners, the Cuban Commando and the Cuban Mercenary (all shirtless in matching camo fatigues) to choke ASW's Blazing Eagle, a masked heavyweight, against the ropes. The Appalachian Dream, Casey King, a dandy from Kentucky sporting tight briefs and a blue sequined jacket, sprays confetti in the face of two attacking brutes but exits early as no-nonsense veteran Shane Storm eliminates him after a body drop. Smokey C—a ponytailed and heavily tattooed scrawny type whose bandana, cut-off jeans, and Phish walk-up music signal his popular pothead gimmick—eventually emerges as the unlikely victor.[1] His more jacked and oiled peers still roll on the mat, rubbing their wounds.

The Pokémon theme song heralds the next match, welcoming to the ring relative newcomer and Boone County champion Huffmanly, "The Leader of #TheYeetMovement," a reference to an internet meme denoting excitement or enthusiasm. At twenty-three, Huffmanly, whose real name is Kasey Huffman, is one of the youngest wrestlers on tonight's card. Though he's long-haired and bearded, his boy-next-door demeanor belies his name; he's a local hero babyface (or face) whose internet and anime references endear him particularly to the kids in the crowd (see plate 7.1).[2] As he circles the ring to the cheering of fans, vaguely Middle Eastern music—possibly ripped from the soundtrack of *Indiana Jones and the Last Crusade*—cuts through the noise, arresting the audience. A chubby henchman in a headscarf, sunglasses, and black suit emerges from the wings and walks down the entrance ramp waving a black flag with a white silhouette of a camel. Kids line the walkway, waving their arms above their heads to mimic the flag. As the curtains part, a mysterious masked man in a black robe and blue briefs appears, staring down the audience, a keffiyeh over his head. He is, we're told by the announcer, "The Syrian Noble Sheik, straight from the hot sands of the Middle East." Clutching a prayer rug and a scimitar, he menacingly approaches the ring. He and Huffmanly scuffle before the referee can jump in, the Sheik wielding his sword against the Boone County champion. An old man in the audience leaps from his seat, offering the unarmed Huffmanly his pocket knife for protection. The henchman grabs the mic from the announcers. "We're going to burn this town down!" he taunts. A man in the crowd yells back, "It's already burnt down, you idiot!" Then the henchman issues the ultimate threat: If the Sheik wins, he will "destroy the American way of life, and make gas prices . . . SKYROCKET!" The crowd screams in revolt.

I'm both disturbed and completely transfixed by this narrative unfolding before me—the assemblage of vague signifiers and ethnic stereotypes to vividly construct an obvious heel.[3] In this too-bright gym with bad acoustics in a small coalfield town, ASW has achieved what all good wrestling strives for: an easily discernible battle of binaries that, through an injection of high camp, transcends the two wrestlers in the ring to stage a moral and political battle between the forces of good and evil. Our boos and jeers are no longer merely the cries of wrestling fans sitting in metal folding chairs in a gym, clutching our Ziploc baggies of bake sale brownies, but universal arbiters of justice.

As Huffmanly stages a comeback to handily defeat his rival and the crowd settles, relieved, I remember the metal plaque I saw hanging in the lobby when I entered the Civic Center this evening. The inscription reads,

JUNIOR HADDAD RECREATION CENTER

IN MEMORY

OF

NATHAN HADDAD JR.

"S.S. CITIES SERVICES TOLEDO"

REPORTED MISSING JUNE 12, 1942

GULF OF MEXICO—WORLD WAR II

"HE GAVE HIS LIFE FOR HIS COUNTRY"

The wall hanging honors the veteran and Boone County native son of a local businessman and immigrant from Lebanon who donated money to build the town pool and park. Its presence in the gym complicates the constructed binary of the All-American hometown hero versus the Middle Eastern other.[4] But this detail is not acknowledged or even implied in tonight's match. There is no irony in wrestling.

ALL STAR WRESTLING is one of at least a half-dozen independent professional wrestling promotions operating across West Virginia in towns like Kanawha City, Dunbar, Hurricane, and ASW's home of Madison.

These companies, like a local dance or theater troupe, are run by a promoter who employs, as independent contractors, a card of local wrestlers who wrestle at each company show. Their contracts are not exclusive, though; wrestlers cross-pollinate, appearing as guest wrestlers on a circuit of other promotions across the state and region. While independent, these circuits work in conjunction with nationally known televised promotions such as WWE, All Elite Wrestling (AEW), or Total NonStop Action Wrestling (TNA), which occasionally sign wrestlers from the independents, like a minor leaguer getting pulled up into the majors. In turn, local promotions often feature retired celebrities from national and regional companies—a serious draw for the promotion, and a way for the former wrestlers to make money after their body is shot, or they can no longer get over with fans, or they just can't give it up.[5] At ASW matches I've seen Gangrel (David William Heath), Sunny (Tammy Lynn Sytch), Tracy Smothers, Ricky Morton, and Jim Cornette and the Midnight Express, among others, make cameos, glad handing and signing autographs—always for a fee.

But independent wrestling doesn't quite have the same glamour and polish, or the dramatic cuts, pyrotechnics, and extravagant costumes, seen in the WWE and other televised promotions. In West Virginia, shows are generally held inside local community centers and armory gyms or occasionally outdoors in grocery store parking lots and small town street festivals. Tickets range from ten to fifteen dollars (at some promotions you pay more to sit in the front rows rather than the bleachers, a difference of about twenty feet) and you can buy them in advance at the local tire shop or weightlifting gym, or by emailing the promoter. The events are family-oriented, most not serving alcohol and prohibiting wrestlers and announcers from using foul language or making vulgar gestures. Locals set up tables in the lobby, selling homemade baked goods and vintage wrestler trading cards, figurines, and signed photographs. Beyond a poster of the grimacing wrestlers striking threatening poses plastered on the yellow cement block wall, there is little other décor. At the beginning of the match, a wrestler walks out to their theme song played over the booming sound system, exciting the crowds with fist pumps and displays of valor if they're a face. If they're a heel, they come out sneering and insulting the marks.[6] But no wrestlers have microphones (unless they steal the announcer's, which happens fairly frequently); they must rely on body language, facial expressions, and well-conceived gimmicks to get fans over. While there are some sculpted bodybuilder types on the independent circuit, many of the local wrestlers in West Virginia do not have the stereotypical wrestler's physique. In ASW, there's a full range of body types represented, from scrawny and short to fit and built, "dad bods" to husky boys: a body positivity exhibition for men.[7]

I attended my first wrestling match—an ASW promotion at the Madison Civic Center—with West Virginia Public Broadcasting reporter Roxy Todd in the summer of 2018. Because Roxy was reporting a story, we had access to the prematch training session and interviewed wrestlers backstage during the show, so, from the outset, my introduction to the sport offered a peek behind the kayfabe curtain. Since then I've attended numerous independent pro wrestling shows in West Virginia—ASW and otherwise—in local rec and civic centers, a mine safety training facility, outdoors at a dance center, and in a city park. You could say I've become a casual fan (though perhaps a strange one, as I pull out my notebook periodically during matches to furiously scribble notes). I've also interviewed various West Virginia wrestlers, ASW promoter Gary Damron, former local televised wrestling show emcee Shirley Love, and former *Beckley Register-Herald* wrestling columnist Gary Fauber. I've also conducted historical research to understand the origins of the sport in West Virginia.

In the past ten years, independent wrestling has boomed in the Mountain State. While Kasey Huffman remembers the early days of ASW drawing only thirty to forty people, today its shows regularly draw crowds of 300–400. This is no small feat in Boone County, with its already small population having declined 14 percent between 2000 and 2018, and employment down 80 percent from 2008 to 2016.[8] Beyond the hustle and hard work of promoter Gary Damron, Huffman can't pinpoint exactly what's to account for the sport's rising popularity, but aside from high school football games and church, few other local events can draw a crowd and bring the community together in one place. The closest movie theater is over twenty miles away. In the county with the highest per capita opioid economic burden in the country—estimated at over $206.5 million for a population of 23,645—having a one-of-a-kind, live, and sober family event like a hometown wrestling promotion is a bright spot in the community.[9] Rocky Hardin, who has been wrestling with ASW for the past ten years as Rocky Rage, says, "It's a town based on coal mines. So everybody's pretty much tight knit, everybody knows everybody, and there's not a lot of stuff for people to do. So when people are at the store and they're like, 'Hey look, there's a [ASW] poster—oh yeah, John said he's gonna be at that show.' And it's like, 'Oh, well I'm definitely going.' It gets people out of the house in a positive light."[10]

A West Virginia Brand: The History of Wrestling in the Mountain State

Independent pro wrestling has a long history in Appalachia, West Virginia in particular, and is rooted in the disenfranchisement and land enclosure of the working class. In his excellent article "Gouge and Bite, Pull Hair and Scratch: The Social Significance of Fighting in the Southern Backcountry," Elliott J. Gorn traces the history of public brawling—which functioned to both settle personal feuds and as scheduled onlooker entertainment—in the Virginia backcountry, from before the Revolutionary War to the antebellum era. Gorn argues that this vicious style of no rules, "rough-and-tumble" fighting took hold in subsistence farm communities in the South and mountains in part due to the violence embedded in the life of the working class—and to some extent even the planter class— through manual work and constant jostling of men in an ever-shifting class hierarchy. This no-holds-barred, particularly southern style of fighting contrasted with boxing's "fair fight," which obeyed Broughton's rules.[11] Gorn writes, "Above all, brutal recreations toughened men for a violent social life in which the exploitation of labor, the specter of poverty, and a fierce struggle for status were daily realities."[12] As class structure became defined and settlements more established, the planter class developed what they considered to be more genteel systems of dueling, and brawling became exclusively associated with the poor and working class in the southern backcountry. Accounts of brutal "eye-gouging" matches along the Ohio River and its tributaries in the territory that is now West Virginia fascinated travel writers at the time, who used these displays of socially acceptable violence as examples of the barbarity of the frontier wilderness and the people who made their homes there.

Irish writer Thomas Ashe describes a gouging match in Wheeling in 1806 in his book *Travels in America*.[13] At a pub in town, he witnessed two men arguing over whose horse was faster. They placed a bet and rode off to the race track, as "two-thirds of the population followed: —blacksmiths, shipwrights, all left work: the town appeared a desert. The stores were shut." Others placed their bets, and when the race results were disputed, two men—a "Kentuckyan" and a Virginian—continued to fight, a ring forming around them. When an onlooker asked if they would rather "fight fair" or "rough and tumble," they chose the latter, the Virginian eventually gouging out both eyes, snapping off the nose, and tearing off the lips of the Kentuckyan. After the latter went off to have his face stitched back together, "the spectacle ended, and the citizens refreshed with whiskey and biscuit, sold on the ground, the races were renewed, and possibly other editions of the monstrous history." His guide later informed him that such public fighting happened frequently, about two or three times a week, and during the spring and fall horse races, such brawls were held for fourteen days straight. This type of violent spectacle was not restricted to Wheeling but "spread down the river" into Kentucky and what is now West Virginia. Gorn notes that the savagery of these rough-and-tumble matches entered the folklore of the period, with New Englanders refer-ring to empty eye sockets as a "Virginia brand," and Kentuckians telling of "battle-royals so intense that severed eyes, ears, and noses filled bushel baskets."[14]

Southern backwoods brag speech directed as verbal insults and full-on spoken duels were another means to threaten or defend the social stand-ing of a frontiersman, subsistence farmer, or boatman. In the early nine-teenth century, boasts of masculine dominance, with audacious claims and comparisons to dangerous animals and powerful inanimate objects, were employed by working-class men turned folk heroes like East Ten-nessee frontiersman Davy Crockett and legendary Ohio and Mississippi River boatman and brawler Mike Fink, who taunted, "I'm half-wild horse and half cock-eyed alligator . . . and I can out-run, out-jump, out-shoot, out-brag, out-drink, an' out-fight, rough-an'-tumble, no holds barred, any man on both sides the river from Pittsburgh to New Orleans."[15] Verbal repartee, physical fights, and the mythology of both externalized the struggles and anxieties felt by frontiersmen. Gorn writes, "The legends [of brawling] were texts that allowed plain folk to dramatize the tensions and ambiguities of their lives; they hauled society's goods yet lived on its fringe; they destroyed forests and game while clearing the land for settlement; they killed Indians to make way for the white man's culture; they struggled for self-sufficiency only to become ensnared in economic dependency. Fight narratives articulated the fundamental contradiction of frontier life—the abandonment of 'civilized' ways that led to the ulti-mate expansion of civilized society."[16] In proving their prowess in the context of a gouging match, brawlers were also demonstrating to their peers their worth as frontiersmen, subsistence farmers, or river boatmen. Champions of rough-and-tumble fighting were storied as heroes in their local communities, a battle-tested vernacular recognition beyond the bounds of the "official" hierarchical control maintained by landholders, boat captains, and wealthy merchants.

The brawling and eye-gouging matches of the antebellum era eventually become more formalized, and official wrestling matches began to be reported in West Virginia newspapers as early as 1889. A 1907 *Bluefield Daily Leader* article gave news of a wrestling match in the city, saying the sport had gone out of favor but was now back in vogue.[17] In 1929 the *Beckley Post-Herald* reported, "Huntington and Charleston are now showing packed houses in wrestling matches and the same will no doubt be true of Beckley once the sport gets a deal hold."[18] During this era, wrestling by both local and itinerant wrestlers took place in armories, skating rinks, opera houses, and Odd Fellows halls in cities like Wheeling, Charleston, Huntington, and Bluefield, but there is some evidence that it also was presented in smaller towns and possibly coal camps.[19] An October 20, 1910, article in the *Bluefield Daily Telegraph* informed readers of "a woman who claims to be the champion wrestler of the world . . . pulling off some big stunts in the coal field," citing stops in the coal boomtown of Pocahontas, Virginia, and the financial hub of the Pocahontas coalfield, Bramwell, West Virginia. I asked historian Ron Eller if he had come across any evidence of wrestling matches in coal camps. Looking through his research files, he found no references to organized wrestling in such a setting, but he said that most of his sources came from larger company towns, where companies did support entertainment in the form of baseball teams and opera venues. "I suspect that there may have been such [wrestling] events in the smaller camps," he said. "After WWII, the organized entertainment venues of the larger camps were generally terminated with the decline of those camps. . . . My general impression would be that nonorganized violence increased during the periods of greatest economic and social change and that organized entertainment efforts by the larger industry were efforts to control such disorder in the workforce and manage production."

"A Soap Opera for Men": Underdogs, Workers, Psychiatrists, and Entertainers of the Squared Circle

As wrestling took hold as organized entertainment, the violence embedded in the sport assumed the form of a pantomime of its previous iteration as a struggle for social standing, while retaining its strong class affiliation. Wrestling in West Virginia today arises out of the cultural context of a similarly imperiled working class, which faces structural economic pressure due to reliance on a dying extractive and destructive monoeconomy that offers few alternatives. In ASW's home of Boone County, once the highest coal-producing county in the United States, coal jobs decreased 60 percent between 2009 and 2015.[20] In the face of the coal industry's decline, few other employment opportunities exist, and when they do, they pay a fraction of what coal jobs did. As people move away for work, the population decline has a ripple effect on the economic well-being of the entire community.[21] The violence of these mining jobs continues to impact both human bodies and the land they live on, in the form of black lung, a high rate of occupational injury, unsafe drinking water, and a desecrated landscape. Miners' pensions and health-care benefits are perpetually threatened by coal company closures and bankruptcy. Meanwhile, pharmaceutical company McKesson allegedly funneled 1.2 million doses of hydrocodone and oxycodone into the county between 2007 and 2012—amounting to 51 doses per resident.[22] Attention from the health-care industry in the community has frequently been focused on extracting profits for corporations, compromising rather than benefiting the health and well-being of residents.

Shirley Love, an Oak Hill native and announcer for the wildly popular *Saturday Nite Wrestlin'*, which WOAY TV in Oak Hill broadcast across southern West Virginia and into Virginia and eastern Kentucky from 1954 to 1977, attributes the sport's popularity in West Virginia to its portrayal of violence. "It's like why is deer hunting so popular in West Virginia? Squirrel hunting? I don't know, it's just [that] the people like violence, whether it's true or not. If you're sitting in a restaurant and there's a fight outside, somebody says, 'FIGHT!' and everybody gets up and goes out and watches it. . . . Violence is a way of life." Love is quick to add that this attraction to violence is not necessarily particular to the state; rather it's human nature to be compelled by such drama. While wrestling may champion violence, it also defies real-life material conditions by asserting control over that violence and converting it to a safe spectacle of entertainment. A babyface with a working-class-hero gimmick, both historically and presently, is portrayed as physically powerful, while a heel, often portrayed as rich, egotistical, or underhandedly powerful, must cheat to win. In his article on the masculine melodrama of wrestling, Henry Jenkins III writes, "The appeal of such a myth to a working class audience should be obvious. In the realm of their everyday experience, strength often gets subordinated into alienated labor. Powerful bodies become the means of their economic exploitation rather than a resource for bettering their lot."[23]

This performative subversion of power allows the audience, particularly male fans, to see themselves reflected in the personas of the wrestlers, who effectively serve as their proxies. Wrestling continues to be dominated by men, mirroring the masculinization of the region through labor—the coal miner, the logger, the steelworker—in the press and popular imagination. Rocky Hardin says, "It's always a story of the underdog. It always has [been] and always will be the easiest thing for someone to get behind. And like I said earlier, it's almost like if you're at the bar and you look over—'Hey look, this [wrestler] looks like a guy I saw at the bar the other night.' Or, 'Hey, this guy could be sitting right next to me.' So it goes back to that. It's easier to relate." This preference for the underdog facilitates both a personal identification with the narrative in the ring, while the entertainment frame establishes a comfortable distance. Fans can observe justice being enacted by exaggerated versions of themselves who physically dominate their enemies. Nearly every wrestler, promoter, or announcer I spoke with says that one of the primary assets wrestling offers its audience is an escape. Shirley Love witnessed this sixty years ago. Elderly people or a mother with ten kids would

> come into the station. And . . . they would be people that you had to almost catch their eye and keep their eye to nod hello or "how are you" or "hi." So they come into the studio and they're very reserved, but get their seat and they just sit there until the wrestling match started. And after about fifteen minutes, they were moving a little bit. Another fifteen minutes they're [pounds table] you know, and another fifteen minutes they're on their feet with [makes jeering expression] good rascalin'. In another fifteen minutes, they're ready to get in there and fight. And when they left they would be, "Yap, yap, yap, yap, yap, yap." So I always wondered how long it would take a psychiatrist to get out of those people what an hour and a half did at the TV station with that *Saturday Nite Wrestlin'*.[24]

Wrestler Jan Madrid, a one-time Fayetteville resident and favorite *Saturday Nite Wrestlin'* heel, said, "We're the greatest psychologists in the world. The average working person can't afford a psychologist, but he can release all that emotion at a wrestling match."[25] The social environment that live wrestling engenders, where fans are free to cheer and shout, paired with an identification with the wrestlers in the ring, can be a catharsis. ASW promoter Gary Damron says, "I've actually had women call me before and say, 'Hey, we come to your show because we've had a bad week, we've had a lot of stress and anger, and coming to your show . . . I can get up and scream and holler and hoot, bad mouth the bad guys when they come out.' And that's a good thing because it's a stress reliever."[26] Talking back to the actual "bad guy"—a boss, an estranged partner, or a hometown nemesis—has real consequences, but that frustration can be channeled and redirected to the wrestling arena. Citing Norbert Elias and Eric Dunning's *The Quest for Excitement: Sport and Leisure in the Civilizing Process*, Henry Jenkins notes that sports popular in working-class communities, like wrestling, boxing, and football (both American and British), offer a sanctioned space for public emotional release, bucking against rules for decorum upheld by upper-class society—an echo of the class association of brawling or "gouging" in contrast to the more polite forms of dueling of the middle and upper classes.[27] Anecdotally, that emotional display, shared in public but contained within the rules of sport, can have mental health benefits. For Kasey Huffman, that's not just for the community of fans but for himself, too. "If it wasn't for wrestling, I really don't know where I would be. Especially suffering with depression and stuff growing up, wrestling was the escape. And I feel like now in West Virginia we can be that escape for other people. I feel like that's our job."[28]

Wrestlers function as entertainers and community psychiatrists, but they are also workers and think of themselves as such. They even adopt the labels of blue-collar work, referring to each other as "workers" and "carpenters." All wrestlers, including those in the WWE, are independent contractors. In the independents, like ASW, it's gig work; it pays very little and is done for the love of the sport. Gary Damron says most independent wrestlers he works with make about forty to fifty dollars per match and rely on merch sales to complement what they bring in directly from the promoter. Pay can fluctuate from show to show and often hinges on a wrestler's specific performance that night, or their popularity with the fans. As a result, there is a level of secrecy kept between wrestlers regarding compensation. Rocky Hardin, who worked previously as a certified nursing assistant but is now wrestling full time, says,

> Some wrestlers might get paid a little more than their friend and if they find that out then there's heat there, so it's one of those subjects where you could be best friends but you don't talk about it . . .

you know what I'm saying? It really just depends too. Like sometimes if you're in something a little bit more hardcore crazy, you
might get a little extra. Or if the crowd's up, if there's more people
out there . . . all of the guys might get a little extra on that too. But
yeah, that's one of the things to where it's not really talked about
among the boys. It's kind of like, when the promoters come in with
the pay, if it's not in an envelope, it's one of those handshakes, pass
it off thing. So yeah, it just depends. I do well, though.

Kasey Huffman works a day job as manager of a small medical business
and wrestles on the weekends. As independent contractors, neither Huffman nor Hardin receive health insurance or other benefits through their
promotion, though they put their bodies on the line at every match. This
level of precarity and physical toll is familiar in the coalfields. While the
outcome is staged, wrestling is extremely physically challenging, even
dangerous. All the wrestlers I talked to expressly told me that despite
the gimmicks, constructed storylines, and choreographed moves, the toll
on their bodies and the injuries are real. Rocky Hardin said, "I've had
one, two, three, four teeth fixed, I have four more cracked in the back,
my knees are shot, my neck's shot, and now you're starting to see people
that's like, 'Hey look, no matter if the finish is predetermined, you guys
are breaking your backs for this.' And that's the cool thing. So people are
starting to understand, like yeah, it might be a worked environment, but
that's a beating that they're taking night in and night out." Huffman, a
former high school soccer player, said, "The fans and the other people
that don't really get wrestling—they consider it like acting—they consider
it, I'm gonna put it in quotations, 'fake,' but it is by far like the most real
thing I've ever done when it comes to a physical standpoint. . . . I feel like
wrestling is a live action movie with no retakes. It's like a play, right? But
it's very physical. But there's still realism to it like when we strike each
other, slam each other—that stuff is real."[29]

The question of what is "real" and what is not is the crux of the sport,
a line wrestlers and promoters are perpetually dancing around and bend-
ing, blending truth and fiction to build intrigue and create plot points.
The sport's drama has been compared to opera, Shakespeare, and a "soap
opera for men."[30] Roland Barthes calls it a morality play and equates it
with French theater. Though as a society we are perfectly comfortable
with the artifice of the stage, the constructed reality of an episodic television show, or a pulp novel, the line between fakery and reality in wrestling

still trips us up—and has for the lifetime of the sport. Freud attributes this inability to discern if a thing or phenomenon is alive or dead, real or fake, as "the uncanny," a feeling he describes as being akin to "the idea of being robbed of one's eyes," an intellectual gouging. Substituting "wrestler" for writer, his description can be read as an accurate summation of kayfabe: "It is true that the writer creates a kind of uncertainty in us in the beginning by not letting us know, no doubt purposely, whether he is taking us into the real world or into a purely fantastic one of his own creation. . . . We must bow to his decision and treat his setting as though it were real for as long as we put ourselves into his hands."[31] As David Shoemaker writes in his book *The Squared Circle: Life, Death and Professional Wrestling*, there is no exact identifiable moment when wrestling began incorporating staged elements; even the more official matches of early "professional wrestling" often had fixed outcomes.[32] The sport became popular in the United States around the turn of the twentieth century as a carnival sideshow, where locals were invited to try their hands at throwing the strong man. These exhibitions were almost always stacked in favor of the wrestler in various ways and were paired with other forms of plebeian theater like vaudeville or circus arts. Richie Acevedo, an Oak Hill native and resident who wrestles as the Cuban Assassin #2 (his father was the Cuban Assassin #1 and a *Saturday Nite Wrestlin'* star), said, "Wrestlers have always crossed over with the vaudeville plays . . . the wrestling card was based on a vaudeville play. Act 1, Act 2, Act 3; Match 1, Match 2, Match 3."[33] As those common theatrical forms faded in popularity, wrestling was a holdover without context, and its dramatic elements became somewhat inscrutable.

Kayfabe and the Thespian Arts of Grimaces, Make Believe, and Mat Pounding

The modern era of West Virginia wrestling began in 1954, when WOAY started broadcasting what was originally named *Saturday Night Wrestling*. Early in the life of the program, the Athletic Commission, citing a 1931 state law that gave it jurisdiction over any professional wrestling and amateur and professional boxing, threatened a court order if the station didn't sanction the matches and pay the commission's referee fee. The next Saturday, the station owner, R. R. Thomas, had Shirley Love precede the show with the disclaimer, "Ladies and gentleman, the following program is not an athletic event. The following program is prearranged for your entertainment."[34] Just to be sure, Thomas abbreviated, "Saturday," changed "Night" to "Nite," and dropped the "g" from the title, which now appeared as "Sat. Nite Wrestlin'" on the marquee, as if those letters bore the semantic weight of the genre, a few pen strokes marking the dividing line between sport and theater. The law was tested again in 1969, when eight wrestlers, a promoter, and a referee were arrested at a match in Bluefield for wrestling and promoting without a license. This was not some elaborate kayfabe storyline but a legitimate legal case. The promoter Warren Schernbach asserted, "The athletic commission is trying to deprive of us our right to entertain the public. Legally we are entertainers, not athletes."[35] The lawyer for the charged argued, "Petitioners herein are not primarily wrestlers. . . . Petitioners are showmen, actors, artist thespians not engaged in any contest of strength, but rather engaged in the thespian arts of facial grimaces, make believe, mat pounding, and use of all the props."[36] West Virginia Supreme Court judges dismissed the case, ruling that the men were actors and entertainers rather than athletes.[37]

But how much are fans aware of wrestling's staged aspects? Outsiders to the sport often assume fans (or even the wrestlers themselves) are dupes. Huffman says that when he tells strangers he's a professional wrestler, they often respond, "You know that's fake, right?" Shoemaker argues, and I would agree, that fans are, and have always been, in on the joke, though some are better at playing along than others.[38] A 1972 feature on the sports page of the *Charleston Daily Mail* headlined "Is Wrestling Real?" explores the question, with quotes from fans who argue on both sides, and wrestlers who deny everything. Everett and Yvonne Nichols, a couple from Clendenin, weigh in as a house divided, "'I like to watch them. Wrestling is just like a western on TV, it's a good show but it's fake.' His wife Yvonne disagrees . . . 'You better believe it's for real. But it makes me so mad. The dirty ones, like that Cuban [the Cuban Assassin #1] (who is billed as the West Virginia Heavyweight Champ) always seems to win.'"[39] Stories depicting the active—even violent—passion of the fans are part of the oral folklore of West Virginia wrestling. Shirley Love recalls an elderly woman emerging from the audience to stab a heel in the leg with her hatpin. During the following match on that night's card, she reappeared, this time spearing the babyface.[40] Love also recounts hearing the story of an old man from Backus, West Virginia, who while watching the show on TV became so enraged at the referee's blind eye that he pulled his shotgun out of the closet and shot the TV. This is, of course, a common trope (Elvis is said to have shot his television set at least once, upon seeing Robert Goulet perform live), but it is also perhaps evidence of how much the fans are knowing participants in the kayfabe of the sport. Whether the grandfather shot his TV or not is irrelevant, but it makes a great story.

Something about this phenomenon aligns stylistically with a particular subversive genre of Appalachian humor that engages with the dynamic of insider and outsider or powerful and powerless. It's not just who's in on the joke and who's out but who's in, who's not, and who knows it. This power-shifting technique is used to turn the tables on the outsider, the pompous, or the powerful, by creating a farce that plays right into their arrogance, obliviousness, or ignorant assumptions. The joke's on them, whether they know it or not.[41] Those who can't laugh at themselves or play along dig themselves into an even deeper hole. Wrestling's outsiders who imagine the fans as gullible patsies are missing the point and, in doing so, exposing their own pretension.

For the whole spectacle of the squared circle to work—what the kayfabe and the fans' buy-in all hinges on—is a good storyline. This is especially true in the independents, which require accommodation of varying skill levels among wrestlers and lack the special effects and big budgets the televised version of the sport can lean on to boost intrigue. Independent promoters like Gary Damron rely on compelling narratives and strong character portrayal to keep fans coming back to the live show each month. They must remember that this is theater. When local wrestling forgets that, and presents lagging narrative arcs, gimmicks that are lazily conveyed, and matches that drag on too long, it doesn't get over. Rocky Hardin told me, "I love being able to go out there and just tell stories. And that's what I tell my trainees. It's like, 'Hey guys, look we're storytellers. At the end of the day, we're storytellers. It's not about me getting all my stuff in, you getting all your stuff in.' It's about going out here and telling a story and when guys forget that, their matches in my opinion—they don't get over as much."

Richie Acevedo also identifies as a storyteller. "I wanted to be a cartoonist or an airline pilot, and instead I became a storyteller. And that's what wrestlers are—we tell stories. And you know, all wrestling matches are mini stories of a big story. So it's like a movie, but like with different chapters, different stories." What Acevedo prides himself on is being a "worker," a wrestler who puts in the work, who knows that selling the story to fans is his highest priority over any personal glory.

How you know you're a worker is, if you [you and your opponent] are in two separate locker rooms and you both only have the same finish, and you go out there and you work something, that's a worker. I don't call my match out in the locker room. I call my match in the ring, okay? I'm an artist. I got a blank canvas—hence the word *canvas* on the ring.[42] I paint my masterpiece, so you get a genuine one-of-a-kind. And today people paint by numbers. . . . But that's why I call myself a worker.[43]

Rather than work out all the moves in advance, Acevedo improvises with his opponent on the fly, using subtle gestures and whispers to communicate the next throw. This to him, is inherent to the artistry of wrestling and his role in crafting that narrative through original creative performance.

Wrestling as a West Virginia Vernacular Tradition

The art of wrestling is a vernacular form, transmitted orally and through observation, live, in television, and online. Acevedo says that wrestling is both part of his family heritage, as well as embedded in the heritage of West Virginia, "like coal mining." He learned the wrestling trade from his father and has passed it on to his son and nephew, who wrestle respectively as the Cuban Commando and the Cuban Mercenary (see fig. 7.1). "We call ourselves the Cuban Dynasty because in all honesty we are the heritage, my son, my nephew, myself. We are the royalty from wrestling. We are the connection to that past."[44] Both wrestling careers and wrestling fandom are often passed down by family members. Gary Fauber, a Montgomery, West Virginia, native and lifelong fan, who wrote a wrestling column for the Beckley newspaper in the 1990s, says he was introduced to it by his mother. "She was familiar with WOAY *Saturday Nite Wrestlin'* here in the area and we actually saw some wrestling on Super Station WTBS, as it was known back then, and she just started reminiscing about things that she had seen and I was just hooked."[45] Huffman says he got his "dad's knowledge when it comes to wrestling" and was "born into it," having watched wrestling with his father since before he can remember. "My dad—I feel like me and him got closer once I started [wrestling] because with my parents getting that divorce at a young age, I really didn't get to see my dad. And he was the one that really got me into it. So now he is like my number one biggest fan."[46]

Though there are a few wrestling schools in West Virginia, wrestling training is often a fairly informal process. Rocky and ASW's trainees

THE CUBAN ASSASSIN

FIGURE 7.1. Family photos belonging to wrestler Richie Acevedo, a.k.a. the Cuban Assassin #2: (top) his father, Angel Acevedo, a.k.a. the Cuban Assassin #1; (bottom) passport photographs of Angel Acevedo's parents, February 19, 2021. Photo by the author.

operate, like Huffman once did, under a loose apprenticeship model, "paying their dues" by traveling with the promotion, and helping set up, sell merch, and assist backstage. They train before matches (the only time there's an accessible ring), learning from seasoned veterans falls and back bumps, the selling of moves, how to do a promo, and how to develop their gimmicks. Brianna Knotts, a Morgantown native who has been training with Rocky and ASW for three months, says, "We don't have a school to go to. We train with Rocky and we follow him to the local shows, so we've traveled to Lincoln County, to Madison, here in Charleston, Hurricane, Marmet. . . . We try to be there at 3:00 to help them set the ring up. And then we stay until the ring comes down, so it's a lot of time and it's volunteer hours, so we're not getting paid. And we're paying to train."[47] She and her boyfriend, who is also a trainee, practice lock-up moves with each other at home between sessions. Even seasoned wrestlers learn (some say steal) from each other on the job, constantly borrowing moves, tag lines, and gimmicks. This is how knowledge is transmitted in wrestling's occupational culture. Acevedo says he stole taglines, popularized them, and now sees WWE wrestlers using them on TV. "For example, everybody would talk about Ricky Steamboat's Arm Drag. Well, he stole that from Jack Brisco. And Jack Brisco stole that from Malenko, Boris Malenko [laughs]. You know, we just take from each other, just one does it better than the other and it just happens to work out."

Some wrestling narratives must be conveyed on the spot, to create an instant dynamic for two wrestlers who have never faced each other before, while other sagas and rivalries unfold across multiple shows, even lasting years. When ASW books older legends, they draw on fans' collective memory of their gimmicks to fill in the gaps of persona and narrative that aren't overtly conveyed in the ring. Rocky says, "There's just something special about the wrestling fans in West Virginia. You know, they grow up with it. It's in their lives. You'll go to Madison and go to Kroger and you'll hear people talk about what happened at ASW in aisle 3, which is pretty cool." Huffmanly, who after his recent matches has been threatened over the PA system by an anonymous voice, says his fans have been demanding that the voice's identity be revealed. "A lot of the fans have been angry saying, 'We need to see him now!' They've been saying that for three months now—they're starting to get mad that they don't know who it is and they're blowing up my social medias, my Facebook, messaging me saying, 'Oh do you know who it is?' Nope! Sure don't!" Beyond just the ring, the plot points and theatrics developed in West Virginia independent wrestling become a common narrative in their respective communities, retold and rehashed in the grocery store aisle, around the dinner table, and in the comments of the wrestler's social media, which today, wrestlers use to expand their interactions with fans and build suspense. Shirley Love said that what made the televised *Saturday Nite Wrestlin'* popular was the interviews he would conduct with local fans between falls. It was not merely the wrestling but also the participatory commentary that made the show so dynamic across the viewing region. "We didn't have a delay on our broadcasting where we could stop it and edit it out," Love said, "so if someone got all fired up, and they usually did, I had to be pretty fast to pull the mic, and a lot of times I wasn't fast enough." He has countless stories of the colorful characters he interviewed at the matches. There was the little old woman who "looked like a Sunday School teacher" and, when asked what she thought of wrestler Jan Madrid, blurted on air, "I'd like to smack that SOB right in the mouth," as well as the young boy sporting a coonskin cap who bragged that his "grandpa found it in a trash dump!"[48]

Love would interact with fans who were watching at home as well, and said he received 75 to 100 fan letters each week when the show was airing. On one occasion, he mentioned on air that he was looking for a good place to go deer hunting the next weekend. A viewer wrote him a letter the next day, and that Sunday took Shirley hunting along Stewart Run on Cheat Mountain, serving him native trout the man had caught from a nearby stream.[49] Once in the spring, Love announced during the broadcast that he'd like to have "a good mess of fresh ramps." The next week, fans brought him several bags of the wild leeks.

> This one Saturday night, somebody brought a big bag and I had left them in the studio inadvertently. You have to remember, the auditorium would stay closed all week and it would get hot and it would get cold, you know, hot and cold air—the heat would come on. And then next Saturday night when we went across, oh Lord, that studio, it was rank! I didn't want to go in . . . much less to go in it to announce the wrestling matches. And the people that started coming in, you could [sniffs] you could see they'd sniff their nose, "What am I smelling?" [laughs].

Wrestling in West Virginia is a community phenomenon, entangled with other forms of vernacular culture—deer hunting in the fall and sharing foraged ramps with neighbors in the springtime, jabs about their potent smell being essential to the tradition. In the 1950s in Bluefield, wrestling matches were followed by a square dance with a local band.[50]

Love tells a story from after his wrestling announcer days:

> I was up in a little place called Hacker Valley, the northern part of Webster County. It's about as far north as you can get without heading south again. There was an old, abandoned farmhouse, beautiful—like an antebellum-type home, and you could tell it was old. But it had fields around it and it had brush and I wanted to find out who owns it to get my rabbit dog and come over and rabbit hunt sometime. So I told the lady, "Ma'am, that farm had to be a beautiful farm one time." Well, she says, "Well, you relate to that farm!" I said, "How would I relate to the farm?" She said that when she was a little girl and her brother was a little boy, the fella who owned it, we'll call him Mr. Brown, Mr. Brown owned the farm and he had the only television in the valley, and he would give her and her brother fifty cents to follow the antenna to the top of the mountain. And she said folks in the community would come up and they would each bring a dish, like chicken and green beans, mashed potatoes, whatever. And she said they had three tables and two of 'em they would put on the porch and one in the yard and they would have, as she described it, dinner on the grounds (that's West Virginia slang). She said she had her little spot over in the corner where she could see the TV set, and they'd all watch *Saturday Nite Wrestlin'*, and she said the porch would be full, where they could peek in the windows and then the inside too.[51]

According to folklorist Alan Jabbour, "dinner on the grounds" or "dinner on the ground" is a communal, "ritual meal held in the cemetery as part of a decoration. . . . The same phrase is used for congregational dinners after church services or during all-day sings of sacred music."[52] For that Hacker Valley community, local televised wrestling was considered an occasion for fellowship and a ritualized meal in community, just as a shape note sing, holiday church service, or Decoration Day. The communion was not only with those there on the grounds but also with a broader network that included Shirley Love, the wrestlers, and the locals interviewed on screen.

Today, Gary Damron takes pride in how his promotion fosters community. "One thing that I'm always told is that the fans that come to our shows, they feel like they're a part of our family. Not just me, but the wrestlers too. I stand here at the door while people are coming in and I greet every person. Because you want them to feel welcomed and you want 'em to feel like, 'Hey, I'm appreciated for going to that.'" The power of the community fostered through independent wrestling is recognized by outside entities looking to tap into the constituency. Shirley Love recalls meeting Jay Rockefeller and many other West Virginia politicians who would make an appearance at *Saturday Nite Wrestlin'* as a campaign stop. ASW is sponsored by a local church. "They love wrestling," Damron says, "and they feel that coming and having a table and passing out cards with their service times on it is connecting with the community. And honestly, since they've started coming here, they've gained like three or four members."

The wrestlers themselves are both modern-day bards and localized folk heroes who enact their own fables, championing the underdog, warning of the danger of an overinflated ego, or pitting good against evil. In his chapter on the construction of nineteenth-century American folk heroes, folklorist Richard Dorson writes, "America's idols all rise from the ranks of the common man and exhibit the traits and manners of unwashed democracy, spitting, bragging, brawling, talking slangily, ridiculing the dandy, and naively trumpeting their own merits,"[53] a prototype of the wrestler. The self-inflating braggadocious claims characteristic of American folk heroes like Fink and Crockett—comparing their strength and physical prowess to those of a vicious predator, a steamboat, or a python—can be traced throughout wrestling's history. In 1959, one such brag was published in a wrestling story in West Virginia's *Bluefield Daily Telegraph*: "Ali Bey is a cruel, sadistic Turk who is erected like a piece of granite and just as tough. He is mean and sneaky and his long arms like a baboar can be used for more cruelty than a poisonous cobra."[54] Today, wrestlers in both independent and televised national promotions do "spots" in which a wrestler grabs the mic, verbally eviscerating his opponent (or the crowd) with exaggerated metaphor and graphic threats. In the late 1990s and early aughts, Gary Fauber's column for the *Beckley Register-Herald* reported on local and televised World Wrestling Federation (WWF) matches. His column, "Figure IV," delivered wrestlers' threats and brag talk, reported on injuries, and on one occasion, relayed a message from the Cuban Commando, who wanted fans to know that he was dedicating his upcoming performance to his grandmother who had just passed away.[55] Like folk heroes, wrestlers are storied by the audience, in conversation, online, and in other forms of representation. At ASW's October 2019 "Halloween Mayhem" show in Madison, I saw at least three children dressed as local wrestlers—one as Kirk Blackman in a tank top and POSER cap, and two as Huffmanly, with blonde ponytail wigs, head-bands, and hands with "YEET" written in sharpie across their palms.

The narratives are not merely one-sided, controlled only by the promoter and wrestlers for consumption by fans; they are also participatory and dialogic. Fans are in conversation with each other during the match, to encourage a louder response or annotate out loud both backstory and the story arc that's unfolding before them in the ring. When Huffmanly was finally challenged by the mysterious voice, who snuck into the ring from behind, masked in a hoodie, a group of kids began repeatedly yelling, "Take Your Mask Off!" Later, when a masked wrestler took on the Barbarian—a National Wrestling Alliance, World Championship Wrestling, and WWF legend and fan favorite—a boy brought back the chant, and a grown woman responded, "You tell him, buddy!" Through their responses, both in person and online, the crowd can directly influence the direction of a storyline—which becomes a communally crafted folk narrative. Rocky Hardin says,

> If we're doing a storyline or we're doing some kind of angle and the fans aren't getting behind that, that's getting scratched. Because at the end of the day it's whatever makes the fans happy. That's what the promoter's gonna go for. A smart promoter listens to the crowd. Just like a wrestler . . . if I'm giving 'em this kind of match and let's say I'm doing chain wrestling, mat wrestling, and the crowd's not into that, okay, well let's switch it up. Let's try some dives and some high flying stuff. If they're not into that, well then, hey look, I'm getting ready to do a comedy spot real quick and it's gonna be, "Haha, look at me, look at Rocky, he's an idiot." But yeah, you have to be able to listen to the crowd and book according to what they want. . . . A promoter will listen to the majority of the crowd and go from there.[56]

Independent wrestling is an amalgam of forms—a place- and community-based vernacular expression that, similar to the hybridity of

West Virginia hot dogs (see chapter 6), also functions in part like popular mass culture. Narratives, a particular language, and knowledge of the local wrestlers and their entangled backstories are transmitted by, participated in, and consumed within a community, but they are also market-driven by an immediate feedback loop. As an entertainment form, live independent wrestling is unusual in that the narrative is often shaped on the spot, according to fan response. Whereas nationally televised wrestling has a longer feedback loop and is informed by television ratings, the indies are much more rooted in a specific community and shaped by local tastes. "It's almost like a public speech that you're wanting interaction with," Brianna Knotts says. "It's not just a one-sided conversation. It's a give and a take. And I feel like there's no other form of entertainment that does that. You go to a movie theater—you don't get to tell the movie what to do. You don't get to tell Broadway or even a concert—like they might play a song [you request], but they already had it planned. But with wrestling, anything goes. Anything can happen."[57]

Ultimately the storylines, who gets booked, and the run of show are determined by the promoter, whose bottom line is money. Shirley Love notes that in *Saturday Nite Wrestlin'*, commercials by advertisers would determine the length of each fall, and sometimes, when advertiser's products were used in the ring, could even influence the outcome of the match.[58] But the promoter's crafting of the angle is heavily influenced by fan response.[59] At each ASW show, Gary Damron closely observes who gets over, who gets heat, and how fans respond to plot development so he can ensure the community will continue to buy tickets and fill seats at shows. In his *Baffler* article "The Art of the Heel," Mike Edison explains, "Wrestling is flawless by design—if a storyline isn't over with the fans, kill it. Never mention it again. If a gimmick isn't working, change it. If your talent isn't going over as a face, do a heel turn. Wrestling writes its own laws and its only concern is its subjects—the fans who watch on TV and buy tickets at the box office."[60] Wrestlers also depend on merch sales as an income stream, and unpopular wrestlers don't sell merch. The dialogic nature of the sport largely accounts for fans' vocality and participation in the kayfabe—they are uniquely aware that their response will shape future cards and storylines. "Whenever I was just considered a fan," Huffman says, "I would try to participate, because you know in that crowd, you're part of the show as well. It's your job to boo the bad guy, cheer the good guy . . . but people in Madison [are] very consistent when it comes to that."[61]

Race, Politics, and the Carnivalesque

Though ASW storylines are of a small, local community, the content of the narratives and wrestlers' gimmicks can be both local and far-reaching, referencing current events, politics, and internet culture. The storyline might not quite be a microcosm or symbol of public opinion, but it's a gesture at it in broad strokes. The Sheik from Syria's flag is not an actual Syrian flag but a black and white camel, a symbol simultaneously simplified and amplified. At an International Combat Sports match in Dunbar, "The Candy Shop" Kevin "Magic" Tyler, who has a male stripper gimmick (he pulled off three pairs of tear-away pants before finally revealing his pink zebra print briefs), teamed up with "The Shake Weight Supreme" Sizzling Stan Stylez, whose entrance involves the suggestive use of a shake weight and Reddi-wip. They were both scantily clad, revealing bulging and oiled muscles. Their opponents, two bears in pink T-shirts, announced as "Gay and Fabulous," sauntered out with pink monkey puppets, slapping each other's butts and flirting with members of the crowd. The largest of the duo tauntingly took off his shirt, shaking his ample belly at Stan and Kevin, threatening to kiss them if he beat them. The fans rallied behind the Gay and Fabulous team, mocking the physically superior male stripper types for their pervy moves and homophobic squeamishness. It's tempting to translate reactions to storylines like this—where a clear binary is being presented, in this case between the effeminate underdogs and hypermasculine strong men—to a discernible political statement. But the performative frame of kayfabe operates under different rules than the real world. This is carnivalesque play, where underdogs of all sorts are championed, nothing is absolute, everything is exaggerated, and opposites are brought together in a carnivalistic mésalliance. Then the binary is flipped, as faces become heels and heels get over. This is not to say that the political import of wrestling is completely illegible, but to cull any direct messages from it, one must consider the performative frame that playfully obscures and complicates its messaging. Cultural historian Michael Denning asserts, "No popular cultural practice is necessarily subversive or incorporated."[62] As with other working-class cultural forms like country music, wrestling has largely been read as politically conservative, but it is not inherently political unless applied as such. Independent wrestling in West Virginia, as I have shown, is a participatory, vernacular assemblage that may be shaped by the individual politics of its wrestlers, fans, and promoters but does not attempt political consensus or represent any particular political ideology. Rather, broad, exaggerated themes and stereotypes clash and coexist in the form.

The "carnivalesque" application can be traced quite literally, to wrestling's history as a carnival sideshow. One can imagine the brawling ring set up among the tents housing the bearded lady, the snake charmer, and the tiny horse. Historians Louis M. Kyriakoudes and Peter A. Coclanis note that these fairs which itinerant wrestlers followed on the southern frontier often included minstrel shows.[63] In his article, "'The Seeming Counterfeit:' Racial Politics and Early Blackface Minstrelsy," Eric Lott describes an illustration of a minstrel show in 1833 that depicts a public brawl happening on the same stage, simultaneous with the blackface performance.[64] Considering the phenomenon of the racialized heel in wrestling, the historical proximity between minstrelsy and wrestling may have influenced the form and its incorporation of the ethnic and racial stereotyped character. At *Saturday Nite Wrestlin'*, wrestlers like the Cuban Assassin who had a racialized gimmick were common. There was Chief Black Eagle (Luis Torres), who wore a floor-length headdress, Chief Red Cloud, and Chief Walking Horse. A 1957 issue of the *Bluefield Daily Telegraph* mentions a wrestler known as "The Jap." In 1958, the paper announced that "The Black Plague," a former Ohio State football player and "the first colored man ever to compete professionally at the sport in Bluefield," would be appearing at an upcoming match in town. A 1959 issue of the same paper refers to the Turkish Assassin as a "Filthy Spick." Though these wrestlers were not performing in blackface as in a minstrel show, they employed their perceived or actual racial or ethnic identity to play an exaggerated character, often in derogatory and culturally appropriative ways.[65] As Roland Barthes says, "It's therefore in the body of the wrestler that we find the first key to the contest." Though he is not writing about race specifically, the body of the wrestler, and all its possible perceived attributes—body type, size, skin color, and appearance, or what Acevedo calls the "cosmetic"—is the foundational material for a gimmick, like the body of an actor typecast in a role. Because wrestlers' signifiers must be immediately clear, racially and culturally stereotyped characters that drew on a collective consciousness were an easy means to achieve that archetypal form or, in Barthes's terms, "as perfection of an iconography." Wrestling has historically been a racially and ethnically diverse sport, but our cultural arsenal of stereotypes, many of which are racist, paired with the nature of the form, which at its root is a money-making endeavor, has encouraged wrestlers of color, foreigners, and those differently abled to exaggerate and capitalize on their differences, or made willingness to do so the price of doing business.

Richie Acevedo (the Cuban Assassin #2), whose father is from Puerto Rico but has Cuban heritage, grew up in Oak Hill, spoke English, French, and Spanish, and was one of the few nonwhite students in his school (see fig. 7.1). He sees his portrayal of the Cuban Assassin as not just a theatrical role but also a means of reclamation of identity and empowerment:

> When I was growing up, you know, you have to understand, my mom was one of the first people around here that was in an interracial relationship, okay? My Spanish side of the family in Puerto Rico, it's a mixture of Black and white. . . . When I was growing up people would pick on me; they would call me "Little Cubie," and they knew I was mixed race. In school you was either Black or white. They didn't have any Spanish people when I was growing up. . . . But I never really got mad or upset about it. And you have to understand something. When I was growing up, when we played as kids, I was always the bad guy or the monster. I was never the hero or the good guy. I was always the bad guy or the monster. It was just me. When we played as kids . . . I didn't mind because I got attention from that. And who wouldn't love attention, especially when you're young? My dad was a bad guy in wrestling, so it just stuck with me, right? I was the bad guy and the monster. And then when I got older I realized that I can say some stuff that is very offensive and not really mean to say something but people would take it offensively if I said something, so I had to really watch out what I say or people want to get in a fight. And they would take the stuff literally. As far as being stereotyped and being the Cuban, I looked like my dad. I act like him in a lot of ways. It just kinda fell in place.
>
> But to me, stereotyping, to use that word—to me people make up their own offensive words. You know, it's like propaganda, you create your own drama, you create your own thing. From wrestling, I learned that we create drama, okay? We're gonna get people angered, we're gonna get 'em mad, we're gonna make 'em happy, we're gonna, you know, you have all those emotions. That's what's great about a wrestling match is you get all those emotions in there. A match should have everything. It should have comedy, it should have drama, it should have action, adventure, you know, and a good finale. Just like a good book, just like a good movie. And I learned

to overlook the stereotype and stuff. I never got tired of it. At the beginning I didn't want to [do it], but after I saw what it can be and what I can do with it, I just took it as my own.[66]

Though not racially charged in the same way, historically in West Virginia and greater Appalachian wrestling, "hillbilly" and "redneck" characters have been prominent, often paired with heels, portrayed as urban, rich, and powerful, who disparage their poor rural counterparts in a class-struggle narrative. Shirley Love remembers the "Scufflin' Hillbillies" tag team, a pair of faces who wore coveralls and guzzled moonshine out of jugs, and wrestler Jan Madrid, who would insult the fans, calling the coal miners "underground farmers." Jim Cornette, who promoted wrestling shows across Appalachia in the early 1990s, was famous for disparaging locals for being "hillbillies out in the sticks."[67] Gary Damron says, "That's what we call cheap heat. It's a way for the bad guy heel to go out and if you want somebody to boo ya, well, what's a better way to do that than go out and say, 'Hey, you're ugly, you're stupid.' You know, or 'This town sucks.'" At a 2019 outdoor match in Charleston featuring several promotions, Ohio's "The Appalachian Outlaw Jock Sampson," himself portraying a regional white stereotype, insulted the local West Virginian fans, saying they were dirty and didn't have running water. These types of gimmicks enact common populist tropes and stage a morality play in pursuit of justice. The underdog is the worker, the poor man, the small guy, the hillbilly, the redneck, or whoever is being insulted at the time, and they will eventually get their due. Damron, Huffman, Knotts, and Hardin all said that these types of racially, ethnically, and culturally stereotyped characters—many of which were rooted in the Cold War era—are waning in popularity today. "It's odd," Huffman said, "because I feel like that type of gimmick, the older generation will like but the younger generation doesn't really care for. Because you know, in the '80s and the '70s that was based off like the stereotypical gimmicks: the Iron Sheik, the Cuban Assassin, Hulk Hogan was this big strong American—the hero. I feel like in today's wrestling . . . as long as that certain person can make a connection to that crowd, I feel like they won't care."[68] Writing about the WWF, Jenkins acknowledges the "mixture of the anti-hegemonic and the reactionary" inherent in the sport. There is male dominance, and violence, and evocation of "racial and ethnic stereotypes that demean groups even where they are intended to promote positive role models," but wrestling also "lends its voice to the voiceless and champions the powerless; . . . in short, wrestling embodies the fundamental contradictions of the American populist tradition."[69] The main values upheld by independent wrestling in West Virginia are those of community, where the narratives are not only shaped by the local audience but kept alive by it, at a time where communities in West Virginia are materially disintegrating through loss of work, population decline, and the ravages of the opioid epidemic.

AS BRIANNA KNOTTS looks ahead to her wrestling career and sees the sport booming in popularity in West Virginia, she hopes that a shift in how wrestling presents and capitalizes on difference, particularly its pervasive populist masculinity, is on the horizon.

> I want to be a strong female persona for girls that will hopefully look up to me and want to do this too. Because I think that's what it's gonna take for the shift of culture in wrestling for women to be taken seriously, and it's happening. I haven't met personally anyone locally that has been like, "Oh, women shouldn't be wrestling," but there's still a lot of animosity toward like intergender wrestling.[70]
>
> Personally, I'm training with all men. There's been a couple younger girls that are between sixteen and eighteen that have kind of dabbled, but I've been for the last three months, pretty much predominantly the only female training. And even at the local shows, I've seen a handful of women's matches. So I feel like as women we really need to lift each other up and show that hey, we have a place to be here, we're not just eye candy. . . . I want to show up, show that I know what I'm doing, and you know, if I have to wrestle men, to me that's fine. And if men are okay with that, because I think women can be just as good as men in this business.

Knotts, who works during the day as a physical therapy assistant, is part of the growing health-care industry in Appalachia, responding to the high percentages of chronic disease, black lung, and the opioid epidemic.[71] As the region changes from a masculinized work force to one of care work predominantly undertaken by women, the archetypal worker shifts from a male coal miner to a female health-care worker, and the iconic site of labor moves from a mine or factory to a hospital or the shifting domestic space of the home health-care worker, perhaps we'll see this reflected—no doubt in wrestling's simplified, exaggerated, carnivalesque, campy way— in West Virginia's squared circle.

CHAPTER 8

Wild, Wonderful, Wasteland West Virginia

Speculative Futures, Vernacular Culture,
and the Embodied Tourism of *Fallout 76*

IT'S A BEAUTIFUL West Virginia evening, with the cicadas buzzing in the trees as the dusk settles in. I'm at a poetry reading at an outdoor venue overlooking the river. The stage backdrop is minimalist and industrial, with a roll-up red garage door, and there are neon signs on each side, one reading, "kill, laugh, love," in Malibu pink and turquoise, the other a yellow and red crest advertising Pickaxe Pilsner. There are about two dozen people here, sitting in the benches and taking turns on stage, and it's admittedly a strange crew. One poet is wearing head-to-toe flannel pajamas and sports a buffalo plaid hunter's cap. There are several in tricorn hats and bomber jackets, one in a bikini top, another in a space helmet and three-piece baby blue suit, and two in matching superhero spandex (one is lean, the other ripped). Some are donning gas masks. Though their attire seems uniquely curated, their overall appearance is grubby and battle-worn, like a steampunk survivalist Burning Man in the backwoods. The poetry is clever, laden with in-jokes and feigned seriousness, but based in personal experience and rooted in place. "I leave the Vault, the sun in my eyes, / Appalachia, my friends, is calling. / But the wonders of the waste will have to wait, / Because the servers [*sic*] not responding."[1] Another poet reads a villanelle parody of Dylan Thomas, titled "Do Not Go Looting in That Bombed Out Place."[2] I've been to quite a few poetry readings in my life, but I've never been to one like this before. Here, everything—the costumes, the cicadas, the macabre neon sign—is taking place virtually, in a postapocalyptic West Virginia as depicted in Bethesda Game Studios' massively multiplayer online game (MMOG), *Fallout 76*.

The story of *Fallout 76*, which was released in the fall of 2018 by the Maryland-based game developer as the eighth installment in its popular postapocalyptic role-playing franchise, is intricate and interlocking, with references to previous installations of the game, but the main atmospheric setting and narrative arc go something like this: Players' avatars emerge from a vault outside of Flatwoods, West Virginia, in the year 2102, twenty-five years after an apocalyptic nuclear war. The members of this Vault 76 are considered to be the best and brightest, chosen by the Vault-Tec corporation to rebuild the world. Upon exiting the vault and entering the wild woods of West Virginia, players receive a message from the Vault Overseer, who charges them with the task of securing three nuclear silos. They soon discover that no other humans, as we know them, have survived the nuclear event.[3] Instead malevolent feral ghouls and mutated animals roam the landscape, assaulting players. Some creatures are common across *Fallout* games, and others, like two-headed opossums, giant ticks, and mangy beavers, are particular to this West Virginia installment. The Scorched—once human, zombie-like figures who operate through a numb, hive-mind consciousness that connects them to other scorched creatures, the Scorchedbeasts in particular—pose some of the biggest threats in the game. Vault members also encounter robots of various iterations, some protecting towns, corporations, and mansions like White Springs, the hotel based on the Greenbrier resort. Players learn that many of these robots were engineered to replace human workers, as with the Motherlode, a mining robot, the Sentrybot strikebreaker, and the DMV bot. This is also the case with the Mole miners, irradiated humans who have developed into squat, aggressive figures, gasping and wheezing in decaying mining suits and unable to speak through their ventilators. Eventually it becomes clear that the goal of the game is to destroy the Scorchedbeast Queen, and in doing so, the entire hive of the Scorched, in order to even have the possibility of rebuilding and repopulating Appalachia and, ultimately, the world.

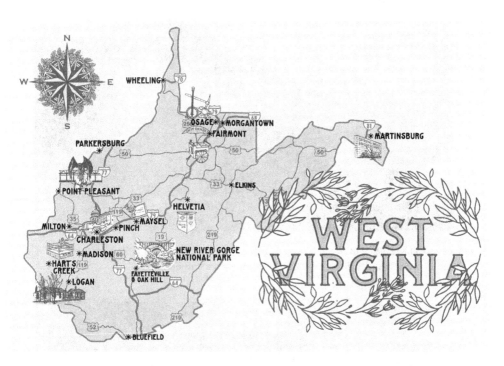

PLATE 0.1. Map of West Virginia. Illustration by Dan Davis.

PLATE 1.1. Scotts Run Museum Coffee Shop regulars gather at the museum on a Saturday, February 18, 2019. Photo by the author.

PLATE 1.2. Singer, bandleader, and shoe repairman Al Anderson outside his shoe repair shop in Scotts Run, West Virginia, April 5, 2019. Photo by the author.

PLATE 1.3. Sarah Boyd Little (left) and Eve Faulkes (right) at Faulkes's home in Morgantown, West Virginia, March 6, 2018. Photo by the author.

PLATE 2.1. Portrait of musician and writer Cora Hairston at the Logan State
Park Museum in Logan, West Virginia, May 3, 2016. Photo by the author.

PLATE 3.1. Eleanor Betler rolls out the traditional Swiss fried pastry *hozablatz* in her home kitchen outside Helvetia, West Virginia, February 5, 2016. Photo by the author.

PLATE 3.2. An effigy of Old Man Winter hangs in the Helvetia Community Hall, awaiting Fasnacht revelers, February 6, 2016. After a square dance in the hall, the revelers will cut him down from the rafters and burn him on a bonfire outside. Photo by the author.

PLATE 3.3. The Hütte Swiss Restaurant, "anchor store" of the community in Helvetia, West Virginia, March 1, 2014. Note the painted coat of arms on the door. Photo by the author.

PLATE 4.1. Rick Wilson on the Milton Old Bank steps, which appear in Breece D'J Pancake's story "The Honored Dead" as the place where the narrator, William Haywood, sits, waiting "for the sun to come up over the hills; wait like I waited for the bus to the draft physical." October 15, 2019. Photo by the author.

PLATE 4.2. Robert Jackson, a childhood friend of Breece D'J Pancake, sits in the pew of the United Methodist Church in Milton, West Virginia, where he last saw Breece, October 15, 2019. Photo by the author.

PLATE 5.1. During the 2018–19 West Virginia teachers' strike, striking public school teachers and employees wore red shirts and bandanas as symbols of solidarity and to evoke the history of labor struggle in the state, March 5, 2018. Photo by the author.

PLATE 5.2. Many striking West Virginia teachers, especially those living near state borders, pointed out that they could travel a few miles to teach in another state and significantly increase their salaries and benefits, February 26, 2018. Photo by the author.

PLATE 6.1. Two Buddy B's hot dogs with chili, slaw, mustard, and onions—the standard toppings included on a "with everything" dog in most places in West Virginia, June 10, 2016. Photo by the author.

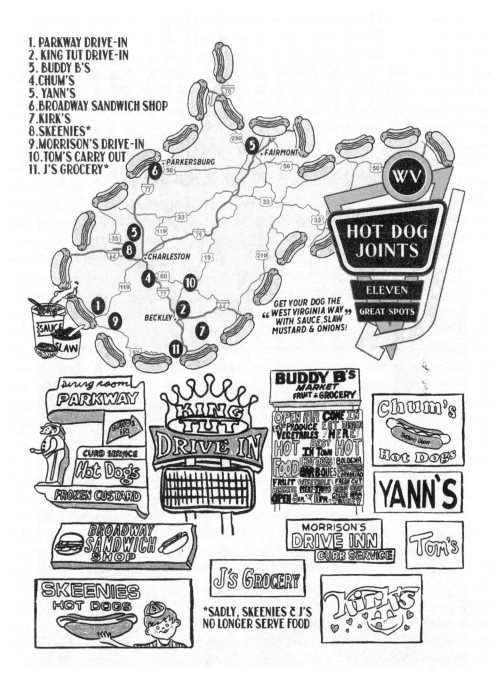

PLATE 6.2. West Virginia map depicting hot dog joints referenced in chapter 6. Illustration by Dan Davis.

PLATE 6.3. Sign claiming "Best in Town Hot Dogs," outside Buddy B's in Sissonville, West Virginia, June 10, 2016. Photo by the author.

PLATE 7.1. Huffmanly jumps off the ropes during a tag team match at ASW's drive-in wrestling show in Winfield, July 18, 2020. The promotion began holding drive-in outdoor events during the COVID-19 pandemic. Photo by the author.

PLATE 8.1. A Fasnacht owl mask depicted in the video game *Fallout 76*, February 17, 2021. Photo by Kristy Henson.

PLATE 8.2. *Fallout 76* gamer and West Virginia resident Kristy Henson created a papier-mâché owl mask inspired by the in-game mask and wore it to the real 2020 Fasnacht event in Helvetia, June 27, 2020. Photo by Lea Michelle Photography—Lea Propst Fedder.

As a nongamer with virtually no gaming skills at my disposal, my field-work in the *Fallout 76* gameworld and gamer network included several guided tours and walk-throughs of the game, the most extensive of which was with John Barton, a West Virginia native, writer, and gamer who published several articles about *Fallout 76* during its debut and attended the release party at the Greenbrier. In his tour, he focused specifically on how the gameworld maps onto places and issues in present-day West Virginia. I also interviewed several *Fallout 76* gamers—some from West Virginia and others from elsewhere whose in-game experience prompted them to visit the state. In addition, I watched Twitch streams of gameplay, followed *Fallout 76* Twitter accounts and the fo76 subreddit, read articles, and reviewed every transcript of in-game holotapes and notes (the primary vehicles through which the game's narrative is communicated to players) posted on the *Fallout 76* wiki.[4]

Almost Almost Heaven: The West Virginia Gameworld of *Fallout 76*

Fallout 76 takes place in a sixteen-square-mile version of West Virginia, a gameworld four times as large as any of the previous *Fallout* games. Though the representation of the state has the iconic *Fallout* style of the retrofuture atomic age, it is unmistakably West Virginia, evident geographically in the rolling hills, lush woods in peak fall foliage, rivers, and subregions like the Cranberry Bog (Cranberry Glades), Ash Heap (coalfields), Toxic Valley (Chemical Valley, or as it's bluntly referred to, "Cancer Valley"), and Forest (Monongahela National Forest). Many of the landmarks in the game are exact or near replicas of their "real-life" counterparts, even if their geographic locations have been rearranged to fit within a condensed square map. At the Mothman Museum in Point Pleasant, players may find a note left for the "real-life" owner, Jeff Wamsley, as well as evidence of a Mothman cult that worshipped out of the basement. The Mothman statue is there too, with its muscular chrome body and glowing red eyes. There's Vault-Tec University in Morgantown, a stand-in for West Virginia University, with game versions of Woodburn Hall and the PRT (Personal Rapid Transit), an electric railway used by WVU students and faculty. In Harper's Ferry, players can pick up loot from a version of the armory that John Brown famously raided in October 1859. Camden Park, the circa-1902 amusement park outside of Huntington, can be found in the game—though *Fallout*'s Widowmaker is modeled after the park's vintage wooden roller coaster the Big Dipper (one player I talked to joked that its virtual version looks much safer). Other game locations based on actual places in West Virginia include the New River Gorge with its iconic bridge, Summersville Lake and Dam (though in the game it has moved northwest, close to Charleston), New Vrindaban—the Hare Krishna temple in Marshall County (called the Palace of the Winding Path in game), Hillbilly Hot Dogs (renamed Hillfolk Hot Dogs), and the Pumpkin House in Kenova, where every fall, the former mayor adorns the porch, roof, and yard of his Queen Anne Victorian house with 3,000 jack-o'-lanterns (one for every person in the town).

The in-game portrayal of Helvetia, the remote mountain village of population fifty-nine, founded in 1869 by Swiss German immigrants, is particularly accurate (see chapter 3). Though the game designers swapped a few building locations, the scale and aesthetic is impeccably simulated and everything is there, down to the hand-painted signs, the historic bootmaker shack, Cheese Haus, Honey Haus, Hütte Swiss Restaurant (called Freya's Restaurant in-game), the Kultur Haus/general store/post office/mask museum, and even the assortment of instruments in the museum that belonged to the original members of the real Helvetia Star Band. Though I had never played the game, when I watched a friend navigate through virtual Helvetia, I was able to direct him where to go based on my familiarity with the real town.

Unlike many video games whose narrative is conveyed in a linear fashion, much like a movie, an MMOG's story unfolds nonchronologically in bits and pieces, through encounters with the gameworld. For the first year and a half after *Fallout 76*'s release, the game lacked active nonplayer characters; instead, its narrative backstory was conveyed entirely through audio holotapes (recordings made by survivors of the nuclear war), audio love letters, and fictional radio stories, as well as by notes (newspaper clippings, diaries, lists, and other ephemera) scattered across the landscape. The contents of these recordings and documents are intertextual, together presenting an overlapping composite of past life in West Virginia, told through a heteroglossia of voices and perspectives. Each player receives the story partially, in a unique order, depending upon their individual movements in the gameworld. In a sense, the player plays the role of a researcher, interpreting the world left behind through a scattered archive of humanity contained in audio recordings, ephemera, and written documents.

In some cases, this story is uttered through oral history by those experiencing nuclear apocalypse who, acknowledging that their civilization was dying, set out to document it. In the "Survivor Story" series of holotapes, the character Dassa Ben-Ami—part of the faction of "Responders" (former health-care workers, emergency medical technicians, and firemen who served as relief workers)—encourages others to record their stories for posterity. Ben-Ami asks questions like a folklorist or oral historian, and on other tapes in the series, the survivors speak directly into the tape, as an autoethnography. "We are your history," he tells the future listener.[5] In another holotape, a member of the Brotherhood of Steel, a militarized survivalist group that deems itself the "guardian of civilization," issues a call for the preservation of all schematics, holotapes, books, and notes, referring to them as "the building blocks of the old world" and "a precious seed," from which the new civilization will be born.[6] As I listened to all of these holotapes and read through notes, I experienced a strange sense of recognition of my own work as a folklorist and documentarian of what will become a heteroglossic, intertwined archive of West Virginia's past. Experiencing this dystopian narrative through voices of the deceased and learning about the narrators' culture and belief system through these documents, one can't help but consider what of our own world would remain as a record of our society after a similar apocalyptic event. What traditions would be retained and what would be disrupted? What current writing, recordings, ephemera, and architecture would constitute the foundation of future civilization? Whose voices would persist and whose would be lost?

Through the tapes and notes, storylines that resonate with events and power structures in both historic and present-day West Virginia are revealed. Narrative themes include the state's aspirational pivot to tourism after industrial fallout, a devastating drug epidemic, wealth inequality and class antagonism, labor struggle, and environmental degradation. We learn that the state was in fact largely untouched by the nuclear war; its destruction was wreaked mainly by extractive industry, corporate greed, and government malfeasance. In the Ash Heap, there are echoes of the Mine Wars history. Mine company robots still roam the smoldering landscape, proclaiming, "Striking is prohibited!" on repeat into the void. Rusting tanks tower over the rubble, not remnants of the nuclear war but rather relics of mine companies' militarization against striking union miners—a futuristic retelling of the Battle of Blair Mountain (called Mount Blair in-game), the largest labor uprising in American history, in which coal companies called in federal troops to suppress the armed miner rebellion. In the narrative of *Fallout 76*, the scabs were not non-union workers but strike-breaking robots. On a wall in virtual Beckley are the graffitied words "Man before Machine," an echo, perhaps, of then senator John F. Kennedy's May 1960 speech "The White House's Answer to West Virginia."[7] There's also an allusion to John Henry's legendary fatal race against the steam drill, which is thought to have taken place in the Great Bend Tunnel in Summers County, West Virginia, between 1870 and 1872.[8] We learn from a holotape that prior to the war, two competing coal companies, Garrahan Mining and Hornright Industrial, had staged a man-versus-machine battle. In their twenty-four-hour mining marathon, Garrahan employed its Excavators, a power armor worn by human miners, while Hornright used its nonhuman auto miners. Though Hornright cheated by sabotaging the power armor, it won by a narrow margin, and declared machines superior to manpower.

This is one thread of a broader game narrative detailing the intensification of automation prior to the nuclear disaster, in which coal companies, steel mills, government agencies, and wealthy employers of domestic workers began replacing their entire human workforce with robots. The town of Grafton was run by a robot mayor, and a ballot measure was up for vote that would replace all government workers in Appalachia with robots by the year 2087.[9] In a holotape left by the Overseer, she says, "Automation used to define life in West Virginia, now it's the only thing left," referring to the robots on autopilot, perpetually performing their duties among the ruins.[10] Mechanization of labor is all too familiar in real-life West Virginia. During the mid-twentieth century, automation in the coal industry—the introduction of automatic loading machines, conveyor belts, and the continuous miner machine—resulted in major job losses, completely transforming the state and its economy over the course of a few decades.[11] That transition is still happening. In 2019, about 14,000 coal miners were employed in West Virginia, down from 64,000 in the 1970s.[12] A 2017 study by the International Institute for Sustainable Development and the Columbia Center on Sustainable Investment estimated that automation will eventually replace 40–80 percent of workers in a mine, meaning automation alone could virtually wipe out the industry in West Virginia.[13]

The story of the West Tek corporation's poisoning of the town of Huntersville's water supply in *Fallout 76* seemingly draws from "real-life" narratives of the decades-long Dupont/PFAS water pollution case in Parkersburg, West Virginia, and the 2014 Elk River chemical spill, in which faulty tanks owned by Freedom Industries leaked 7,500 gallons of crude 4-methylcyclohexane methanol (MCHM) into the Elk River, leaving

300,000 residents without safe water.[14] The subplot also alludes to the twining of corporate and governmental interests through the Appalachian Regional Commission's economic development grants, and a perpetual cycle of scarcity that leaves impoverished rural communities with little power.[15] In *Fallout 76*, West Tek and the federal government offered the town of Huntersville a rural development grant to establish a West Tek Research Development Center, promising along with it the installation of a much-needed wastewater treatment plant and new sewer lines in the struggling rural town. Unbeknownst to the community, West Tek used Huntersville's citizens as a test population for its Forced Evolutionary Virus (FEV) through the town's water supply, framing the subsequent ill effects as the flu. The poisoned citizens mutated, eventually resulting in the Snallygaster creatures who roam the gameworld and attack players. Many West Virginians' trauma and fear of an unsafe water supply is personified here as a literal monster.

In the predisaster world of *Fallout 76*, even traditional culture has been appropriated by machines. Prior to the nuclear war, the virtual town of Helvetia invested in a fleet of protectron robots to "keep its traditions alive" and reduce the workload on a small community. This mirrors a concern in real-life Helvetia, as its population ages and young people move away for work. Though the town's Cheese Haus is equipped with a full industrial cheese making kitchen, the town has not had a resident cheese maker in over twenty years and as of 2016, was home to only one milk cow (the recipe for Helvetia Cheese requires a fresh supply of milk).[16] In-game, Helvetia traditions like cheese making, honey making, and music making are no longer practiced by humans but are carried on by robots, presenting the ethical and theoretical question of the potential role of mechanization, digitization, and cyborgs in sustaining cultural heritage. In the holotape "Helvetia Protectron Updates," a mechanic updating the robots confides, "The robots will now decide on their own how often we celebrate Faschnacht [*sic*]. Jensen is aware of my concerns, about frequency and the unpredictable environmental factors. . . . Jensen says it will be better for tourists."[17] As I explain in chapter 3, Fasnacht, in real-life Helvetia, is an annual pre-Lenten festival in which locals and festivalgoers don homemade masks and parade with lanterns from one dance hall to the other, square dance to the Helvetia Star Band under an effigy of Old Man Winter, and, at midnight, cut him from the rafters and burn him on the bonfire while serenading each other with "Country Roads." Though Fasnacht was initially celebrated as a quiet, private event by locals, when town matriarch Eleanor Mailloux helped revive the event in the late 1960s, she reconceived of it as a festival intended to both reinforce the cultural heritage of Helvetians and lure tourists to the secluded town at the end of winter, providing a much-needed economic boost to the town's few businesses and volunteer-run organizations. Initially, the new iteration of Fasnacht brought with it tensions between visitors who came to party and Helvetians—older residents in particular. As the festival has become more embedded over time in the community's cultural life, those issues have subsided, but the negotiations needed when communities open up their cultural celebrations to tourists remain. Through its stylized lens and postapocalyptic projections, *Fallout 76* takes up these real-life tensions between internal and external motivations and the contested arena of cultural heritage tourism.

As I argued in the book's introduction, the construction of heritage commodities for tourist consumption has a long history in Appalachia, complicit with the privatization of public lands and enclosure of the commons.[18] Cultural heritage practices have also been threatened by extractive industry, environmental degradation, and climate change. The balancing act between the two is illuminated in the *Fallout* narratives in Helvetia as well as in the minor storyline of the Lewisburg Basket Festival. In a holotape, the character Dave Jones, president of the Appalachia Arts Foundation, welcomed attendees of the town's annual basket festival, commenting, "As you all know, it's a little smaller this year. Good quality wicker is a bit harder to come by these days, but I'm proud of what we've been able to organize." Though in *Fallout* the lack of access to quality wicker may be due to irradiation or toxic waste, this is not an extreme exaggeration of reality. Ramp foragers, ginseng diggers, white oak basket makers, and other traditional wildcrafting practitioners I've interviewed have told me that they're no longer able to access wild materials and land where they once foraged due to the razing of mountaintops or enforcement of property rights by absentee timber and coal companies. Mary Hufford's 1992–99 ethnographic project for the American Folklife Center, "Tending the Commons: Folklife and Landscape in Southern West Virginia," thoroughly documents the community resources lost through logging and mountaintop-removal mining.[19]

Amid the destruction and exploitation in *Fallout 76*'s reimagining of West Virginia is a visual and auditory beauty that mirrors the physical place. With the dappled light shining through the forest, wind blowing across the grasses, and brilliant fall color, the gameworld can be quite stunning, capturing sensory experiences particularly familiar to West Virginians. When West Virginia native, writer, and gamer John Barton took me on a walkthrough of the game, he seemed perpetually in awe of how the game developers evoked the feeling of his home state, through the sound of the wind, birds, frogs, cicadas, the sweeping mountain vistas, and the flora. He said players from elsewhere were particularly arrested by the sounds. "When the game came out there were people walking into areas and they went . . . 'damn!' because they thought they were about to be attacked by everything because this noise was everywhere and it was constant! It's like, 'No, it's cicadas! That's normal, that's West Virginia.' They're like, 'That's just weird!' 'No, that's just normal.'"

On the *Fallout* reddit forum, players from West Virginia often comment on the accuracy of the game soundscape, which changes relative to the player's location. As Barton toured me through various locations in the game, he periodically stopped to remark upon the startlingly accurate simulation of the West Virginia landscape. "The thing about the forest is—that's north central West Virginia. Like forget that you're in a game and just look at the landscape, the leaf change, you actually start getting in and looking at what trees and vegetation are available going through the woods."[20] By twining the sounds and sights of the corporeal West Virginia with a resonant narrative that itself is based so deeply in place thematically, the designers have conveyed a phenomenon particular to the state: how intimately its culture is rooted in the land. The family homeplace serves as both a psychic and material bedrock, social life is built on kinship networks, and cultural traditions rely on a microlocal commons: a fiddle tune in one holler sounds different than the same tune just over the mountain, ginseng diggers know how to manage the plant community so their harvests will sustain season after season, and on Decoration Day each year, neighbors meet in the community graveyard to picnic and tend family plots.[21] All is sustained by good stewardship of both land and human relationships. Barton says, "The designers captured what it meant to be in West Virginia. There is not a land or a people or a state anywhere else that have the connection to the land that you see in West Virginia so that people would care to rebuild. You know? Like anywhere else you have a huge natural disaster, 'Okay, we're going somewhere else. We're leaving!' Not 'Oh there's going to be giant monsters and nuclear fallout and whatever else? Great! We're building this place back!' It doesn't work anywhere else."[22] It is not merely the postapocalyptic narrative or the scenic portrayal of West Virginia that resonates with players but also the coexistence of these two realities: the land's beauty and its simultaneous destruction; a contradiction acutely familiar to West Virginians.

Tomorrow's People: The Uncanny, Local-Color Writers, and Imagining Appalachia's Future

Fallout 76 achieves a haunting mimesis of West Virginia. Real-life locales are portrayed with such detailed accuracy, but they are projected twenty-five years into the future after the fall of a functional civilization. This West Virginia is devoid of other people aside from the players from Vault 76, but the staggered gait of the diseased Scorched serves as a reminder of the havoc wreaked by industry. West Virginia cryptids such as Mothman, the Flatwoods Monster, and the Grafton Monster—born in real life from local anxieties over environmental pollutants, disenfranchisement, and the inexplicable "other"—appear out of nowhere during gameplay. The mountain drawl we hear on recordings of past human residents has been replaced by robots who stalk the landscape, repeating their programmed lines in the Queen's English. Ephemeral materials like paper, textiles, and perishables that would have been present in places like the Mothman Museum or the state capitol are absent or decayed. Somehow this state of deterioration does not highlight the differences between the in-game portrayal and today's West Virginia but rather emphasizes their similarities. Many actual West Virginia cities, like Welch, Bluefield, and Charleston, were built for a much larger population than resides there now, the historic downtown hotels and multistory bank buildings are all vestiges of a time when the promises of extractive industry had not yet been so conspicuously broken.[23] Entire tops of mountains that existed twenty years ago are now completely lopped off. Players from West Virginia often point out that the roads in the game are eroded just as much as they are in real life.

In his essay "The Uncanny," Freud describes the terror of doubling as "something familiar which has been repressed," or the feeling "produced by effacing the distinction between imagination and reality," coupled with the sense of that doubling being out of time, a regression to a previous, infantile mental state of *repetition-compulsion*.[24] The hollowed out, "out of time" feeling conjured by vacant spaces, a dwindling population, and desecrated landscapes is one West Virginians know deeply. The post-apocalyptic West Virginia of *Fallout 76* can feel like a warning, or a premonition, the uncanny feeling of "something fateful and unescapable."[25]

Experiencing the game as a West Virginia resident, it becomes clear that *Fallout 76*'s evocative and familiar portrayal of the state's postapocalyptic future, in fact, reveals the tensions of its present reality. In his essay, "Progress versus Utopia; or, Can We Imagine the Future?," political theorist Fredric Jameson writes, "Imagining of the future may always have some aspect of the uncanny—hope or dread." What science fiction effectively does, he explains, is to defamiliarize the familiar and reorganize it in such a way that by envisioning our future, we are for once able to "experience our own present." Through this process of estrangement—that experience of regression inherent to the uncanny—science fiction allows us to conceptually transform our present reality "into the determinate past of something yet to come."[26]

Together the scattered documents in *Fallout 76* construct a portrait of a place where workers are powerless victims caught in a system of corporate and governmental corruption that leaves the people with no good options. Though these stories are fictionalized into at times comedic melodrama, their fully rendered depiction of one version of West Virginia's not-so-distant future is effective at laying bare the contradictions of present-day reality not only in the state but across the country and around the world. What does the imaginary of West Virginia make available to the game developers' story? Why did they choose this place, specifically, to set their postapocalyptic narrative? I tried on numerous occasions and through various avenues to get in touch with Bethesda game developers to ask these questions and never received a response, but in published interviews, developers mention spending about a week in the state to scout locations, and that the biodiversity, terrain, diverse landscapes of both heavy industry and forest, and the "remote" nature of West Virginia particularly appealed to them.[27] Pete Hines, Bethesda's senior vice president of global marketing and communications said, "Most of the planet doesn't really know a whole lot about West Virginia, so in a lot of ways, it's a blank canvas where you're not bringing a lot of assumptions."[28]

To contextualize this question of what a West Virginia imaginary offers to game developers, we might look to a past example of how Appalachia was used as a setting for the literary narratives of local-color writers in the years between 1870 and 1890. As historian Henry D. Shapiro explains in *Appalachia on Our Minds: The Southern Mountains and Mountaineers in the American Consciousness, 1870–1920*, these writers, who were not from the area but capitalized on their tangential knowledge of it, portrayed Appalachia as a discrete region of the southern mountains, and exploited it as an oppositional "other," outside of American progress and unity—a "strange land inhabited by a peculiar people."[29] These sketches were published in monthly magazines like *Harper's*, *Lippincott's*, and *Scribner's* and were written for a genteel middle-class mass readership, offering that audience a glimpse of a yet unassimilated "exotic corner" and affirming the dominance and centrality of its own middle-class cultural milieu. Shapiro writes, "The lessons [of local-color sketches] taught were two: the monolithic character of modern, middle-class American culture, and the pastness of the past."[30]

As local-color writers used the Appalachian region to assure East Coast middle-class readers that they were in fact "the center of the universe and the true bearer[s] of American culture." The Bethesda game developers of *Fallout 76* find in West Virginia a fitting screen on which to project overarching anxieties of late capitalism—deindustrialization, resource extraction, environmental destruction, and automation. Though these are issues faced by societies around the globe, their effects manifest more blatantly in "sacrifice zones" like West Virginia. While local-color writers exploited the imaginary of Appalachia to convey "the pastness of the past," portraying the region as a place and time that progress had not yet reached, *Fallout 76* uses Appalachia to mess with time; in its virtual West Virginia, the past, present, and future collide. The Freudian "out of time" feeling evoked by corporeal West Virginia provides an ideal canvas for the midcentury atomic age aesthetic *Fallout* applies to all its futuristic virtual renderings. Where local-color narratives constructed Appalachian degradation and degeneracy and framed them as a lapse in progress, the *Fallout 76* narrative frames degradation as an *advance* in progress, situated within a cultural and geographic "other" that has borne the brunt of industrial pollution, economic decline, and worker exploitation. "Yesterday's people," as Appalachians were called by Jack Weller in his 1965 book of the same title, are repositioned as "tomorrow's people"—the "best and the brightest" of Vault 76.[31] This is different from the exploitative media portrayals that the region has long been subject to; there is no hillbilly cosplay here (aside from, perhaps, the option for players to apply "coal miner smudge" to their avatars' faces), no Appalachian poverty porn.[32] Through their futuristic postapocalyptic sci-fi reimagining of West Virginia, the Bethesda game developers, who—aside from one developer at a sister company who tested a late-stage version of the game—are not from the state, levy a critique of the hegemonic structures that have depleted the state's resources, including its people. But while the terms and chronology have been rearranged in the developers' virtual rendering, Appalachia still serves as a narrative "other" —the "blank canvas," as Pete Hines called it, upon which dominant middle-class anxieties are projected—the imaginary sacrifice zone where capitalism's battles will be staged and contained.

The expansive gameworld and open sandbox nature of gameplay in *Fallout 76* allows players to experiment with whether the outcome of this future leans more toward the hope or the dread in Jameson's binary. The game offers a space where players can explore and direct an alternative future that puts West Virginia at the center; the rebirthplace of civilization. "In Vault 76 our future begins," the game trailer intones.[33] In her essay "How *Fallout 76* Can Help Us Rebuild West Virginia," Elizabeth Catte writes, "To create and interact with this different version of West Virginia is to imagine it liberated from its destructors, and that can be potent, particularly for those of us who live in the region. What if, instead of our collective fantasies of punishing Appalachia, we dreamed of its resurrection?"[34] In this reading of the game narrative, *Fallout 76* is neither utopic nor dystopic but rather postdystopic, poised on the edge of possibility. The game allows players to enact these hypotheticals: What if, in bearing the brunt of capitalism's horrors, the canary in this system of abuse of power, West Virginia is in fact the fertile crescent of a reimagined world? Moving beyond the rejection of the stereotype of Appalachians as "yesterday's people," an inherently backward demographic stuck in a perpetual culture of poverty, what might emerge from this speculative reframing of the population as "tomorrow's people," who, in standing at the edge of the world, are uniquely positioned to reenvision its rebirth? What possibilities might this framing produce and in what ways is it potentially detrimental?

In the final chapter of his book *Ramp Hollow: The Ordeal of Appalachia*, historian Steven Stoll suggests that one future for Appalachia might lie in a "reconstituted commons."[35] He writes in the form of proposed legislation, "This landscape [of commons communities] will provide the ecological base for hunting and gathering, cattle grazing, timber harvesting, vegetable gardening and farming. The ecological base will be owned as a conservation easement or land trust under the authority of the states and/or counties where each community resides."[36] This designation, he says, would "preserve and encourage a makeshift economy that has been practiced for two centuries among mountain farmers." *Fallout 76*'s gameworld and narrative is built on the paradox of West Virginia as both commons and commodity. The game's backstory is of a commons destroyed by unregulated industry, nuclear disaster, and subsequent conflict. The gameworld the players inhabit now is a return to that commons and a subsistence way of life that is in fact deeply rooted in real-life West Virginia but is now repackaged into a futuristic imaginary. This is not necessarily the revolutionary commons that Stoll imagines but a narrative experiment. The commons of *Fallout 76* is one under threat by mutants, cryptids, and machines still enacting corporate plots. Though robots on autopilot continue to enforce some private land rights, most of the land is free rein—the gameworld is a West Virginia that has been returned to the frontier it once was. Survival depends on the player's ability to "harvest" food and resources like mutfruit, blackberries, and silt beans (the in-game version of a half-runner bean) that grow wild, meat from mutated and irradiated animals, and equipment such as armor and weapons. Some natural products, like Mothman eggs, can be harvested and commoditized to be sold in exchange for materials for self-defense, sustenance, or building Construction and Assembly Mobile Platforms (C.A.M.P.s). The player is a frontiersman or woman or, perhaps more appropriately for West Virginia, a mountaineer, charged with rebuilding Appalachia and, in turn, the world. In a sense, this reading could be viewed as a future revisioning of the "myth of emptiness," long employed by colonizers and corporations to present landscapes, including those in Appalachia, as being devoid of people and "unproductive" so that settlers and industry could encroach on the land.[37]

Anthropologist Arjun Appadurai describes the potential of works of the imagination to be "a collective platform from which to project notions of resistance, irony, selectivity, and in general, *agency.*"[38] What are the stakes of *Fallout 76*'s use of West Virginia as a speculative imaginary? How do the players make use of that collective platform and what impact does that have on the actual place of West Virginia or public consciousness about the actual place? Shapiro argues that local-color narratives about Appalachia, which numbered 90 sketches and over 125 short stories published in the genre's heyday of 1870–90, effectively "established Appalachia as a discrete region in the public consciousness, in but not of America," and "had consequences beyond the pages of the magazine . . . to the degree that it became the basis for private or public action."[39] What public and private actions might the narrative of *Fallout 76* prompt? The answer lies in one arena where comparisons between local-color texts and the *Fallout 76* video game fray—in the differences between the more passive role of the reader and the gamer's agency in shaping a game's narrative. The virtual embodiment and interactive nature of MMOGs make the form particularly evocative. Players do not merely read this futuristic narrative but inhabit it, through unique yet common sensory, aesthetic, and social in-game experiences. And unlike local-color fiction, which was oriented toward a readership outside of Appalachia, through *Fallout*, an audience from both outside the state and within it can inhabit roles in the narrative. In order to consider what impact the game might have on the culture of West Virginia, we need to understand the community of players of *Fallout 76*—what their interaction is with each other, and what constitutes their relationship with both the corporeal and the virtual versions of West Virginia.

Vault Dwellers: The Vernacular Culture and Social Life of *Fallout 76*

By the end of 2018, the year *Fallout 76* was launched, the game had sold 1.4 million copies, and as of January 2020, about 400,000 players were active across all platforms.[40] At the time of this writing, the PlayerCounter website, which gives real-time updates on how many players are currently playing online, generally reports between 22,000 and 35,000 people playing the game at any given time.[41] Together these players make up a loose network, or a "community of practice," as Constance Steinkuehler writes in her article on MMOGs.[42] They share and are united by a common narrative and aesthetic reality, though their experiences are individualized. As players share and act upon those individualized experiences of the game's collective imaginary, the story of the game no longer merely constitutes that "official" narrative written by the game developers but also becomes a folk narrative that is shared among players and is variable, as each player interprets, inhabits, and cocreates the narrative and its manifestation in the gameworld. Both folk narratives and video game experiences gather, as Kiri Miller argues in her work comparing the *Grand Theft Auto* video game and *Grimm's Fairy Tales*, "a dispersed audience around a common experience."[43] Likewise, *Fallout 76* players narrate and share their own experiences in the game and outside of it, the metanarrative itself functioning as a creative expression. For example, the friends who led me on a tour of *Fallout 76* often recount the in-game story to each other of how "Katie jumped off the New River Gorge Bridge . . . and LIVED," and attempt the same feat themselves. On the *Fallout 76* subreddit, players swap similar stories of their virtual escapades and informally develop their own common language. And on Twitter, players share virtual photos of their avatars taken at locations throughout the gameworld. In turn, those stories, images, and language inform future play within the game.

The network of *Fallout 76* players has developed its own vernacular norms and culture that expand and shape how the "official" narrative constructed by Bethesda is virtually embodied. For one, an ethic of collaboration has emerged among them. In an interview, Bethesda game designer Ferret Baudoin commented, "We had whole plans for ways to let players murder each other, and they just wouldn't do it. We have a weird, wonderful audience that would rather help each other even when they have the other options."[44] John Barton explained, "If you're talking about massive multiplayer online games, it's very much a Darwin structure, it's survival of the fittest. . . . Within this game that's not the case. You've got people that actively look to help each other, especially new players, and are donating some of the best equipment to the game, not just to new players that are friends of theirs but to completely random level ones."[45] He feels that this collaborative code echoes West Virginians' hospitality and culture of care—an ethic of the commons that the game makes available but that has ultimately been developed and perpetuated by game players. These vernacular rules dictate how players interact with each other and the approach of respect they bring to the shared resources in the in-game environment.

In her book *Play between Worlds*, which explores the MMOG *EverQuest*, T. L. Taylor argues that rather than being passive recipients of a narrative, video game players are actually cocreators "in producing a meaningful experience and artifact," engaged in participatory and dialogic media.[46] She views MMOGs as simultaneously spaces of social life, public spheres, and sources of cultural production. In *Fallout 76*, this is most evident in the culture that has emerged around the building, embellishing, and sharing with other players (both in-game and outside of it) from one's C.A.M.P. Barton says that, curiously, many players build their C.A.M.P. not in the most strategic locations but rather on plots of land with the most scenic views. Players appreciate the aesthetics of the in-game landscape, and their experience of it directs their gameplay just as much as the game's prescribed quests. The collectively run Twitter account @HOAWasteland "Wasteland Estates HOA (Homeowner's Association)" shares players' C.A.M.P. photos for evaluation by the collective and hosts Twitch streams where players lead the account owners and other viewers on tours of their respective C.A.M.P.s.[47] Players have constructed wildly creative C.A.M.P.s—some built as bars, yoga studios, music venues, and multistory midcentury modern homes. One player created a replica of the *Star Wars* Death Star, another the hotel from *The Shining*. Though not necessarily intended by the game developers as such, players have designed and used these C.A.M.P.s. as social spaces where players commune informally in-game or participate in poetry readings, comedy nights, and friendly roasts of other players. Kiri Miller says that the way players interact with a video game is not in fact a process of consumption but rather a performance in the folkloric sense, "different every time it is enacted."[48] In *Fallout 76*, players assume an avatar, curate that avatar's attire and appearance, and have agency to improvise and cocreate the world they inhabit through their builds, mods, social events, and vernacular norms.

The vernacular expression performed by players in *Fallout 76* is of particular import because it is rooted in an actual place. The gameworld maps closely onto the natural and built environment of West Virginia, which serves as the touchpoint, both virtually and in real life, for the folk group of its players. Additionally, the prescribed quests in *Fallout 76* are minimal and fairly easily accomplished. After players complete those tasks, namely detonating nuclear bombs to kill the Scorchedbeast Queen, they spend most of their time in the game's open sandbox, engaging in creative projects like building their C.A.M.P., staging virtual photos, or exploring the large gameworld. Mike Mallow, a native and resident of Pendleton County, West Virginia, says that simply exploring the in-game portrayal of his home state of West Virginia has been his main purpose in playing *Fallout 76*. "Really for much of the game, I have not done missions or anything like that, I have just wanted to look around. And that's probably what two-thirds of my gaming experience has been is just exploring. And I'm still discovering new things, and that's what's really incredible about it. . . . I guess I like the isolation of the game partly too, that's kinda my thing."[49] Devoid of nonplayer characters (NPCs) for gamers to interact with, the virtual place of West Virginia is, in a sense, *Fallout 76*'s main character, as the entity that players spend most of their time interacting with. Whereas local-color writers avoided specific description of the physical place of Appalachia, using instead the remoteness and isolation of the "strange land" as a blank canvas on which to depict characterization of its "particular people" and the drama of social relationships, *Fallout 76* developers have faded characters into the background as disembodied voices accessible only through holotapes and notes scattered across the landscape, and bring the "strange land" of West Virginia into the foreground as a stand-in for its "particular people."

"They Even Have Wood Piles Set Up Where They're Supposed to Be": *Fallout 76* Tourism and the Psychic Merging of Virtual and Physical West Virginia

The centrality of place in *Fallout 76* manifests in the vernacular culture of the network of players in how they value knowledge of the geography and culture of real-life West Virginia. That familiarity has currency in the virtual realm, informing players' experiences of the gameworld. Conversely, the virtual simulation of West Virginia inspires players to seek out experiences in the actual place on which the game is based. In some instances, players conflate the two iterations of West Virginia. T. L. Taylor writes, "To imagine we can segregate these things—game and non-game, social and game, on- and offline, virtual and real—not only misunderstands our relationship with technology, but our relationship with culture."[50] Players do not interact with the West Virginia of the gameworld and the West Virginia of the physical world as separate entities with finite borders; instead, these worlds are like oil slicks, overlapping and bleeding into each other conceptually and experientially. Folkloristically, this psychic merging of experience in virtual and physical space has particular bearing on how an imaginary of West Virginia is being formed among a mixed insider and outsider network of players (from the state and from outside of it) and may contribute to the codification of a particular vernacular narrative about the culture, folklore, history, and landscape, and aesthetic of West Virginia.

Even before *Fallout 76* launched, players from outside the state began visiting. Restaurant owners, museum directors, and Visitor's Bureau officials report regular visits by players on *Fallout 76* tours of West Virginia, crisscrossing the state to experience the real-life counterparts of multiple in-game locations. Common sites for players to visit include the Mothman Museum, the Greenbrier, Helvetia, the Green Bank Observatory, Morgantown, and Flatwoods. *Fallout 76* literally provides these tourists with a map to guide their trip and offers a narrative frame in which to situate aspects of the state's culture, history, and folklore. Though the West Virginia Department of Tourism has no estimates of how many have visited the Mountain State because of *Fallout 76*, tourism commissioner

Chelsea Ruby reported an increase in hotel occupancy between June 2017 and 2018, which she believed may have been in anticipation of the game, and she noted increased web traffic and searches for sites featured in-game.[51] Helvetia resident Clara Lehmann says the small Randolph County village has seen a significant bump in *Fallout 76*–related visitors, throughout the year and for Helvetia's public celebrations. The town's February 2020 Fasnacht celebration was the festival's biggest yet, drawing over 600 people, and more than doubling the profit of the year prior. She estimates that 30 percent of the attendees were *Fallout 76* gamers new to the event and says the game has brought more visitors of a different, younger demographic than the town typically draws.

The players I talked to who were inspired to visit West Virginia after playing *Fallout 76* all said that though they have played other *Fallout* installments based on actual locations such as Washington, D.C. (*Fallout 3*), Boston (*Fallout 4*), and other games mainly set in major urban areas, this is the only game that has prompted them to seek out a physical experience. Porter Lyons, a *Fallout 76* gamer and Ohio native and resident who has done two tours of in-game locations in real-life West Virginia, speculates on this phenomenon:

> I wonder if it's just the fact that West Virginia is sort of off the beaten path in terms of states. It's not really talked about as much on a national scale. . . . When we hear West Virginia I think most people probably think . . . "I'm sure a lot of these locations are still pretty well preserved and true to their character and form and not manipulated by progress and [laughs] innovation and things like that, like so many historical places have." So yeah, I think just going back to that idea of mystique and the character that West Virginia has. I think that's very appealing for *Fallout* players.[52]

Some feelings, though, can't be conveyed through a screen. When Lyons visited, he felt that places in West Virginia were steeped with more intrigue and mystery than the game evokes. "Having visited some of the destinations before the game came out," he said, "I had these ideas built up in my head of what it might look like in-game. I think they got some locations pretty spot on based off of what I had seen before going. However, I think I was a little let down [by the game] in terms of some of the feelings that I suppose you get actually being in West Virginia, and being in those locations in-game. Being at the locations physically in real life, there's this sense of mystique and wonder and oddity . . . that the game isn't quite able to capture as well as I feel like they could have."

Other visitors found that their experiences in physical West Virginia also impacted their perception of the game, as well as how they interact socially with other players in-game. Mark Fields, an Ohio native who made two trips to West Virginia with his gamer son after playing *Fallout 76*, said, "After we went to West Virginia I had actually talked to a couple people in the game about having visited and a little bit about how things in the game are represented. . . . I was able to share a little bit about actual West Virginia to people. I talked to some guy in Texas, somebody else in Washington State. I think I talked to some kids in Canada one day about it."[53] Experiences in physical West Virginia become a sort of social capital in conversations in-game and outside of it, in both virtual and physical spaces. "Based on the Twitter community that I'm following, they seem like they are engaged and interested in what West Virginia is," Mike Mallow said. "Because I'm always quick to be like, 'Well I'm from, I live a half hour away from most of these places.' And they seem excited by that fact."[54]

Players from West Virginia, those familiar with the state, or others visiting for the first time have developed their own vernacular quest in which they compare the fictionalized virtual versions of places to their actual counterparts. This happens both in the game and in real life. The owner of the YouTube channel Rifle Gaming, which has nearly 700,000 followers, reviews in-game locations relative to their physical versions, remarking in one video that the Bethesda game developers "even have woodpiles set up where they're supposed to be."[55] Clara Lehmann said that she met a couple from northern West Virginia who were on a *Fallout 76* tour. "They commented that Helvetia was the most like the game that they had visited so far, which made them very happy. There was a wild excitement in their eyes, I kid you not."[56] She's noticed that for the most part, players who have made the long drive up the mountain to Helvetia in a sort of *Fallout* pilgrimage show genuine respect and curiosity for the state and its communities.

Some West Virginia gamers say that through the game, they've learned things about their home they didn't know before, and it's encouraged them to explore more of the state in real life. Kristy Henson, who grew up in Ohio but now lives in Buckhannon, West Virginia, says, "I have not been all throughout West Virginia, so I've pretty much been to Marshall [University] and Charleston and Buckhannon and Morgantown [laughs].

. . . My boyfriend's natively from Clarksburg, West Virginia . . . so anytime [his family and friends] talk about anything, I [used to] have no idea what they're talking about, but now that I've been playing the game, I've been to all the cities, so I'm like, 'Okay, I've been there in *Fallout*, okay, it has this landmark . . . ' So that's how I travel through the state [laughs]."[57] The simulation of places in-game mentally maps directly onto the real-life counterparts, blending in players' mental conceptions of them. Mike Mallow said that playing the game inspired him to visit Spruce Knob, West Virginia's highest peak. Though the mountain is located in his home county, it took *Fallout* to get him up there. He also hiked up Seneca Rocks, a place he hadn't been since seventh grade, though he sees it every day on this commute to work. In-game, he chose to locate his camp there. "I was like, that's my home and that's where I want to be at. I've moved around different places, but I've always come back to Seneca Rocks."[58] Though Seneca Rocks is a familiar landmark, the game grants him open access to it through a virtual commons that doesn't exist in the physical world. Reddit user Yeoldecatwench commented, "I've lived in WV for about 16 years now and have learned so much about the state from this game. It's been so exciting to learn about a freaking giant teapot and the history of Blair Mountain because I've googled so many landmarks in this game! I even built my C.A.M.P. under the New River Bridge on the spot where my fiancé proposed to me :)" Another reddit user commented, "Beckley native here. My dad was from Parkersburg. . . . You're right the atmosphere is spot on. It's nice being able to immerse myself in home."[59] Players familiar with West Virginia seek out the digital counterpart of places to which they have an emotional attachment.

The gamers I talked to all reported that their virtual experiences in the West Virginia of *Fallout 76* encouraged further exploration of the real-life locations; the one informing and deepening the other, adding new dimensions to physical places, and illuminating the experience of them virtually. Nick Bowman, a media studies professor at Texas Tech University and a former West Virginia resident, reports that *Fallout 76* has indeed altered players' perceptions of and facilitated attachments to West Virginia. "Among our findings included the development of a 'sense of place'—a meaningful and emotional connection with the artifacts and places portrayed in the game. Players, including many nonnative West Virginians, reported an increased knowledge and recognition of West Virginia locations, as well as a deeper understanding of the state's culture and folklore." In fact, through his statistical analysis, Bowman and

FIGURE 8.1. Mike Mallow's *Fallout 76* avatar plays a duet with a friend during one of the game's Fasnacht events, August 25, 2020. Photo courtesy Mike Mallow.

his colleagues found that after two months of regular *Fallout* play, "non-native West Virginians felt a sense of place for West Virginia on par with natives of the state."[60] Norwegian Anders Isaksen commented on a West Virginia Public Broadcasting piece about Bowman's study:

> I am a Norwegian living in the city of Bergen, Norway. Since late 2018 I have been playing Fallout 76 and I have to admit that I have developed a love for West Virginia. I have never been to the USA but it [*sic*] I were ever to get a chance to visit your wonderful country West Virginia is high on my list of places I want to travel to. Your local culture, folklore, nature and people seem absolutely lovely. Without the game you and your amazing state would just be a word on a map. Now it is in my heart. Country Roads take me home <3[61]

Reddit user NTC13 commented, "As an Australian, I've actually had thoughts about moving to West Virginia after playing FO76. I really love mountains, forestry, rivers and lakes and WV seems like a good place for those." Participation in the game, with its immaculate attention to detail, developed narrative, and sensory experience, seems to provoke a desire for a physical experience in West Virginia. If, as Jameson says, science fiction helps us to understand not necessarily the future but the present, an embodied experience in modern-day West Virginia contextualizes the future postapocalyptic West Virginia players have inhabited in-game.

But the West Virginia sense of place that *Fallout 76* reportedly seeds in its players could ultimately be a misrepresentation. The game's immaculate spatial simulation may indeed foster a strong emotional attachment to the physical place of West Virginia, through which some cultural understanding is conveyed. But the simulation stops at people—the landscape is depopulated, the people are dead, the culture is disembodied. While players may develop factual knowledge of the state's culture and be able to orient themselves geographically, the game offers no opportunity to understand or develop a meaningful relationship with a virtual representation of the people and communities who constitute that culture and inhabit those spaces. Similar to how West Virginia culture and community are represented on signs and literature in the New River Gorge, as I discussed in the introduction, the narrative about the state that *Fallout 76* codifies may be one of depopulation, abandonment, and disembodiment. As we examine how *Fallout* tourists from elsewhere are now interacting with real West Virginians in their communities and cultural spaces, the potentially false understanding of place that these players may have developed is an important factor to consider.

"The Robots Will Now Decide . . . How Often We Celebrate Fasnacht": The Contentious Arena of Cultural Heritage Tourism

What is the impact of this increased tourism and psychic blending of physical places in West Virginia with their postapocalyptic virtual counterparts? How does it affect not only players' conceptions of the state but also communities in the state itself? In March 2019, Bethesda Softworks held an in-game Fasnacht event in Helvetia, based on the actual town's cultural tradition, in which players engaged in a quest with the mission of assisting the protectron "artisan" robots during a masked lampion parade. When players completed the quest, they were rewarded with one of several masks including those depicting a jester, owl, witch, or a "toothy man" (perhaps inspired by the "toothy man" masks worn in actual Helvetia Fasnachts past). The event was a popular social gathering. After the quest, players assembled in different houses in virtual Helvetia, talking about their in-game experiences and playing the Helvetia Star Band instruments hanging on the wall (see fig. 8.1). After participating in that in-game event, the following year, gamers Porter Lyons, Kristy Henson, and Mark Fields traveled to Helvetia to attend the real-life 2020 Fasnacht. There they met other gamers from as far away as California and others from within West Virginia who had also been inspired by their virtual experience. At least five of the gamers, including Kristy, created papier-mâché masks based on the Bethesda-designed in-game masks, wearing them in the real-life masked lampion parade and square dance held under the effigy of Old Man Winter. Kristy, who made her own version of the *Fallout 76* owl mask, said she went dressed as her in-game avatar (see plates 8.1 and 8.2). In this sense, players are extending their in-game "performances" to the real-life geographic, social, and cultural spaces on which the game itself was initially modeled. The in-game aesthetic is now being replicated by players in the physical world and influencing the real-life traditional culture of the town of Helvetia, so immaculately represented in the virtual space. Folk narratives are beginning to overlap and hybridize through the mass cultural entity of *Fallout 76*.

Carol Appadurai Breckenridge writes of these "zones of contestation" as hybridized cultural forms of modernity, "in which national, mass, and folk culture provide both mill and grist for one another," engaging in "mutual cannibalization" by co-opting and corrupting each other.[62] Clara Lehmann mentioned that one player from West Virginia proposed that Helvetia hold a special parade for the gamers during Fasnacht. The community decided that it did not want to alter its cultural traditions in such a way, but it is considering offering a walking tour that would allow gamers and other attendees access to buildings often shuttered during the winter. Lehmann said that overall, this increased tourism due to *Fallout 76* has been generally positive; the windfall from the bustling 2020 Fasnacht will help the community install a new roof on its historical museum, an expense the town has been saving up for for three years. But there is some worry that a spike of visitors to the tiny, remote town, particularly during Fasnacht, could overwhelm the capacity of Helvetia's volunteers and disturb its solitude. Lehmann told me, "As you can imagine, we can only handle so many tourists to this small village as there just aren't enough of us, and we intentionally live out here for the joy of the isolation." *Fallout* tourism could create a cycle of cannibalization where players are ultimately corrupting the places and traditions the game is inspired by and so closely mirrors.

Considering its thousands of active players, *Fallout 76* has the potential to economically benefit West Virginia through increased tourism.

Governor Jim Justice and the state Tourism Office welcome the potential boost. Justice said in a 2018 press release, "It's finally time the rest of the world sees what a gem West Virginia is. For years, I've been saying we have it all: beautiful scenery, the best people you could ask for and more. And now, we get to share a piece of that with people all over the world through the unique lens of this video game." Tourism commissioner Chelsea Ruby added, "Our goal is to welcome each and every one of the game's players to Almost Heaven." For now, the uptick in visitors brought by *Fallout 76* seems fairly manageable, but even a small increase in visitor numbers, which might not have a significant impact on West Virginia as a whole, could, as Lehmann points out, overwhelm small community-run events. The game could in fact exacerbate some of the issues its narrative illuminates, effectively compromising both the control local communities have over how their cultural traditions are practiced and their ability to sustain those traditions.[63] This trap is not new in Appalachia; in fact it ties back to the construction of an Appalachian imaginary developed by local-color writers. As C. Brendan Martin chronicles in his book *Tourism in the Mountain South: A Double-Edged Sword*, many local tourism industries built on the culture of the mountains have destroyed or disrupted that very culture, whether in the commodification of heritage crafts created specifically for tourist consumption, land development that raises real estate prices and pushes out locals, or the environmental pollution resulting from that development.[64] Will the robots soon decide how often we celebrate Fasnacht?

John Barton and others within the state have raised questions about cultural extraction, citing concerns that *Fallout 76* may be yet another scenario where a corporation from elsewhere, in this case Bethesda Softworks, profits from West Virginia's resources, while West Virginians see little or even negative material benefit. This too has been a pattern in the tourism industry in the mountains, where most of the profits are siphoned away to outside developers while locals in the service sector (see chapter 6) or the tourism industry are mostly kept in precarious low-wage seasonal work.[65] In terms of access to the portrayal of West Virginia within *Fallout 76* itself, Barton has pointed out that many West Virginians, particularly residents in the most rural counties, may not actually be able to play the game that's based on their home, due to the state's insufficient broadband coverage (West Virginia ranks forty-fourth of the fifty states in terms of access).[66] Though the game offers a social sphere in which players have creative agency within a virtual imagined West Virginia, entry to that space requires access and the sticker price of forty to sixty dollars plus the cost of equipment. As such, *Fallout 76* functions among players as both commons and commodity where players are free to participate in and cocreate the world established for them by game developers—if they're able to pay the price of entry.

"People Are Now Coming Back to West Virginia"

In April 2020, Bethesda Softworks launched *Wastelanders: Fallout 76*, the much anticipated game expansion that was widely considered to be a direct response to player criticism that the game, with its lack of any extended directives or NPCs to interact with, was boring. "People are now coming back to West Virginia," Bethesda's website advertises. Those people are members of two factions, the Settlers and the Raiders, who come to Appalachia in search of the gold suspected to be buried in a vault somewhere in the mountains.[67] Players are given the opportunity to join a faction and assist in this quest.

What is incongruous about the *Wastelanders* expansion is that it is strangely devoid of any grounding in or elaboration of the game's "West Virginia-ness" that was so precisely developed and presented in *Fallout 76*'s initial iteration. Most of the NPCs don't seem to be from the region or have a particular stake in it, and new locations and quests aren't particularly West Virginia–specific but could feasibly exist in any of the *Fallout* games. No longer the main character, West Virginia has faded into the background as just a setting in which to stage this more generic gameplay. In *Fallout 76*'s tug of war between the paradox of West Virginia as both commons and commodity, the developers have appeared to fall squarely in the camp of commodity, through the narrative of resource extraction in the outsider Raiders' and Settlers' quest for gold, but also in their treatment of the place as merely a background in which to set their product.

But the players seem to have a different idea. "It kinda came and went," says Porter Lyons. "The communities I belong to in-game, we really don't talk about *Wastelanders* much anymore. It was irrelevant after the first couple weeks and everybody's kinda gone back to . . . playing the game as they did before." He said that *Wastelanders* introduced more weapons and other items for players to collect, and locations for virtual photographers to take pictures, but the players he knows have all returned to exploring the landscape, sharing what they've collected, taking photos, building C.A.M.P.s, and communing with other players in-game. For the players, this play within the commons is what they're attracted to; the future of West Virginia they're interested in is one of hope, not dread. Meanwhile, events and locations that map onto real-life West Virginia continue to be a draw. Porter told me, "When they relaunched it [Fasnacht] this year, that was one of the most popularly attended events again! Almost everybody on a server was at Helvetia and participating in this, which isn't the most stimulating event from a gameplay [perspective]. But I think why people enjoy it so much is because it feels so inspired by something that exists in real life, in real-life Helvetia."[68] As players from outside and inside the state bring that curiosity to locations in real-life West Virginia, perhaps their understanding of the place will become more twined with the real creators and stewards of the traditions and places they have come to love virtually—the actual people and culture living and breathing and evolving in West Virginia today.

We're Fighting for Our Future

Toward a Visionary Folklore

Unless we write recipes for future kitchens,
there's no reason to think we'll get food we like.

—G. A. COHEN

Can any one of us here still afford to believe that efforts
to reclaim the future can be private or individual?

—AUDRE LORDE

ANNE WASHBURN'S 2012 *Mr. Burns: A Post-electric Play* is a postapocalyptic imagining of the vernacular narratives of a future America.[1] It asks, What common stories will unite us? What songs will we all know? What narratives from the present will eventually become the folklore of the future? The first act is set in "the very near future," immediately following a catastrophic nuclear event. The curtain opens with a group of strangers gathered around a campfire, collectively trying to reconstruct the lines and narrative of *The Simpsons*' "Cape Feare" episode.[2] In recalling this pop cultural reference point common to the randomly composed group (one of them admits that he never actually watched *The Simpsons*, he just knows lines because his ex-girlfriend was an overly zealous fan), they're attempting to distract themselves from the respective trauma they've all recently experienced, though they can't help but occasionally interrupt the narrative of Bart and Homer with their personal stories of the apocalyptic incident. An outsider happens upon their bonfire, and following an initially tense confrontation, they welcome him into the group after he offers, as an olive branch, a Sideshow Bob line they'd been trying to remember. The second act is set seven years later; in the time that's passed since, the strangers have formed a theater troupe that travels to encampments across the desecrated, postelectric United States, performing theatrical imitations of *The Simpsons* episodes with lines and plots they've been able to reconstruct among themselves and buy or barter off others. The third act jumps ahead once again, this time seventy-five years into the future. The initial characters from the previous acts are no longer present, but instead we witness a religious ceremony of sorts, in which *The Simpsons'* "Cape Feare" episode, those original personal accounts of the catastrophic event, and pop songs and "commercials" from the theatrical performance, have now merged in some sort of mythological ceremony transmitted through oral tradition. Though we know the ritual performance is based on material less than a hundred years old, it feels ancient, a deeply embedded, sacred cultural narrative. As a postapocalyptic speculative fiction, the play envisions future evolutions of cultural heritage and how modern pop culture may twine with vernacular culture and personal narrative in a "zone of contestation" to take on a hybridized form, eventually becoming ritual, myth, or religion.

Mr. Burns: A Post-electric Play asks us to consider the evolution of cultural forms and our present role—whether active or passive—in shaping the folklore of the future. Folklorist Henry Glassie elaborates on his conception of tradition as "the creation of the future out of the past. A continuous process situated in the nothingness of the present, linking the vanished with the unknown; tradition is stopped, parceled, and codified by thinkers who fix upon this aspect or that in accord with their needs or preoccupations."[3] Glassie frames tradition as a temporal concept, a moving target constantly churning. Folklorists and scholars who study traditions necessarily arrest expressive practices in their present moment, but that means we're always working from a mere snapshot of culture in motion. While Glassie's conception is commonly cited in the field, a directive urging a forward-thinking approach to vernacular culture that recognizes the necessity of prior contributions, his emphasis is still weighted in the past. If the present is "nothingness," what is the value of that moment as the past transformed into the future? Are the actions taken in that present not important? Do we just send traditions off, like some message in a bottle tossed into the sea with a wing and a prayer that they might weather the onslaught of time's storms and gales to eventually land fully intact upon some future shore?

To do the work of a folklorist is inherently to believe in the future. We record voices, document events and objects of vernacular culture, and share those stories in order to create a record of community life, practices, creative work, and perspectives, many of which are marginalized or suppressed by dominant narratives. We place these recordings, documents, and writing in archives and libraries, carefully labeling them with metadata so future descendants of those artists and communities, researchers, and the general public might one day use them to understand what it was like to live here in this place, to be us or them, in this moment. But in our fieldwork and ethnographic relationships we don't often pay enough heed to that future beyond "sustainability," or mere survival of current forms. By bringing Glassie's conception of tradition as the basis of the future into conversation with Fredric Jameson's assertion—that science fiction in truth tells us little about the future but a lot about the present, illuminating how our current reality will ultimately be historicized—we can imagine how a notion of what I'm calling "visionary folklore" might be fruitful.

This concept is related to Barbara Kirshenblatt-Gimblett's emerging notion of "anticipatory heritage," which operates "in anticipation of the future when the present will be past"—an imperative for cultural workers to collect the present as it's unfolding. Though I didn't encounter Kirshenblatt-Gimblett's conception of anticipatory heritage until after this manuscript was largely written, it describes, to some extent, the framework within which I have approached my fieldwork in West Virginia, and the presentation of a selection of that work in these chapters. What I'm calling visionary folklore, though, is the next step, chronologically speaking; rather than conceiving of heritage as a "mode of cultural production that has recourse to the present," as Kirshenblatt-Gimblett says of anticipatory heritage, visionary folklore can be viewed as having recourse to the future—a future that is contested.[4] How might a future-focused framework help us be more attuned to present conditions? What current narratives will constitute the base of future folklore? What must we fight for in the present so that future communities may retain their sovereignty and have agency over how their traditions are transmitted?

My suspicion is that adopting a future-minded approach to cultural work will have liberatory effects for communities in the present too. As visionary poet Audre Lorde writes in her reflection on the lessons of the civil rights and Black Power movements, "We are making the future as well as bonding to survive the enormous pressures of the present, and that is what it means to be a part of history."[5] Future-building, she asserts, is a collective and creative project that in turn lends hope to the present, making it endurable.

In his chapter, "Critical Folklore Studies and the Revaluation of Tradition," in the collection *Tradition in the Twenty-First Century: Locating the Role of the Past in the Present*, Stephen Olbrys Gencarella engages with Glassie's temporal concept of tradition in proposing a "critical folklore studies." Gencarella presents the model of tradition and betrayal, positioning the concepts not as antonyms but as necessary counterparts in the process of cultural reproduction. He writes, "Every opportunity to pass something on is also an opportunity to betray that passing."[6] Acknowledging that "tradition" is not inherently good, Gencarella argues that tradition bearers, communities, and networks are constantly negotiating what aspects of tradition will be transmitted, and what will be shed or "betrayed." Current debates over the removal of Confederate and colonial monuments in the United States, including here in West Virginia, are one example of how official and state memory is often contested, but this process is also happening in cultural communities, as the chapters of this book have shown. The members of Scotts Run Museum—who not only regularly enact a counternarrative of their community but also have drafted a specific vision for its future—offer the most direct example of this, but there are others. Writer Shirley Campbell carefully preserved her autobiographical songs and poems in a notebook as a statement of identity and tangible artifact of her creative labor for a future reader. Home cooks and residents of Helvetia consider just what is at the core of their cultural traditions, allowing recipes, material culture, and communal celebrations to be revived, retained, and mutated so that those traditions might survive. And in Milton a dedicated pair of friends twine text and place to experience the writings of beloved hometown writer Breece D'J Pancake as a placemaking project, lending layered meaning to their hometown. These community members are invested in creating and maintaining shared cultural reference points in hopes they might leave behind a trace, a road map, a legacy, for the future vernacular culture of West Virginia. As Washburn's rendering warns, though, while the intentional actions of tradition bearers are important in this process, which aspects of tradition endure and which aspects are cast off for the ages is determined not only by the conscious choices of their communities of origin but also is greatly impacted by the material conditions, environment, and ideological currents (not to mention mere happenstance) of the society in which they occur.

The postapocalyptic narrative of *Fallout 76*, in which players inhabit a world ravaged by the atrocities of capitalism and are charged with rebuilding a society and culture out of what remains, suggests that we must consider the material conditions of cultural communities. Gencarella proposes that "folklorists must turn their attention to inciting crises in traditions that prohibit social justice." I'm reluctant to wholeheartedly agree, as I believe that such a drastic intervention in a community-based tradition by a folklorist would need to be approached delicately and specifically, and is potentially problematic, putting too much power into the hands of one folklorist's subjective assessment and interfering with communities' self-determination of their own tradition making. But I'm interested to see the ethical protocol for such an interference further outlined. I argue instead that as a next step beyond documentation, contextualization, and presentation, folklorists, myself included, should be more attuned to the future life of traditions beyond sustainability, and actively work in collaboration with communities to combat the outside destructive forces, such as privatization, extraction, and austerity, that disrupt them and block their agency to negotiate the transmission of their traditions. Glassie gestures at this when he asserts that the antonym of *tradition* is not *change*, but *oppression*. "Oppressed people are made to do what others will them to do. They become slaves in the ceramic factories of their masters. Acting traditionally, by contrast, they use their own resources—their own tradition, one might say—to create their own future, to do what they will themselves to do. They make their own pots."

But it is becoming ever harder for people to make their own pots. The deracinating forces of capitalism and its atrocities of extraction, environmental destruction, disease, poverty, and climate change that can act upon the creative practices of cultural groups are so powerfully disruptive that they are often the primary etic causes of the death of tradition. In West Virginia, witness, for example, the local community whose members for generations dug ramps on a certain hillside—a site of community practice and shared memory—now lost due to land being privatized or altogether ravaged by a coal company.[7] Or the new communities of

Haitian, Burmese, Puerto Rican, and Ethiopian refugees and immigrants who work long night shifts at the local chicken processing plant in the rural small town of Moorefield, where there are language barriers among workers and few places and little time to gather in community and engage in cultural practices.[8] Or consider the community graveyard of a former Black coal camp in Logan County, where locals once gathered every Memorial Day to picnic and decorate the graves of their relatives, before it was destroyed when the gas company ran a pipeline through, cracking graves and disturbing remains.[9] These sorts of disruptions seem to be occurring at an accelerating rate, particularly in a place like West Virginia, where the population, especially in rural areas, is declining faster than in any other state, the majority of land is owned by outside private companies and investors, and many of the livable wage-paying jobs that do exist demand long hours and grueling, often dangerous work, leaving little time or energy for other pursuits.[10] Recently, the COVID-19 pandemic has exacerbated outstanding and intertwined social issues including unemployment, poverty, poor health, addiction, racism, and structural reliance on a rapidly declining extractive and destructive monoeconomy.[11] In the wake of the pandemic (if it's possible to speak of the end of it), it will become all the more necessary for folklorists and cultural workers invested in the sovereignty of marginalized and oppressed populations to take a visionary approach to cultural work. To do so, our work must be in collaboration with communities and be based in material analysis. As Gencarella writes of his critical folklore studies, "It would not seek utopia but rather struggle to make the future better, redress past injustices, and improve the present for as many people as possible." Perhaps, though, a bit of a utopian spirit would yield a beneficial and productive outlook for folklorists, inspiring us to work in collaboration with communities to not only envision collective futures but create them together, by fighting for improved material conditions for everyone.

What might this look like in practice? Collaborative ethnographic methodology suggests that folklorists work with communities and practitioners to engage in that dialogue, draft a collective vision, and identify an action plan. Questions that could be included in fieldwork interviews include, What is the future you envision for your community and its cultural traditions? What resources and structures need to be in place to ensure your community and its cultural practices thrive now and in the future? And what do you need in order to achieve that future? In his article "Theorizing Public Folklore Work," Gregory Hansen cites several examples of how public folklorists have leveraged their fieldwork to advocate for local cultural communities, including lobbying for traditional basket makers' rights to access and sustainably harvest grasses in endangered wetlands, helping foster a renaissance of dying art forms like Baltimore screen painting, and other productive cultural interventions that have benefited the well-being of practitioners and their respective traditions.[12] However, as evident in the Scotts Run Museum members' vision which calls for among other goals, affordable housing, some of the necessary advocacy that will help secure the sustainability of cultural communities for the future may lie outside the scope of the usual work of arts and humanities nonprofits and philanthropic grants. This may include fighting for new and expanded social programs such as universal healthcare, a mandated livable wage, child tax credits, affordable housing, unconditional basic income, debt relief, mutual aid networks, and other infrastructural and policy shifts that will directly benefit the material conditions of communities and practitioners we work with.[13] Such programs could undoubtedly assist in the cohesion of cultural communities, granting resources, time, space, and well-being that will allow them to fully engage in their respective creative practices.

In addition, public folklorists and cultural workers who engage with local communities to "amplify voices in a democratic polity" could make more efforts to communicate the value of our collaborative methodology as a model for bottom-up participatory democracy and grassroots community engagement across positionalities, which can be applied to other contexts. Just as striking West Virginia teachers reimagined the space of the state capitol as one where policy that determines the life and work conditions of a group of workers was shaped by those workers themselves, entities that could benefit from planning methods that work in collaboration with the communities they impact include local planning and zoning offices, community development commissions, rural development offices, tourism boards, arts and cultural organizations, and community-engaged educational programs. Surely, the work of these organizations and government agencies involves and impacts folklife in various ways; public folklorists can leverage that intersection as an entry point to advocate for the inclusion of the voices of cultural communities regarding specific policies which may impact their self-determination and ability to sustain their cultural traditions. As Mary Hufford writes in her article "Deep Commoning: Public Folklore and Environmental Policy on a Resource Frontier," which addresses the potential applications of public folklore within environmental policy specifically in the Appalachian coalfields, "public folklorists and heritage workers on resource frontiers will need to embrace the task, described by Tim Winter, of 'understanding the various ways in which heritage now has a stake in, and can act as a positive enabler for, the complex, multi-vector challenges that face us today, such as cultural and environmental sustainability, economic inequalities, conflict resolution, social cohesion, and the future of cities'."[14]

To undertake this type of holistic work is to acknowledge what may be obvious: that the sustainability of expressive culture is inextricable from the material sustainability of the community from which it emerges. Further, we might borrow the concept of "intergenerational justice," which is most often used in the context of the climate change movement, and apply it to our notions of cultural heritage and cultural equity. What does intergenerational justice look like in terms of cultural traditions? Sociologist Erik Olin Wright writes of the term, "Future generations should have access to the social and material means to live flourishing lives at least at the same level as the present generation."[15] Those social and material means include those with which communities are able to practice and perform their cultural traditions, and folklife is a crucial aspect of a flourishing life. Commitment to visionary folklore and cultural intergenerational justice would reify a core value of the field of folklore: that our collective futures—of folklorists, artists, tradition bearers, cultural communities, and vernacular art forms—are inherently twined, all part of a diverse, just, equitable, and pluralistic society. As Mark Nowak reminds us in *Social Poetics*, his book on worker poetry workshops, "Solidarity is simultaneously a historical condition, a contemporary action, and a future aspiration. Solidarity, deep within its definition, embraces all three tenses: the past, the present, and the future."[16] So too must the field of folklore.

In the meantime, as old traditions die, communities are adapting, responding, and reshaping to birth new expressive forms. What I've witnessed through my work in West Virginia and what much of this book explores is that though some traditions may be disrupted or even destroyed by extractive industry, climate change, and structural inequality, communities are responding to and at times resisting these deracinating and destructive forces with new forms of expressive culture. In the aftermath, isolated individuals link their fates and new creative futures can be born together. As scholar and activist Lynne Segal writes, "Understanding the lineages of loss . . . can supply the tools for pondering what remains afterwards, and hence for both a possible 'rewriting of the past as well as the reimagining of the future.'"[17] West Virginia teachers striking against austerity measures and privatization built collective power through their signs, chants, T-shirts, and memes. Faced with the widespread lack of personal protective equipment in the midst of a pandemic, sewists took to their machines to stitch masks and distribute them to local first responders through veteran-run mental health peer support networks. Unable to gather and hold indoor events for months due to COVID-19 quarantine restrictions, All Star Wrestling hosted drive-in matches outside a local dance studio. When the Scotts Run Museum regulars could no longer gather at their regular Saturday coffee shop, Eve Faulkes worked with her students to develop a "Together Even When Apart" care package to distribute to the network. It included yard signs, a set of greeting cards to send to each other, a journal to document how they were coping, and information on how to register to vote and keep safe during COVID. Local businesses hosted hot dog sales to cover their lost income and employees' medical expenses. Porchsitters of Appalachia, a mutual aid group that formed in Boone County during the pandemic, assists in collective self-provisioning, giving away food, seeds, vegetable plants, and garden tools to local families and sharing information on gardening, food preservation, and traditional herbal medicine. A post on the group's Facebook page asks, "Do you believe it is possible to think radically regarding food, food access, and local food sustainability in Boone County? What does envisioning our food culture look like? What could the future of food look like in our communities?"[18] As ever, West Virginia communities offer potent examples of how expressive culture fortifies identity and creates shared narratives that the collective can apply to further resist structural inequality and oppression. Tradition, as they see it, is indeed the fight for the future.

Acknowledgments

THIS BOOK is the physical manifestation of many conversations and dialogues with artists, practitioners, community leaders, colleagues, friends, texts, and cultural expressions. I am enormously grateful to everyone who took the time to sit down with me for an interview or share their experiences, stories, creative work, perspectives, suggestions, edits, and resources. The book would not have been possible without your generosity, trust, work, and brilliance.

First, thank you to all of my consultants (and their family members), whose lived experience, stories, knowledge, creative work, and constructive feedback are the subject of these chapters: Richie Acevedo; Al Anderson; the anonymous West Virginia teachers and the anonymous United Mine Workers of America member I spoke to on the West Virginia state capitol steps; John Barton; Eleanor Betler; Betty Biggs; Lou Birurakis; Dylan Bishop; Marie and Junior Burrell; Jerimy Campbell; Shirley Campbell; Emily Comer; Mary Jane Coulter; Gary Damron; Kelli Douglas; Gary Fauber; Eve Faulkes; Mark Fields; Charli Shea Fortney-Heiskell; Cora L. Hairston; Diana Hamilton; Ella Hanshaw; Rocky Hardin; Kristy Henson; Karla Hilliard; Ernest Hoeffer; Kasey Huffman; Robert Jackson; Kelly Kerney and Ethan Bullard; Brianna Knotts; Clara Lehmann and Jonathan Lacocque; Sarah Boyd Little; Amy Lough; Shirley Love; Porter Lyons; Mike Mallow; Charlene Marshall; Dave McKay; Stanton Means; Jay O'Neal; John Propst; Elaine Purkey; Sharon Rollins; Jessica Salfia; George Sarris; Linda "Bunch" Smith; Bill Valos, Lynn Valos, and Troy Valos; Dave Whipp; and Rick Wilson.

I'm grateful to Eric Waggoner, the board members, program committee members, and my former coworkers at the West Virginia Humanities Council for recognizing the value of this project and supporting it with time, encouragement, and feedback. Thank you, too, to everyone who has supported or participated in the work of the West Virginia Folklife Program.

Thank you to everyone at UNC Press, including Mary Carley Caviness, Kim Bryant, Lindsey Starr, and copyeditor Alex Martin. Special thanks to my wonderful editor Lucas Church, who asked important questions of this manuscript, and whose vision and guidance was invaluable in shaping this book into its final form. Thank you to my readers for their engaged and thoughtful feedback, particularly the brilliant Mary Hufford, whose dedicated and integrative work, particularly in West Virginia, inspired me early on to pursue the work of public folklore and continues to teach me so much. In many ways this book rests upon the strong foundation she has built for critically engaged public folklore work in the Mountain State and beyond.

I'm indebted to my amazing unofficial readers: Sophie Abramowitz, Tijah Bumgarner, Danille Christensen, Mike Costello, Amy Dawson, Adam Harris, Rosemary Hathaway, Jesse Montgomery, Nick Murray, Jessica Salfia, Tom Sexton, Travis Stimeling, Kim Stryker, Emily Wallace, Jessie Wilkerson, and Rick Wilson, who gave their time to read proposal and/or chapter drafts and offered crucial edits, suggestions, and resources. I hope I can return the favor someday.

I'm grateful to Erica Abrahams Locklear, Barbara Ellen Smith, Stephanie Williams, and especially Elizabeth Engelhardt for those initial conversations and votes of confidence for this project. Marcie Cohen Ferris and Bill Ferris, Rebecca Gayle Howell, Robert Gipe, Emily Wallace, and Ashley Melzer also offered their guidance throughout as I navigated the writing and publishing process—thank you.

The Gerald E. and Corrine L. Parsons Fund Award from the American Folklife Center at the Library of Congress supported initial research into existing West Virginia folklife documentation; sincere gratitude, as always, to the AFC staff for their time, guidance, and knowledge.

The Turkey Land Cove Foundation offered me time and space to write—a much appreciated and productive respite during those first uncertain weeks of the pandemic.

Thank you to Charleston Creativity Connections for their support to fund the creation of maps and color printing, to Dan Davis for the incredible original maps, and Annie Howe for the gorgeous cover art that brings the chapter subjects to life so perfectly.

My wonderful friends supported my work in a multitude of ways, from feeding my cats when I was away writing to general encouragement. I'm especially grateful to Dan Davis and Hillary Harrison (and the *Fallout 76* party crew), Elaine McMillion Sheldon and Curren Sheldon, Tijah Bumgarner and Dan Carlisle, Mike Costello and Amy Dawson, Molly Born and Zander Aloi, Becky Wright (and her friend Jessica Hurley), Ryan Babbitt, and the Eastham Jammers.

Thank you to my family and the Ambrose-Montgomery family for all their support. And thank you to Jesse, who makes everything—including this book—so much better.

Notes

A NOTE ON COLLABORATIVE ETHNOGRAPHIC METHODOLOGY AND
WRITING AS PUBLIC FOLKLORE PRAXIS

1. Mary Hufford citing Sandra Gross-Bressler on the American Folklife
Preservation Act. Hufford, "Deep Commoning," 12–13.

2. Hansen, "Theorizing Public Folklore."

INTRODUCTION

1. Though the circumstance of West Virginia's birth is often attributed
to nineteenth-century mountaineers' rejection of slavery, it was above all an
economic strategy by the founders to assert control over the valuable land of
Virginia's western counties. See Stoll, *Ramp Hollow*, 132–36.

2. Harlan, "Booker T. Washington's West Virginia Boyhood."

3. Cherniack, "Hawks Nest Tunnel Disaster." See also Catherine Venable
Moore's essay "The Book of the Dead," inspired by and included in the 2019
West Virginia University Press edition of Muriel Rukeyser's book of poems by
the same name. Moore, "The Book of the Dead."

4. The stretch of Route 60 from Gauley Bridge to Ansted is also the setting
for Breece D'J Pancake's haunting story "Time and Again." Pancake, *The Stories of Breece D'J Pancake*.

5. National Park Service, "Basic Information."

6. National Park Service, "Places."

7. Hufford, "Breaking the Time Barrier," 9.

8. Hufford, "Ethnographic Overview and Assessment."

9. National Park Service, "Tourism to National Parks of Southern West Virginia Creates Nearly $70 Million in Economic Benefits"; National Park Service, "History and Culture."

10. Ben-Amos, "Toward a Definition of Folklore in Context."

11. Stefano, "Folklife at the International Level."

12. Bauman, "The Philology of the Vernacular," 32.

13. Noyes, "Humble Theory."

14. Abrahams, *Everyday Life*, 143.

15. Hufford, "Working in the Cracks," 166.

16. Murphy, "Toward a Bright Future."

17. National Endowment for the Arts, "State Partnership Agreements."

18. Milnes directed the Augusta Heritage Center at Davis and Elkins for twenty-five years, served as the representative folklorist for the state, and, in his tenure at Augusta, amassed an archive of over 2,000 hours of audio and video documentation and produced a wealth of books, films, and albums, generally focused on West Virginia's music and dance traditions, storytelling, herbal medicine, and local German and Swiss communities.

19. Baron and Spitzer, "Cultural Continuity and Community Creativity in a New Century," vii.

20. Lassiter, *The Chicago Guide to Collaborative Ethnography*, 16.

21. Steven Stoll writes of how the industrialist elites in Charleston and Wheeling welcomed the deforestation of West Virginia in the name of timber, coal, oil, railroad, and real estate profits and "civilization, historical progress, and social order." Stoll, *Ramp Hollow*, 169.

22. John Lilly's 2005 project, "An Introduction to West Virginia Ethnic Communities," Matt Meacham's 2005 West Virginia Humanities Council study of musicians and music infrastructure in West Virginia's Third Congressional District, and Gerry Milnes's extensive fieldwork conducted through the Augusta Heritage Center, were all helpful guides for my fieldwork. Lilly, "An Introduction to West Virginia Ethnic Communities."

23. Fortunately, the rally was effectively shut down by local activist groups and unable to gain a foothold in the region. Klibanoff, "Inside White Nationalists' Longshot Plan to Win Over Appalachia."

24. According to the *Guardian*, in the 2010 Census, 9 percent of Black people in the United States were not counted. The Urban Institute estimates that somewhere between 1.1–1.7 million Black Americans will be undercounted in the 2020 Census. In West Virginia, officials were also concerned that the population in general would be undercounted because of the Census's move to mostly online reporting. Mona Chalabi, "How the US Census Misses People of Color—and Why It's So Harmful," *Guardian*, February 27, 2020, www.the guardian.com/us-news/datablog/2020/feb/27/2020-us-census-black-people -mistakes-count; Amelia Ferrell Knisely, "As Census Survey Moves Online, WV

at Risk of Undercounting, Losing Federal Funds," *Charleston Gazette-Mail*, October 7, 2019, www.wvgazettemail.com/news/as-census-survey-moves-online-wv-at-risk-of-undercounting-losing-federal-funds/article_2116860f-838f-58df-870a-5059eacd0ec5.html.

25. According to the West Virginia Humanities Council's *West Virginia Encyclopedia*, there was "no resident native population at the time of white settlement," but this statement is contested and hinges on a settler-colonial understanding of occupancy and ownership. More research is needed on historical and current Native American tribal groups and cultural communities in the Mountain State. Maslowski, "Indians"; Knollinger, "Wild, Wondering West Virginia."

26. Brown reports that the number of Black coal miners in West Virginia "accounted for three-quarters of the region's black population by 1940—the census year that boasted the region's greatest black population density of the century." Brown, *Gone Home*, 6, 22–23.

27. According to the 2000 Census, the minority population in West Virginia increased 31.9 percent since 1990, while the non-Hispanic white population decreased 0.5 percent, and from the 2000 census to the 2010 census, the white population in the state decreased from 95 percent to 93.9 percent, while nonwhite populations increased. In the 2020 census, the white population in the state decreased 7.4 percent, while the Black and African American population increased 4.3 percent (2,689 residents), and the Hispanic and Latino population increased 56.4 percent (12,559 residents). The overall diversity index increased from 13.1 percent to 20.2 percent from 2010 to 2020. Pollard, "A 'New Diversity'"; Census Viewer, "Population of West Virginia"; US Census Bureau, "West Virginia Population Declined 3.2% from 2010 to 2020."

28. Kirshenblatt-Gimblett, "Mistaken Dichotomies," 36.

29. Weller, *Yesterday's People*; Frost, "Our Contemporary Ancestors in the Southern Mountains"; Schrag, "Appalachia."

30. Williams, *The Country and the City*, 35.

31. Steiner, "Regionalism in the Great Depression."

32. Hufford, "Carnival Time in the Kingdom of Coal."

33. Beryl Crowe defines the commons as "a fundamental social institution that has a history going back through our own colonial experience to a body of English common law which antedates the Roman conquest. That law recognized that in societies there are some environmental objects which have never been, and should never be, exclusively appropriated to any individual or group of individuals." Crowe, "The Tragedy of the Commons Revisited," 53.

34. Hufford, "Working in the Cracks."

35. See Stoll, *Ramp Hollow*, for a thorough and brilliant exploration of the relationship between the enclosure of the British commons and enclosure of agrarian land in Appalachia.

36. Martin, *Tourism in the Mountain South.*

37. Stoll, *Ramp Hollow*, 242.

38. The 1978 Appalachian Land Ownership Study found that these conglomerates owned nearly 40 percent of the land and 70 percent of the mineral rights in the land surveyed. Eller, *Uneven Ground*, 199.

39. Geographer Clyde Woods notes the use of depopulation as a development strategy in the Mississippi Delta too, citing Judith Porter's interview with a plantation bloc leader as described in her 1992 article "What Works and What Doesn't? Perceptions of Economic Development among Delta Leaders." When she asked the leader what his vision was for the Delta's future, he replied, "Ten years down the pike, I see beautiful fields of cotton and soybeans, the growth of industry, and a program to encourage out-migration, which will solve a lot of problems." Woods, *Development Arrested*, 270.

40. Hufford, "Reclaiming the Commons," 108.

41. Eller, *Uneven Ground*, 6.

42. Glassie, "Tradition," 295.

43. Hafstein, "Folklore Talks."

44. Folklorist Dorothy Noyes defines the "surround" as the "spatiotemporal, material, linguistic, and gestural frameworks of social interaction." Noyes, "Aesthetic Is the Opposite of Anaesthetic," 148–49.

45. Hufford, "Breaking the Time Barrier," 9.

46. Hafstein, "Folklore Talks."

47. Kurin, "Presenting Folklife in a Soviet-American Cultural Exchange," 190.

48. Ryden, *Mapping the Invisible Landscape*, 45.

49. Ryden, 213.

50. Federici, *Re-enchanting the World*, 3; Noyes, "Group," 29.

51. Turner, "The Witch in Flight."

52. Proschan, "Field Work and Social Work," 150.

53. Eller, *Uneven Ground*, 223.

54. Ono and Sloop, "The Critique of Vernacular Discourse," 22.

CHAPTER 1

1. The Scotts Run Museum Coffee Shop regulars generally spell it "Scotts Run" without the possessive apostrophe, though in some texts it is spelled "Scott's." I defer to the community's spelling here.

2. See Noyes, "Group," 16–17; and Noyes, "The Social Base of Folklore."

3. Lewis, "America's Symbol of the Great Depression in the Coal Fields." Immigrants from Mexico arrived later and were also documented by FSA photographers.

4. Stoll, *Ramp Hollow*, 220; Martin, "West Virginia Mine Wars."

5. Lewis, "America's Symbol of the Great Depression in the Coal Fields," 1–2.

6. Birurakis, interview with author, February 23, 2019.

7. Little, interview with author, March 16, 2018.

8. Fortney-Heiskell, interview with author, March 23, 2019.

9. Hickok, *Reluctant First Lady*, 136–37.

10. Roosevelt, *This I Remember*.

11. Photos accessible through US Resettlement Administration, Library of Congress, Photos, Prints and Drawings.

12. Lewis, "America's Symbol of the Great Depression in the Coal Fields," 8.

13. She continues, "I do not believe if most of us knew the conditions under which some of our brothers and sisters were living that we would rest complacently until we had registered the fact that in this country the day is past when we will continue to live under any governmental system which will produce conditions such as exist in certain industries and in certain parts of the country." Roosevelt, "Ratify the Child Labor Amendment," 4.

14. Hoffman, *Eleanor Roosevelt and the Arthurdale Experiment*, 17.

15. Cook, *Eleanor Roosevelt*, 139. For more information on the entities involved in this contested decision, I recommend Patterson, "A New Pattern of Life."

16. Lewis, "'Why Don't You Bake Bread?'"

17. Patterson, "A New Pattern of Life," 74.

18. Hoffman, *Eleanor Roosevelt and the Arthurdale Experiment*, 21.

19. Clapp, "Arthurdale," 26. This was a report prepared by Clapp for Eleanor Roosevelt, John Dewey, and others involved in education at Arthurdale.

20. Clapp, *Community Schools in Action*, 217–47.

21. Clapp, "Arthurdale," 26.

22. Patterson, "A New Pattern of Life," 106; Clapp, "Arthurdale," 27.

23. Whisnant, *All That Is Native and Fine*.

24. According to Eleanor Roosevelt's "My Day" newspaper columns. Roosevelt, "My Day."

25. Sarris, interview with author, April 5, 2019. Though creating an all-white community out of one that was previously diverse was not Eleanor Roosevelt's intention, she ultimately conceded to the protests. She recommended the founding of a community of fifteen homesteads for Black miners. While a 350-acre plot was optioned for construction, it was never built. Cook, *Eleanor Roosevelt*, 140.

26. Birurakis, interview with author, February 23, 2019.

27. Julian, "'I Am Going to Tell the Story,'" 33.

28. Evans, *Women Selling Ice Cream and Cake*.

29. Roosevelt, *This I Remember*, 1949, reprinted in *A Taste of History, with Ethnic Flavor*.

30. Little, interview with author, March 16, 2018.

31. Coulter, interview with author, May 7, 2019.

32. Little, interview with author, March 16, 2018.

33. Marshall, interview with author, March 23, 2019.

34. Marshall, interview with author, March 23, 2019.

35. Little, interview with author, March 16, 2018.

36. Anderson, interview with author, April 5, 2019.

37. "Gov. Moore Will Open I-79 Segment," *Charleston Gazette*, October 10, 1970.

38. Anderson, interview with author, April 5, 2019.

39. Ben Conley, "Scotts Run PSD Update," *Dominion Post* (Morgantown, W.Va.), July 9, 2013, www.tmcnet.com/usubmit/-code-scotts-run-illegal-/2013/07/09/7260986.htm.

40. Anderson, interview with author, April 5, 2019.

41. Noyes, "Group," 19.

42. The current museum is the third iteration of the Scotts Run Museum. The previous museums closed due to building issues and mismanagement. See Coulter, interview with author, May 7, 2019.

43. Noyes, "Group," 23.

44. Faulkes, interview with author, April 11, 2019.

45. Marshall, interview with author, March 23, 2019.

46. *Songs of Scotts Run.*

47. Federici, *Re-enchanting the World*, 3.

48. Scotts Run Museum and Trail, website.

49. Nearly eighty years after the disaster, in May 2021, Scotts Run Museum members unveiled a sign memorializing the lives of the fifty-six miners who died in the explosion of the Christopher No. 3 Mine at Osage. The sign was supported by the Lynch Foundation and the Monongalia County 4-H Leaders Association. Scotts Run Museum, May 23, 2021.

50. Scotts Run Museum and Trail, website.

CHAPTER 2

1. Glassie, Murphy, and Peach, *Ola Belle Reed and Southern Mountain Music on the Mason-Dixon Line.*

2. "Nora Carpenter Traditional Music Collection."

3. Hilliard, "'Written and Composed by Nora E. Carpenter.'"

4. Sawin, *Listening for a Life*, 1.

5. Jones, *Live.*

6. Campbell, interview with author, March 16, 2016.

7. Campbell, "I Never Dreamed," July 14, 1971.

8. Campbell, "The Telephone," undated.

9. Campbell, "The Victory," undated.

10. Campbell, "A Mother's Prayer," September 14, 1986.

11. Campbell, "Mom," October 20, 1986.

12. Campbell, "Mothers, Sisters, Wives," undated.

13. James Bovard, "The '85 Farm Bill Will Hurt Exports," *New York Times*, December 12, 1985, www.nytimes.com/1985/12/12opinion/the-85-farm-bill-will -hurt-exports.html.

14. Campbell, "Old MacDonald," October 3, 1985.

15. Campbell, "Mexico City Earthquake," September 29, 1985, and "Wheels of Justice," August 28, 1985.

16. Hanshaw, interview with author, November 20, 2018.

17. Kelly Kerney, personal correspondence with author, August 30, 2020.

18. Kelly Kerney, personal correspondence with author, July 12, 2021.

19. Hairston, interview with author, May 3, 2016.

20. Hairston, *Faces behind the Dust*; Hairston, *Hello World*.

21. Purkey, "One Day More."

22. Fones-Wolf, "Ravenswood Strike."

23. Purkey, *Mountain Music, Mountain Struggle*.

24. Purkey.

25. Sean Duffy, "Celebrating the Musical Women of Coal Country: Karen Collins, Elaine Purkey Remember Hazel Dickens," *Weelunk* (Wheeling, W.Va.), August 26, 2019. https://weelunk.com/celebrating-the-musical-women-of-coal -country-karen-collins-and-elaine-purkey-remember-hazel-dickens.

26. Fox, *Real Country*, 108.

27. See Smith, "The Household Searchlight Recipe Book."

28. Clark, "Letters from Home."

29. Kodish, "Fair Young Ladies and Bonny Irish Boys," 133.

30. Rosenberg, "It Was a Kind of Hobby."

31. Silverstein and Urban, "The Natural History of Discourse."

32. Campbell, interview with author, April 26, 2016.

33. Bauman and Briggs, "Poetics and Performance as Critical Perspectives on Language and Social Life."

34. Campbell, interview with author, April 26, 2016.

35. Campbell, interview with author, April 26, 2016.

36. Christensen, "Materializing the Everyday."

37. Bloom, "I Write For Myself and Strangers."

38. Campbell, interview with author, March 16, 2016.

39. Christensen, "(Not) Going Public."

40. Rosenberg, "It Was a Kind of Hobby," 329.

41. Campbell, "Dear Shirley," June 17, 1986.

42. Fox, *Real Country*, 126–28.

43. Campbell, "Disgruntled Poet," January 30, 1972.

44. Campbell, "Oh, to Be," August 27, 1971.

45. Sawin, *Listening for a Life*, 6.

46. Campbell, "Words," June 22, 1986.

47. Sawin, *Listening for a Life*, 26.

48. Purkey, interview with author, October 27, 2016.

49. Purkey, interview with author, October 27, 2016.

50. Purkey, "America! Our Union!," in *Mountain Music, Mountain Struggle*.

51. Turino, *Music as Social Life*, 4.

52. Fox, *Real Country*, 125.

53. Fox, 241.

54. Sawin, *Listening for a Life*, 200.

55. Hairston, interview with George Mason Folklore Field School, May 24, 2018.

56. "Lean on Me" was written by Bill Withers, a coal miner's son and native of Raleigh County, West Virginia—less than a hundred miles from where Hairston is from.

57. Sawin, *Listening for a Life*; Christensen, "(Not) Going Public," 73.

58. Sean Duffy, "Celebrating the Musical Women of Coal Country: Karen Collins, Elaine Purkey Remember Hazel Dickens," *Weelunk* (Wheeling, W.Va.), August 26, 2019.

59. Virginia Myrtle Ellis, aka Aunt Jennie Wilson (1900–1992), was a claw-hammer banjo player from Logan County, West Virginia. Spence, "Aunt Jennie Wilson."

60. Turino, *Music as Social Life*.

61. Fox, *Real Country*, 31.

CHAPTER 3

1. Sutton, *Helvetia*.

2. A local 1875 newspaper article reports on Helvetia's forty-seven-member brass band. "Neighborhood Items," *Weston Democrat*, May 24, 1875.

3. Betler, interview with author, February 5, 2016.

4. For more on Helvetia's seasonal celebrations, see Hilliard, "One Year in Helvetia."

5. Mailloux, *Oppis Guet's Vo Helvetia*, 3.

6. In April 1917, several West Virginia newspapers reported that a riot erupted in Helvetia after a German flag had been hoisted in town. The following month, Helvetia held a patriotic rally "as a further evidence of the village's patriotism." "Rioting Follows Raising of German Flag in W.Va.," *Wheeling Intelligencer*, April 12, 1917; "War at Helvetia," *Raleigh Herald* (Beckley, W.Va.), April 13, 1917; *West Virginian* (Fairmont, W.Va.), May 28, 1917.

7. Mailloux, *Oppis Guet's Vo Helvetia*.

8. The questionable solution: "For a couple of hours shower in cold water. In case there is still no sign of life, add a cupful of salt and continue for another hour." Mailloux, *Oppis Guet's Vo Helvetia*, 61.

9. Mailloux, *Oppis Guet's Vo Helvetia*, 22.

10. Glassie, "Tradition," 177.

11. The Balli sisters are the subject of the documentary *Swiss Family Balli*. Rice, *Swiss Family Balli*.

12. Sutton, "Walter Aegerter."

13. Hilliard, "Something Good from Helvetia."

14. Hilliard, "Fat Tuesday"; Balic, "Fritters," 276–77.

15. Isin, "Moulds for Shaping and Decorating Food in Turkey," 184; Isin, *Sherbet and Spice*, 10–11; Balic, "Fritters," 276–77.

16. See Porch Railings document held in the Helvetia Genealogy Archives, http://helvetiawv.com/Genealogy/Index.html.

CHAPTER 4

1. Paul Hendrickson, "The Legend of Breece D'J Pancake," *Washington Post*, December 10, 1984, www.washingtonpost.com/archive/lifestyle/1984/12/10/the -legend-of-breece-dj-pancake/cd125f05-b96b-4c89-9bf6-620fddbf441f.

2. In her essay about Breece in the special issue of *Appalachian Heritage*, Grace Tooney Edwards writes that Breece recommended she teach Chuck Kinder's *Snakehunter* in her Appalachian literature course and lent her a copy. Edwards, "Breece D'J Pancake."

3. Pancake, *The Stories of Breece D'J Pancake*. For more on Breece's life, see Douglass, *A Room Forever*.

4. Seybert, "'He'll Always Be a Part of Us.'"

5. Edward Relph, quoted in Ryden, *Mapping the Invisible Landscape*, 39.

6. Ryden, 45.

7. Wilson, "Done Too Soon," unpublished.

8. Pancake, "Trilobites," in *The Stories of Breece D'J Pancake*, 22–23.

9. In October 2021, Rick wrote to let me know that the Old Bank steps had been torn down.

10. Helen Pancake in Douglass, *A Room Forever*, 24.

11. Edwards, guest editor's note on "A Loss of Tone," 36.

12. Though there are no outright political references in "A Room Forever," Rick Wilson says that the Huntington flop hotel that inspired the story's setting was next to the used bookstore that sold AMP pamphlets and Wobbly materials. Slifer, "1970s Activist Publishing in West Virginia."

13. Ryden, *Mapping the Invisible Landscape*, 48.

14. Bernard, "Here's What I Hate about Writer's Houses."

15. For a recent example, in the Apple TV+ show *Dickinson*, Emily Dickinson is seen embarking on a carriage ride with the character Death, then going home to pen the words, "Because I could not stop for Death / He kindly stopped for me; / The carriage held but just ourselves / And Immortality." *Dickinson*, season 1, episode 1, "Because I Could Not Stop," November 1, 2019.

16. Helen Pancake letter to Tommy Schoffler.

17. Pancake, "The Honored Dead," in *The Stories of Breece D'J Pancake*, 122.

18. Pancake, "Trilobites," in *The Stories of Breece D'J Pancake*, 138.

19. Ryden, *Mapping the Invisible Landscape*, 40.

20. Douglass, *A Room Forever*, 19.

21. Pancake, "Trilobites," 21.

22. Rick is referring to *Stranger with a Camera*, the documentary of a 1967 murder of a Canadian filmmaker by an East Kentucky landowner, now a foundational document of Appalachian studies for its consideration of the insider/outsider dynamic in media representations of the region. Barret, *Stranger with a Camera*.

23. According to Helen Pancake, Company Hill was named such because it was owned by the C&O Railroad. The site also appears in Breece D'J Pancake's stories, "The Honored Dead," and the unpublished "A Loss of Tone."

24. Bolles, "Inside the Harlan County Coal Miner Protest."

25. Jackson, interview with author, October 15, 2019.

26. Jackson.

27. Pancake was likely twenty-six, the age he was when he died.

28. Jackson, interview with author, October 15, 2019.

29. Barbour, "Breece Pancake, an Appalachian Voice."

30. Edwards, "Breece D'J Pancake."

31. Breece D'J Pancake letter to C. R. and Helen Pancake.

32. Douglass, *A Room Forever*, 74.

CHAPTER 5

1. Catte, Hilliard, and Salfia, *55 Strong*.

2. Salfia, introduction, 8.

3. Boettner, "Does West Virginia Invest Enough in Education?"

4. Here, I am drawing upon the work of political theorist Nancy Fraser and historian Tithi Bhattacharya. Fraser explores how "capitalist society harbors a deep-seated social-reproductive 'crisis tendency' or 'contradiction,'" in that the waged economy relies on social reproduction, historically undertaken by women, as an uncompensated background condition that all labor depends on, while simultaneously destabilizing that work, rendering it impossible. Fraser, "The Crisis of Care?," 22.

5. Silvia Federici writes, "'everyday life' is not a generic complex of events, attitudes, and experiences searching for an order. It is a structured reality, organized around a specific process of production, the production of human beings, which, as Marx and Engels pointed out, is 'the first historical act' and a fundamental condition of all history." Federici, "From Crisis to Commons," 175–76.

6. Anonymous West Virginia public school teacher, interview with author, February 26, 2018.

7. Anonymous West Virginia high school student, interview with author, February 26, 2018.

8. Here, I am drawing upon Tithi Bhattacharya through her interview on *The Dig* podcast and in her book *Feminism for the 99%*, coedited with Cinzia Arruzza and Nancy Fraser. Bhattacharya, "Feminism for the 99% with Tithi Bhattacharya"; Arruzza, Bhattacharya, and Fraser, *Feminism for the 99%*.

9. Bady, "West Virginia Snow Days."

10. As folklorist Frank Proschan writes, "Social functions and deepest meanings of folk traditions are often displayed most clearly and compellingly at times of social stress." Proschan, "Fieldwork and Social Work," 150.

11. The protest gatherings outside local schools in 2018 were not technically picket lines as generally defined. Because superintendents in every county closed schools each day of the work stoppage, there were in actuality no picket lines to be crossed. Most teachers and school service employees did use the term *picket line* to refer to their protest gatherings at both the Capitol and their local schools, which is why I put it in quotation marks when writing about the teachers' strike. In 2019, however, the superintendent of Putnam County was the only superintendent out of the fifty-five who refused to close schools, creating for those two days a literal picket line, where teachers who did not report to work were not paid. A Putnam County Schools spokesperson reported that only 25 percent of staff and 10 percent of students were present in the building. Teachers and school employees on the picket line said that the number of students inside was actually much lower than 10 percent. On the first day of the 2019 strike, no bus drivers reported to work. Jack Flatley, "Strike Fund to Focus on Putnam School Employees Who Held Picket Lines," *WV Metro News*, February 21, 2019, http://wvmetronews.com/2019/02/21/strike-fund-to-focus-on-putnam-school-employees-who-held-picket-lines.

12. Katie Campbell, "Red for Ed Movement No Longer a Revolution, but It's Still Alive," *Arizona Capitol Times*, May 3, 2019, https://azcapitoltimes.com/news/2019/05/03/red-for-ed-movement-no-longer-a-revolution-but-its-still-alive.

13. O'Neal, interview with author, February 27, 2018. In July 2020, the Kanawha County Board of Education changed the name of Stonewall Jackson Middle School to West Side Middle School. Ryan Quinn, "Stonewall

Jackson Middle Will Be Renamed West Side Middle," *Charleston Gazette-Mail*, July 16, 2020, www.wvgazettemail.com/news/education/stonewall-jackson -middle-will-be-renamed-west-side-middle/article_56cac2ee-70ee-579f-bf71 -9f1b9056693a.html.

14. Anonymous West Virginia middle school student, interview with author, March 2, 2018.

15. Anonymous member of United Mine Workers of America, interview with author, February 27, 2018.

16. Anonymous West Virginia elementary school teacher, interview with author, February 27, 2018.

17. National Conference of State Legislatures, "Legislators by Generation."

18. Jake Jarvis, "Senate President Says WV Teachers on Strike Are Being 'Disrespectful,'" *WV News*, February 26, 2018, www.wvnews.com/news/wvnews /senate-president-says-wv-teachers-on-strike-are-being-disrespectful/article _0664fca2-1504-58a3-8321-f21472fb5bf4.html.

19. Perry Casto, in Catte, Hilliard, and Salfia, *55 Strong*, 37.

20. Casto, 36.

21. Thompson, *Customs in Common*, 467.

22. Alford, "Rough Music or Charivari."

23. E. P. Thompson writes that rough music only works "if (first) the 'victim' must be sufficiently 'of' the community to be vulnerable to disgrace, to suffer from it: and (second) if the music does indeed express the consensus of the community—or at least of a sufficiently large and dominant part of the community." In the case of the strike, teachers used rough music to "punch up" and subvert authority. While it may not have been effective in shaming Carmichael, it did assert the teachers' charge and affirm their solidarity, both publicly and for the network itself. Thompson, *Customs in Common*, 490.

24. Alford, "Rough Music or Charivari," 516–18.

25. Salfia, "How 'Strike Tacos,' Delivery Pizza, and Bagged Lunches Fueled an Activist Movement."

26. Pepperoni rolls, consisting of Italian white bread and pepperoni, originated with Italian coal mining families in the northern coalfields of West Virginia as a shelf-stable meal for underground miners. They were commercialized in Fairmont and are now a popular and iconic food item across the state.

27. Salfia, "How 'Strike Tacos,' Delivery Pizza, and Bagged Lunches Fueled an Activist Movement."

28. Stephen Smith, Wilma Lee Steele, and Tina Russell, "We Are Proud to Be 'Rednecks': It's Time to Reclaim That Term," *Guardian*, April 14, 2018, www .theguardian.com/us-news/2018/apr/14/redneck-pride-west-virginia-protests -strikes/; Todd, "Do You Know Where the Word 'Redneck' Comes From?"

29. Slocum, Hathaway, and Bernstein, "Striking Signs," 367.

30. West Virginia's Right-to-Work Law was deemed unconstitutional in February 2019 but was upheld by the state supreme court in April 2020. Carter, "West Virginia Supreme Court Upholds Right-to-Work Law"; Mark Curtis, "West Virginia Right-to-Work Law Overturned," WTRF (Wheeling, W.Va.), February 28, 2019, www.wtrf.com/news/west-virginia-headlines/west-virginia -right-to-work-law-overturned/; Jake Jarvis, "Right-to-Work Lawsuit Could Be Argued in Front of WV Supreme Court This Year," *WV News*, April 21, 2019, www.wvnews.com/news/wvnews/right-to-work-lawsuit-could-be-argued-in -front-of-wv-supreme-court-this-year/article_32a7c3ef-5a3c-54c4-8387-ac846 08a79b9.html.

31. Graeber, "The Center Blows Itself Up."

32. Dickens, "They'll Never Keep Us Down." The song also appears on Dickens's 1980 album *Hard Hitting Songs for Hard Hit People.*

33. Bailey, "Battle of Blair Mountain."

34. Brandon Wolford, in Catte, Hilliard, and Salfia, *55 Strong*, 46.

35. In 1990, West Virginia public school teachers struck for eleven days in a fight for higher salaries and reforms to public education in the state. Teachers eventually won a pay raise, additional training and support, and policies that allowed them more direct involvement in school operations. Wilson, "1990 Teachers' Strike."

36. Gregg Wingo, "Marijuana Is West Virginia's Next Billion Dollar Industry," *Fayette Tribune* (Oak Hill, W.Va.), February 24, 2018, www.fayettetribune.com /opinion/marijuana-is-west-virginia-s-next-billion-dollar-industry/article _eefeddb6-197f-11e8-ac70-3b7f4fb85675.html.

37. At least two vocal critics of the teachers' strike have been voted out of office in the years since. In the spring of 2018, state senator Robert Karnes, a longtime opponent of unions who commented during the strike that teachers were holding students "hostage," lost to Republican primary opponent Bill Hamilton, who had been supportive of the teachers' strike and against right-to-work. On Election Day 2018, Karnes was still trolling teachers on Twitter. However, Karnes was again elected to the state senate in November 2020. In June 2020, Senate president Mitch Carmichael lost the Republican primary to Amy Nichole Grady, a teacher endorsed by the West Virginia chapter of the American Federation of Teachers. Izaguirre, "Teacher Beats West Virginia Senate President after Protests"; Jilani, "West Virginia Republican Said Teachers Won't 'Have Any Significant Effect' on Elections."

38. Holder, "'Don't Make Us Go West Virginia on You.'"

39. Jay O'Neal, in Catte, Hilliard, and Salfia, *55 Strong*, 22.

40. Quoted in Salfia, introduction, 92.

41. Thompson, *Customs in Common*, 487.

42. Karla Hilliard, in Catte, Hilliard, and Salfia, *55 Strong*, 92.

43. Ryan Quinn, "Governor Signs Ed Bill, Opening WV to Charter Schools, Upping School Funding," *Charleston Gazette-Mail*, June 28, 2019, www.wvgazette mail.com/news/education/governor-signs-ed-bill-opening-wv-to-charter-schools-upping/article_26bf088b-e8b3-5f26-a375-4609b154fe67.html.

44. Thompson uses the phrase "symbolic vocabulary" to refer to the various techniques under the umbrella of rough music employed by communities to enact popular justice. Thompson, *Customs in Common*.

45. Kelli Douglas, interview with author, February 26, 2018.

CHAPTER 6

1. The "hot dog" pastry is a specialty of Spring Hill Pastry Shop in South Charleston.

2. "Stanton," telephone conversation with author, June 3, 2016.

3. Russell Yann passed away in January 2021 at the age of eighty-nine. Yann's continues to remain open. Anthony Russell Yann Jr. obituary, *Times West Virginian* (Fairmont, W.Va.), January 19, 2021, https://obituaries.timeswv.com/obituary/anthony-russell-yann-jr-1081464500.

4. Harold, "Marmet's Yellow Slaw Offers a Tasty Twist on the Standard West Virginia Hot Dog."

5. "'Hot dog and cold hog' was an expression used by a vendor of wienerwurst and ham sandwiches," the article reports. "Notes of the Fair," *Wheeling Daily Intelligencer*, September 8, 1897.

6. King, *Hot Dog*.

7. "'Hot Dog' Man Arrested, Shows He Is Not "Stuck," *Daily Telegram* (Clarksburg, W.Va.), September 27, 1916. I could find no other record of "Gus Lopez" in the Clarksburg newspaper during this era, but several articles from 1907 and 1911 mention a "G. B. Lopez," a member of the local Italian society who once had his rooster stolen by another "foreigner." "Protested Are News Reports," *Daily Telegram* (Clarksburg, W.Va.), November 28, 1911; "Red Rooster Cause of a Larceny Case," *Daily Telegram* (Clarksburg, W.Va.), June 20, 1907.

8. "More than 20,000 'Hot Dogs' Sold in Charleston Each Day," *Charleston Daily Mail*, October 31, 1920; "Hot Dog," *West Virginian* (Fairmont, W.Va.), May 23, 1922.

9. US Census Bureau, "Census of Population and Housing."

10. Ross, "The Scotts Run Coalfield from the Great War to the Great Depression."

11. An October 27, 1922, article in the *West Virginian* compares "certain foreigners" who own and frequent immigrant-owned restaurants and dives to "bloated poisonous spiders." "Take This Difficulty to the State," *West Virginian*

(Fairmont, W.Va.), October 27, 1922. Many other articles warn of the radicalism and communism of foreigners. "New Fire Engine Is Recommended by Kiwanis Club," *West Virginian* (Fairmont, W.Va.), June 28, 1922.

12. "Hot Dog Wagon Doomed to Oblivion in Fairmont if City Fathers Take Action," *West Virginian* (Fairmont, W.Va.), May 23, 1922.

13. "Sidelights," *West Virginian* (Fairmont, W.Va.), May 24, 1922.

14. "Newsstand Permit Granted Stemple," *West Virginian* (Fairmont, W.Va.), June 26, 1922.

15. "'Hot Dog' Man Arrested, Shows He Is Not "'Stuck,'" *Daily Telegram* (Clarksburg, W.Va.), September 27, 1916.

16. This dual clientele eventually influenced business logistics. Bill Valos said, "A. J. built the Broadway Sandwich Shop and two brick apartments attached to his shop. These were used in later years to feed school kids lunch out of so as to leave space for his adult workers and trade. This made workers happy." Valos, e-mail message to author, March 9, 2020.

17. Valos.

18. "Jailers Crush Fruit to Find Saw Blades," *Raleigh Register* (Beckley, W.Va.), January 28, 1949.

19. I was not able to find this particular article in the *Charlotte Observer* archives, but I note the story here as it is now part of West Virginia hot dog folklore.

20. West, "The Best Curb Girl in Logan County."

21. The owner of the Hinton Dairy Queen, Tommy Vance, told me that their franchise agreement was grandfathered in as a "non-systems food store," meaning they are allowed to sell Dairy Queen ice cream but have to establish their own menu of food products. This is what allows the store to sell the homemade chili, made from the original recipe of the owners who operated it in the 1950s. Though he said that the Dairy Queen corporation doesn't particularly favor this type of agreement, it "allows you to put your personal touch in the food and store and just the whole experience." Vance, telephone conversation with author, February 12, 2020.

22. McKay, interview with author, July 9, 2019.

23. *Raleigh Register* (Beckley, W.Va.) and *Beckley Post-Herald*, 1949–75.

24. Couto, "It Takes a Pillage"; "In Coal Country, the Mines Shut Down, the Women Went to Work and the World Quietly Changed," *New York Times*, September 14, 2019, www.nytimes.com/2019/09/14/us/appalachia-coal-women-work-.html.

25. Ludke, Obermiller, and Rademacher, "Demographic Change in Appalachia." According to the Appalachian Regional Commission, "distressed areas" are "those census tracts in at-risk and transitional counties that have a

median family income no greater than 67% of the U.S. average and a poverty rate 150% of the U.S. average or greater." Appalachian Regional Commission, "County Economic Status and Distressed Areas in Appalachia."

26. Bureau of Labor Statistics, "CPI Inflation Calculator."

27. US Census Bureau, Quick Facts.

28. See Emily Wallace's work on the history of pimento cheese and oral historian Sara Wood's work on slug burgers. Wallace, "It Was There for Work"; Wood, "A Hamburger by Any Other Name."

29. McKay, interview with author, July 9, 2019.

30. Noyes, "Aesthetic Is the Opposite of Anaesthetic," 148–49.

31. West Virginia Hot Dog Blog, "What Is a West Virginia Hot Dog?"

32. Noyes, "Aesthetic Is the Opposite of Anaesthetic," 150.

33. In his groundbreaking article on the triviality barrier in children's folklore, Brian Sutton-Smith identifies the perception of a cultural form as being "fun" to be one of the primary barriers of triviality in cultural study. Sutton-Smith, "Psychology of Childlore."

34. I should note that the Virginia Folklife Program did commendably award a 2016–17 apprenticeship grant to master hot dog purveyor Joey Mirabile Sr. of Richmond and apprentice Logan Caine. Virginia Folklife Program, "Joey Mirabile Sr. and Logan Caine."

35. Deetz, *In Small Things Forgotten*, 8.

36. Steelhammer, "Flood of 2016."

CHAPTER 7

1. In wrestling lingo, a "gimmick" is the wrestler's on-mat persona.

2. A "babyface" or "face" is a "good guy" or hero wrestler.

3. A "heel" is the common wrestling term for a "bad guy" or villain.

4. "Boone War Memorial Fills Major Recreational Need," *Post Herald* (Beckley, W.Va.), June 30, 1954.

5. "Getting over" means to be popular with fans, inspiring cheers for babyfaces and boos for villains.

6. A "mark" is either a fan who believes some or all of the events in wrestling or a fan who is particularly devoted to a certain wrestler, promotion, or professional wrestling in general.

7. While there are occasional women's matches in West Virginia independent wrestling promotions, there is usually at the most one scheduled per card. Women's wrestling does seem to be on the rise, however.

8. US Census Bureau, Quick Facts; Leins, "West Virginia Is Dying and Trump Can't Fix It"; Bowen et al., "An Overview of the Coal Economy in Appalachia."

9. Eric Eyre, "Report: Boone County Leads US in Per-Capita Opioid-Related Costs," *Charleston Gazette-Mail*, March 21, 2018, www.wvgazettemail.com /news/health/wv_drug_abuse/report-boone-county-leads-us-in-per-capita -opioid-related/article_ebca6051-eb47-5a22-b566-8929b4ad7d9c.html.

10. Hardin, interview with author, September 10, 2019.

11. In 1743, British prizefighter Jack Broughton published *Broughton's Rules: Rules to Be Observed in All Battles on the Stage: As Agreed by Several Gentlemen at Broughton's Amphitheatre*, which effectively formalized the sport of boxing. Up until then the sport had no official code or weight classes and was generally fought barehanded, with wrestling permitted. Broughton, *Broughton's Rules*; Olver and Wallenfeldt, "Boxing."

12. Gorn, "'Gouge and Bite.'"

13. Ashe, *Travels in America*.

14. Gorn, "Gouge and Bite,'" 27.

15. Gorn, "'Gouge and Bite,'" 29. Captain John Fink, who was born "four miles above Wheeling, on the river" and worked on the Wheeling ferry, claimed to be a relative of Mike Fink's and says Fink "laid up his boat near us" on his last trip in 1815, before heading west to work on the Mississippi. Mike Fink would have been working (and brawling) all along the Ohio, which now forms the northeastern border of West Virginia, with Ohio and Pennsylvania. Howe, *Historical Collections of Ohio*, 322.

16. Gorn, "'Gouge and Bite,'" 33.

17. "Wrestling Match to Be Pulled Off," *Bluefield Daily Leader*, December 4, 1907.

18. "Capana Plans Mat Bout for Beckley Fans," *Post-Herald* (Beckley, W.Va.), April 22, 1929.

19. Ron Eller, email to the author, December 20, 2019.

20. US Census Bureau, Quick Facts; Leins, "West Virginia Is Dying and Trump Can't Fix It"; Nancy Peyton, "Boone County Rises, Falls in Coal's Clutches," *State Journal*, March 11, 2017, www.wvnews.com/statejournal/boone -county-rises-falls-in-coal-s-clutches/article_9186e110-d1b2-5333-819a-1eed65 f2dcb6.html.

21. Amelia Ferrell Knisely, "Coal Decline Forces Boone to Slash Jobs; More Budget Cuts Expected," *Charleston Gazette-Mail*, September 4, 2019, www. wvgazettemail.com/news/southern_west_virginia/coal-decline-forces-boone -to-slash-jobs-more-budget-cuts/article_b760c89d-9594–5f46-abda-603ab2c 61c7a.html.

22. Roni Caryn Rabin, "McKesson, Drug Distribution Giant, Settles Lawsuit over Opioids in West Virginia," *New York Times*, May 2, 2019, www.nytimes .com/2019/05/02/health/mckesson-opioids-west-virginia.html.

23. Jenkins, "Never Trust a Snake," 41.

24. Love, interview with author, January 24, 2020.

25. *Charleston Gazette*, April 24, 1971.

26. Damron, interview with author, January 15, 2020.

27. Jenkins, "'Never Trust a Snake,'" citing Elias and Dunning, *Quest for Excitement.*

28. Huffman, interview with author, September 17, 2019.

29. Huffman; Harold, "Live from Oak Hill."

30. Gary Fauber, "Figure IV," *Beckley Register-Herald*, April 25, 1999. In this piece, Shirley Love, emcee for Saturday Nite Wrestlin', is quoted as saying, "I was everybody's Saturday Night Opera." Harold, "Live from Oak Hill."

31. Freud, "The Uncanny," 7.

32. Shoemaker, *The Squared Circle*, 9–10, 28–29.

33. Acevedo, interview with author, December 4, 2019.

34. Mannix Porterfield, "Handguns, Hairpins, and Hairy Chests: In an Era of Experimentation for Television, Wrestlin' Show Fit Right In," *Beckley Register-Herald*, December 26, 2004; Harold, "Live from Oak Hill."

35. "Ten Wrestlers Are Arrested," *Raleigh Register* (Beckley, W.Va.), August 20, 1969.

36. "State Supreme Court Hears Wrestlers' Plea," *Post Herald* (Beckley, W.Va.), September 4, 1969.

37. Associated Press, "Wrestlers (?) Win in Supreme Court," *Post Herald* (Beckley, W.Va.), September 5, 1969.

38. Shoemaker, *The Squared Circle*, 28–29.

39. Sam Hindman, "Is Wrestling Real? Fans Say Yes and No, But Agree There Is Nothing Quite Like It!," *Charleston Daily Mail*, April 3, 1972.

40. Mannix Porterfield, "Handguns, Hairpins, and Hairy Chests: In an Era of Experimentation for Television, Wrestlin' Show Fit Right In," *Beckley Register-Herald*, December 26, 2004.

41. Legendary West Virginia old-time musician Frank George tried to pull one over on me in this fashion. After I'd spent a full afternoon interviewing him, when I pulled out the release form for him to sign, he exclaimed, "Well you know I can't read!"

42. In wrestling parlance, the mat on the floor of the ring is referred to as a "canvas."

43. Acevedo, interview with author, December 4, 2019.

44. Acevedo.

45. Fauber, interview with author, October 3, 2019.

46. Huffman, interview with author, September 17, 2019.

47. Knotts, interview with author, October 30, 2019.

48. Love, interview with author, January 24, 2020.

49. Porterfield, *A Man Called Shirley.*

50. "World Championship at Stake Here Tonight; Other Top Bouts Carded," *Bluefield Daily Telegraph*, October 27, 1956.

51. Love, interview with author, January 24, 2020.

52. Jabbour and Jabbour, "*Decoration Day in the Mountains*—Author Q & A."

53. Dorson, *American Folklore*, 201.

54. *Bluefield Daily Telegraph*, May 23, 1959.

55. Gary Fauber, "Figure IV," *Beckley Register-Herald*, April 25, 1999.

56. Hardin, interview with author, September 10, 2019.

57. Knotts, interview with author, October 30, 2019.

58. Porterfield, *A Man Called Shirley*, 37, 45.

59. *Angle* is another term for storyline in wrestling slang.

60. Edison, "The Art of the Heel."

61. Huffman, interview with author, September 17, 2019.

62. Denning, "The End of Mass Culture," 14.

63. Kyriakoudes and Coclanis, "The 'Tennessee Test of Manhood.'"

64. Lott, "'The Seeming Counterfeit.'"

65. In the Netflix show *GLOW*, a fictionalization of the 1980s-era Gorgeous Ladies of Wrestling circuit, the promoter, played by Marc Maron, pushes the character Arthie, an Indian American medical school student, to develop such a gimmick. When asked what her "type" is, she earnestly replies, "Intelligent and whimsical!" He responds, "No. No. [Be a] terrorist or genie or some sort of other evil Arab." An African American character, Tamme Dawson, feels perpetually plagued by her gimmick, uncomfortable with her negative stereotyping of Black women in her portrayal of "The Welfare Queen." *GLOW.*

66. I hoped to talk to other West Virginia wrestlers who played racially or ethnically stereotyped characters for their perspective, but other than Richie Acevedo's father, Angel, who now lives in Canada, the other wrestlers who played racial or ethnic characters with *Saturday Nite Wrestlin'* are no longer living. At matches I've attended, ASW and otherwise, wrestlers of color are a small minority, and none that I know of, other than the Sheik from Syria (who is white and not local), has a racially or ethnically stereotyped gimmick.

67. Cornette, promo on Smoky Mountain Wrestling.

68. Huffman, interview with author, September 17, 2019.

69. Jenkins, "Never Trust a Snake," 64.

70. Wrestling between men and women.

71. Campbell Robertson, "In Coal Country, the Mines Shut Down, the Women Went to Work and the World Quietly Changed," *New York Times*, September 14, 2019, www.nytimes.com/2019/09/14/us/appalachia-coal-women -work-.html.

CHAPTER 8

1. "Servers Not Responding," via Wasteland Estates HOA Twitter, accessed March 27, 2020, https://twitter.com/HoaWasteland/status/1112517593405906944.

2. Via Dead Rabbit Girl, March 28, 2019, https://twitter.com/deadrabbitgirl/status/1111386605606985728.

3. This was the case prior to the Wastelanders Expansion, released on April 14, 2020, about a year and a half after *Fallout 76* was released, which updated bugs and introduced nonplayer characters.

4. *Fallout* Wiki.

5. "Survivor Story: Dassa Ben-Ami," *Fallout* Wiki.

6. "Preservation of Technology Holotape," *Fallout* Wiki.

7. Kennedy said, "It is happening in other industries undergoing automation—in this case, the mechanization of the mines, both a blessing and a curse—for automation, machines replacing men, is one of the growing new problems the next President cannot avoid." From Kennedy, "The White House's Answer to West Virginia."

8. Lane, "Great Bend Tunnel."

9. "Sam Blackwell: 'No' on Measure 6," *Fallout* Wiki.

10. "Overseer's Log: Firehouse," *Fallout* Wiki.

11. Eller, *Uneven Ground*, 16–20.

12. Worland, "Coal's Last Kick"; McCormick, "West Virginia's Coal Powered the Nation for Years."

13. Hiroko Tabuchi, "Coal Mining Jobs Trump Would Bring Back No Longer Exist," *New York Times*, March 27, 2017, www.nytimes.com/2017/03/29/business/coal-jobs-trump-appalachia.html.

14. Casto, "Elk River Chemical Spill."

15. Steven Stoll writes of the failure of the Appalachian Regional Commission to improve the material conditions of Appalachian residents and its success in paving the way for expanded extractive industry. Stoll, *Ramp Hollow*, 262–63.

16. In 2020, Sandy Burky, Michalla Metzner, and several others began making a modified Helvetia cheese at home using milk sourced from a neighboring county, but the Helvetia Cheese Haus does not currently have a resident cheesemaker.

17. "Helvetia Protectron Updates," *Fallout* Wiki.

18. Martin, *Tourism in the Mountain South.*

19. Hufford, "Tending the Commons."

20. Barton, interview with author, February 21, 2020.

21. Edwards, "Stewards of the Forest."

22. Barton, interview with author, February 21, 2020.

23. The population of West Virginia has declined 40 percent since 1950,

and it is losing population faster than any other state. West Virginia Department of Health and Human Resources, "A Look at West Virginia's Population by Decade."

24. Freud, "The Uncanny."

25. Freud, 11.

26. Jameson, "Progress versus Utopia"; Suvin, "Estrangement and Cognition."

27. Bethesda Softworks' Pete Hines listed the developers' criteria as they scouted a location for *Fallout 76*: "It needs to be remote; they needed to have some biodiversity, and regions that felt very different." Good, "West Virginia Is So Ready for Its *Fallout 76* Close-Up."

28. Quoted in Webster, "Why West Virginia Was the Perfect Setting for a New *Fallout* Game."

29. Shapiro, *Appalachia on Our Minds.*

30. Shapiro, 15.

31. The eastern Kentucky–based Trillbilly Worker's Party podcast uses the term "tomorrow's people," somewhat in jest, to refer to this particular phenomenon of the Appalachian population bearing the brunt of capitalism's atrocities, and how that experience is subsequently used as a talking point by cavalier politicians. Trillbilly Worker's Party, "Episode 73."

32. In several interviews, Bethesda game developers express their distaste for "red neck post-apocalyptic." Design director Emil Pagliarulo said, "That was really important for us, to not stereotype the people or the culture and to not go down that road, and to treat it with respect." Good, "West Virginia Is So Ready for Its *Fallout 76* Close-Up."

33. Bethesda Softworks, *Fallout 76* Official Trailer.

34. Catte, "How *Fallout 76* Can Help Us Rebuild West Virginia."

35. Stoll, *Ramp Hollow*, 271.

36. Stoll, 272–73.

37. In her article, "Deep Commoning: Public Folklore and Environmental Policy on a Resource Frontier," Mary Hufford cites Andrew Sluyter's notion of the "myth of emptiness," in reference to colonization of the Veracruz area of Mexico from the fifteenth century on, and applies it to twenty-first-century environmental review reports in West Virginia that present the land in question as previously being unproductive and unpopulated, so that it may be used by the "productive" coal industry. Hufford, "Deep Commoning," 12–13.

38. Appadurai, *Modernity at Large.*

39. Shapiro, *Appalachia on Our Minds*, 18.

40. Strickland, "*Fallout 76* Sold 1.4 Million Digital Copies"; "*Fallout 76* Player Count Report."

41. PlayerCounter, "*Fallout 76* Live Player Count."

42. Steinkuehler, "Learning in Massively Multiplayer Online Games."

43. Miller, "Grove Street Grimm," 121.

44. Quoted in Valentine, "Bethesda Wants to Bring Humanity to *Fallout* through NPCs."

45. Barton, interview with author, February 21, 2020.

46. Taylor, *Play between Worlds*, 133, 159.

47. The @HOAWasteland Twitter account was deleted in 2020, seemingly due to interpersonal issues among the collective.

48. Miller, "Grove Street Grim," 264; Kapchan, "Performance," 122.

49. Mallow, interview with author, March 18, 2020.

50. Taylor, *Play between Worlds*, 153.

51. Steven Allen Adams, "Post-apocalyptic West Virginia: Wild and Wonderful *Fallout 76*," *Intelligencer/Wheeling News-Register*, August 26, 2018, www.the intelligencer.net/news/top-headlines/2018/08/post-apocalyptic-west-virginia -wild-and-wonderful-fallout-76.

52. Lyons, interview with author, March 18, 2020.

53. Fields, interview with author, March 18, 2020.

54. Mallow, interview with author, March 18, 2020.

55. Rifle Gaming, "Here's Why I'm Downgrading into This Trailer."

56. Lehmann, email to author, April 15, 2020.

57. Henson, interview with author, March 25, 2020.

58. Mallow, interview with author, March 18, 2020.

59. clueing_4looks, "Being from West Virginia," *FO76* subreddit, July 31, 2019, www.reddit.com/r/fo76/comments/ck9c8z/being_from_west_virginia.

60. Bowman, Banks, and Rittenour, "A Longitudinal Analysis (Two Months) of *Fallout 76* Players."

61. McCormick, "'Sense of Place' *Fallout 76* Research to Be Published in New Scientific Journal."

62. Breckenridge, *Consuming Modernity*, 5.

63. "Gov. Justice Announces New Partnership with Bethesda Softworks."

64. Martin, *Tourism in the Mountain South*.

65. Martin, 136.

66. West Virginia ranks forty-fifth out of fifty states in broadband coverage. Broadband Now, "Internet Access in West Virginia."

67. This gold is intended to become the new currency in the gameworld of Appalachia and eliminate trading among the Vault dwellers.

68. Lyons, interview with author, June 26, 2020.

CONCLUSION

1. Washburn, *Mr. Burns*.

2. The Cape Feare episode itself draws on cultural allusions to both *Cape Fear* movies (1962 and 1991), *Night of the Hunter*, and Alfred Hitchcock's *Psycho*, among others.

3. Glassie, "Tradition," 176.

4. Kirshenblatt-Gimblett, "Folklore Talks."

5. Lorde, "Learning from the 60s," 144.

6. Gencarella, "Critical Folklore Studies and the Revaluation of Tradition," 53.

7. Based on an interview with Ernest Hoeffer, a lifelong ramp digger in Helvetia, West Virginia. Hoeffer, interview with author, April 30, 2016.

8. Here I draw from fieldwork with immigrant workers in the Pilgrim's Pride chicken plant in Moorefield, West Virginia, and an interview with Hardy County English for speakers of other languages teacher Amy Lough. Lough, interview with author, February 25, 2020.

9. From a personal account relayed by Cora Hairston in an interview with the author and the George Mason Folklore Field School. She said, "So the cemetery is located up on the hillside where my little community still is, and it was desecrated by a bulldozer. It was through the gas company. I think they were putting in pipelines. And we had to fight. We fought for 10 years more with them, the desecration of them. And it's never been restored, can never be restored. They have my father's tombstone turned backwards. I don't even think it's on the right grave. They have some tombstones placed where I know those gentlemen that were supposed to be there are not on that side. They were on the other side. Just missed . . . so we fought them and finally it was solved." Hairston, interview with the George Mason Folklore Field School, May 24, 2018.

10. O'Leary, "The Where and the How of West Virginia's Population Decline." Boettner, "Who Owns West Virginia in the 21st Century?"; Patrick, "The Poultry Plant That's Changed the Face of This Appalachian Town."

11. A May 2020 piece in the *Guardian* reports that since the beginning of the COVID-19 pandemic in March 2020, the coal industry has experienced the highest decline in sixty years, with over 6,000 miners losing their jobs in March and April and coal production on track to decline 22 percent by the end of the year. Michael Sainato, "The Collapse of Coal: Pandemic Accelerates Appalachia Job Losses," *Guardian*, May 29, 2020, www.theguardian.com /us-news/2020/may/29/coal-miners-coronavirus-job-losses.

A July 9, 2020, report in the *Guardian* reports that opioid overdoses are rapidly accelerating during the coronavirus pandemic. The piece quotes a former director of the West Virginia Office of Drug Control Policy: "The number of opioid overdoses is skyrocketing and I don't think it will be easily turned back. Once the tsunami of Covid-19 finally recedes, we're going to be left with the social conditions that enabled the opioid crisis to emerge in the first place, and those are not going to go away." Chris McGreal, "'Opioid Overdoses Are Skyrocketing': As Covid-19 Sweeps Across US an Old Epidemic Returns," *Guardian*, July 9, 2020, www.theguardian.com/us-news/2020/jul /09/coronavirus-pandemic-us-opioids-crisis. The West Virginia Center on

Budget and Policy reports that over 130,000 West Virginia residents have filed unemployment claims since the beginning of the COVID-19 pandemic, and 60,000 West Virginians are now uninsured due to job loss. Allen, "60,000 West Virginians Have Likely Lost Health Coverage over the Past Month."

12. Hansen, "Theorizing Public Folklore," 38–39.

13. According to a study by the Urban Institute, COVID-related federal relief programs such as the federal stimulus, expanded unemployment benefits, and the Supplemental Nutrition Assistance Program reduced poverty in West Virginia by over 70 percent, affecting an estimated 301,000 West Virginians. O'Leary, "Federal Relief Programs in West Virginia Cut Poverty by 71 Percent."

14. Hufford, "Deep Commoning," 2.

15. Wright, *How to Be an Anti-capitalist in the 21st Century*, 15.

16. Nowak, *Social Poetics*, 253.

17. Segal, *Radical Happiness*, 52–53.

18. Porchsitters of Appalachia, Facebook post, April 13, 2020, www.facebook.com/porchsitters2020/photos/a.102257631431453/118725186451364/?type=3&theater.

Bibliography

PRIMARY SOURCES

Newspapers

Arizona Capitol Times
Beckley (W.Va.) Post Herald
Beckley (W.Va.) Register-Herald
Bluefield (W.Va.) Daily Leader
Bluefield (W.Va.) Daily Telegraph
Charleston (W.Va.) Daily Mail
Charleston (W.Va.) Gazette-Mail
Daily Telegram (Clarksburg, W.Va.)
Dominion Post (Morgantown, W.Va.)
Fayette Tribune (Oak Hill, W.Va.)
Guardian
Intelligencer/Wheeling (W.Va.)
    News Register
New York Times

Raleigh Herald (Beckley, W.Va.)
Raleigh Register (Beckley, W.Va.)
State Journal (Clarksburg, W.Va.)
Times West Virginian (Fairmont,
    W.Va.)
Washington Post
Weelunk (Wheeling, W.Va.)
West Virginia Public Broadcasting
West Virginian/Fairmont West
    Virginian
Weston (W.Va.) Democrat
Wheeling (W.Va.) Intelligencer
WV Metro News
WV News

Oral History and Fieldwork Interviews

All interviews were conducted by the author unless otherwise noted. Nearly
all of the interview recordings and transcripts are accessible through the
West Virginia Folklife Collection, housed by the West Virginia and Regional
History Center at West Virginia University Libraries.

Acevedo, Richie. Oak Hill, West Virginia, December 4, 2019, transcript.

Anderson, Al. Osage, West Virginia, April 5, 2019, transcript.

Anonymous member of the United Mine Workers of America. Charleston, West Virginia, February 27, 2018, transcript.

Anonymous West Virginia elementary school teacher. Charleston, West Virginia, February 27, 2018, transcript.

Anonymous West Virginia high school student, Charleston, West Virginia, February 26, 2018, transcript.

Anonymous West Virginia middle school student. Charleston, West Virginia, March 2, 2018, transcript.

Anonymous West Virginia public school teacher. Charleston, West Virginia, February 26, 2018, transcript.

Barton, John. Charleston, West Virginia, February 21, 2020, transcript.

Betler, Eleanor. Helvetia, West Virginia, February 5, 2016, transcript.

Birurakis, Louis. Osage, West Virginia, February 23, 2019, transcript.

Campbell, Shirley. Charleston, West Virginia, March 16 and April 26, 2016, transcript.

Coulter, Mary Jane. Osage, West Virginia, May 7, 2019, transcript.

Damron, Gary. Madison, West Virginia, January 15, 2020, transcript.

Douglas, Kelli. Charleston, West Virginia, February 26, 2018, transcript.

Fauber, Gary. Beckley, West Virginia, October 3, 2019, transcript.

Faulkes, Eve. Morgantown, West Virginia, April 11, 2019, transcript.

Fields, Mark. Conducted remotely, March 18, 2020, transcript.

Fortney-Heiskell, Charli Shea. Morgantown, West Virginia, March 23, 2019, transcript.

Hairston, Cora L. Logan, West Virginia, May 3, 2016, transcript.

Hairston, Cora L. Interview by George Mason, Folklore Field School, May 24, 2018, transcript.

Hanshaw, Ella. Seville, Ohio, November 20, 2018, transcript.

Hardin, Rocky. Charleston, West Virginia, September 10, 2019, transcript.

Henson, Kristy. Conducted remotely, March 25, 2020, transcript.

Hoeffer, Ernest. Helvetia, West Virginia, April 30, 2016, transcript.

Huffman, Kasey. Charleston, West Virginia, September 17, 2019, transcript.

Jackson, Robert. Milton, West Virginia, October 15, 2019, transcript.

Knotts, Brianna. Charleston, West Virginia, October 30, 2019, transcript.

Little, Sarah Boyd. Morgantown, West Virginia, March 16, 2018, transcript.

Lough, Amy. Moorefield, West Virginia, February 25, 2020, transcript.

Love, Shirley. Oak Hill, West Virginia, January 24, 2020, transcript.

Lyons, Porter. Conducted remotely, March 18 and June 26, 2020, transcripts.

Mallow, Mike. Conducted remotely, March 18, 2020, transcript.

Marshall, Charlene. Morgantown, West Virginia, March 23, 2019, transcript.

McKay, Dave. Beckley, West Virginia, July 9, 2019, transcript.
O'Neal, Jay. Charleston, West Virginia, February 27, 2018, transcript.
Purkey, Elaine. Harts, West Virginia, October 27, 2016, transcript.
Sarris, George. Morgantown, West Virginia, April 5, 2019, transcript.
"'Stanton." Telephone conversation. June 3, 2016.
Vance, Tommy. Telephone conversation. February 12, 2020.

Recorded Songs and Albums

Dickens, Hazel. "They'll Never Keep Us Down." In Barbara Kopple, dir.,
    Harlan County, USA. Cabin Creek Films, 1976.
———. "They'll Never Keep Us Down." *Hard Hitting Songs for Hard Hit
    People*. Rounder Records, 1980. Audio CD.
Jones, Grandpa. *Live*. Monument, 1970. SLP18138. LP.
Purkey, Elaine. *Mountain Music, Mountain Struggle*. Marimac Recordings,
    1996. CD-4011. Audio CD.
———. "One Day More." On *Classic Labor Songs from Smithsonian Folkways*.
    Smithsonian Folkways Recordings, 2006. Audio CD.
Songs of Scotts Run. Zone 8 Recording, 2017. Audio CD.

SECONDARY SOURCES

Abrahams, Roger D. *Everyday Life: A Poetics of Vernacular Practices*.
    Philadelphia: University of Pennsylvania Press, 2005.
Alford, Violet. "Rough Music or Charivari." *Folklore* 70, no. 4 (1959): 505–18.
Allen, Kelly. "60,000 West Virginians Have Likely Lost Health Cover-
    age over the Past Month." West Virginia Center on Budget and Policy,
    April 23, 2020. https://wvpolicy.org/60000-west-virginians-have-likely
    -lost-health-coverage-over-the-past-month-2.
Appadurai, Arjun. *Modernity at Large: Cultural Dimensions of Globalization*.
    Minneapolis: University of Minnesota Press, 1996.
Appalachian Regional Commission. "County Economic Status and Dis-
    tressed Areas in Appalachia." Accessed August 14, 2020. www.arc.gov
    /appalachian_region/CountyEconomicStatusandDistressedAreasin
    Appalachia.asp.
Arruzza, Cinzia, Tithi Bhattacharya, and Nancy Fraser. *Feminism for the
    99%*. New York: Verso, 2019.
Ashe, Thomas. *Travels in America, Performed in 1806: For the Purpose of Explor-
    ing the Rivers Alleghany, Monogahela, Ohio, and Mississippi, and Ascertaining
    the Produce and Condition of Their Banks and Vicinity*. London:
    Printed for Richard Phillips, Bridge-Street, by John Abraham, Clement's
    Lane, 1808.

Bady, Aaron. "West Virginia Snow Days." *Popula*, February 25, 2019. https://
popula.com/2019/02/25/west-virginia-snow-days.

Bailey, Kenneth R. "Battle of Blair Mountain." *e-WV: The West Virginia Encyclopedia*, June 29, 2018. www.wvencyclopedia.org/articles/532.

Balic, Adam. "Fritters." In *The Oxford Companion to Sugar and Sweets*, edited
by Darra Goldstein, 276–77. New York: Oxford University Press, 2015.

Barbour, Russ. "Breece Pancake, an Appalachian Voice." WPBY-TV and West
Virginia Educational Authority, 1989. DVD.

Baron, Robert, and Nick Spitzer. "Cultural Continuity and Community Creativity in a New Century." In *Public Folklore*, edited by Robert Baron and
Nick Spitzer, vii–xviii. Jackson: University Press of Mississippi, 2007.

Barret, Elizabeth. *Stranger with a Camera*. Whitesburg, Ky.: Appalshop, 2000.
DVD.

Bauman, Richard. "The Philology of the Vernacular." *Journal of Folklore
Research* 45, no. 1 (January–April 2008): 29–36.

Bauman, Richard, and Charles L. Briggs. "Poetics and Performance as Critical Perspectives on Language and Social Life." *Annual Review of Anthro-
pology* 19 (1990): 59–88.

Ben-Amos, Dan. "Toward a Definition of Folklore in Context." *Journal of
American Folklore* 84, no. 331 (1971): 3–15.

Bernard, April. "Here's What I Hate about Writer's Houses." *New York Review
of Books*, August 11, 2011. www.nybooks.com/daily/2011/08/11/heres
-what-i-hate-about-writers-houses.

Bethesda Softworks. *Fallout 76* Official Trailer, June 10, 2018. www.youtube
.com/watch?v=M9FGaan35s0.

Bhattacharya, Tithi. "Feminism for the 99% with Tithi Bhattacharya." Interview by Daniel Denvir. *The Dig: A Podcast from Jacobin*, March 6, 2019.
Audio. https://thedig.blubrry.net/podcast/feminism-for-the-99-with
-tithi-bhattacharya.

Bloom, Lynn Z. "'I Write for Myself and Strangers': Private Diaries as Public
Documents." In *Composition Studies As A Creative Art*, 171–85. University
Press of Colorado, 1998.

Boettner, Ted. "Does West Virginia Invest Enough in Education? A Closer
Look at the Data." West Virginia Center on Budget and Policy, June 6,
2019. https://wvpolicy.org/does-west-virginia-invest-enough-in
-education-a-closer-look-at-the-data.

———. "Who Owns West Virginia in the 21st Century?" West Virginia
Center on Budget and Policy, December 9, 2013. https://wvpolicy.org
/who-owns-west-virginia-in-the-21st-century-2.

Bolles, Sydney. "Inside the Harlan County Coal Miner Protest." *Rolling Stone*,

September 3, 2019. www.rollingstone.com/politics/politics-features
/harlan-county-coal-miner-blockade-879324.

Bowen, Eric, Christiadi, John Deskins, and Brian Lego. "An Overview of
the Coal Economy in Appalachia." Commissioned by the Appalachian
Regional Commission. January 2018. www.arc.gov/assets/research
_reports/CIE1-OverviewofCoalEconomyinAppalachia.pdf.

Bowman, Nicholas D., Jaime Banks, and Christine Rittenour. "A Longitudinal Analysis (Two Months) of *Fallout 76* Players." Open Science Framework, March 24, 2020.

Breckenridge, Carol A., ed. *Consuming Modernity: Public Culture in a South
Asian World.* Minneapolis: University of Minnesota Press, 1995.

Broadband Now. "Internet Access in West Virginia." Accessed April 20, 2020.
https://broadbandnow.com/West-Virginia.

Broughton, Jack. *Broughton's Rules: Rules to Be Observed in All Battles on
the Stage: As Agreed by Several Gentlemen at Broughton's Amphitheatre.*
London: C. Sessions, 1994.

Brown, Karida L. *Gone Home: Race and Roots through Appalachia.* Chapel
Hill: University of North Carolina Press, 2018.

Bureau of Labor Statistics. "CPI Inflation Calculator." Accessed October 31,
2021. www.bls.gov/data/inflation_calculator.htm.

Campbell, Shirley. "Collected Poems and Songs." Unpublished manuscript.

Carter, Mark A. "West Virginia Supreme Court Upholds Right-to-Work
Law." *National Law Review* 10, no. 113 (April 22, 2020). www.natlawreview
.com/article/west-virginia-supreme-court-upholds-right-to-work-law.

Casto, James E. "Elk River Chemical Spill." *e-WV: The West Virginia Encyclopedia*, June 11, 2018. www.wvencyclopedia.org/articles/2428.

Catte, Elizabeth. "How *Fallout 76* Can Help Us Rebuild West Virginia." *In
These Times*, August 28, 2018. https://inthesetimes.com/article/21368
/fallout-76-west-virginia-appalachia-post-apocalyptic-video-game.

Catte, Elizabeth, Emily Hilliard, and Jessica Salfia, eds. *55 Strong: Inside the
West Virginia Teachers' Strike.* Cleveland: Belt, 2018.

Census Viewer. "Population of West Virginia: Census 2010 and 2000 Interactive Map, Demographics, Statistics, Quick Facts." Accessed September 9, 2019. http://45.79.181.212:8080/state/WV.

Cherniack, Martin G. "Hawks Nest Tunnel Disaster." *e-WV: The West Virginia Encyclopedia* December 20, 2016. www.wvencyclopedia.org/articles
/338.

Christensen, Danille. "Materializing the Everyday: 'Safe' Scrapbooks,
Aesthetic Mess, and the Rhetorics of Workmanship." *Journal of Folklore
Research* 54, no. 3 (September–December 2017): 233–84.

———. "(Not) Going Public: Mediating Reception and Managing Visibility in Contemporary Scrapbook Performance." In *Material Vernaculars: Objects, Images, and Their Social Worlds*, edited by Jackson Jason Baird, 40-104. Bloomington: Indiana University Press, 2016.

Clapp, Elsie Ripley. "Arthurdale—A School." Washington, 1936.

———. *Community Schools in Action*. New York: Viking, 1939.

Clark, Amy D. "Letters from Home: The Literate Lives of Central Appalachian Women." *Appalachian Journal* 41, no. 1/2 (2013): 54-76.

Cohen, G. A. *If You're an Egalitarian, How Come You're So Rich?* Cambridge, Mass.: Harvard University Press, 2000.

Cook, Blanche Wisen. *Eleanor Roosevelt*, vol. 2, *1933-1938*. New York: Penguin, 1999.

Cornette, Jim. Promo on Smoky Mountain Wrestling, February 1, 1992. www.youtube.com/watch?v=wURKR9uyEgw.

Couto, Richard A. "It Takes a Pillage: Women, Work, and Welfare." *Race, Gender & Class* 10, no. 1 (2003): 670-78.

Crowe, Beryl. "The Tragedy of the Commons Revisited." In *Managing the Commons*, edited by Garret Hardin and John Baden, 53-65. San Francisco: W. H. Freeman, 1997.

Deetz, James. *In Small Things Forgotten: An Archaeology of Early American Life*. New York: Anchor, 1996.

Denning, Michael. "The End of Mass Culture." *International Labor and Working-Class History*, no. 37 (1990): 4-18.

Dorson, Richard. *American Folklore*. Chicago: University of Chicago Press, 1959.

Douglass, Thomas E. *A Room Forever: The Life, Work, and Letters of Breece D'J Pancake*. Knoxville: University of Tennessee Press, 1998.

Edison, Mike. "The Art of the Heel: For God and Country, Wrestling and Donald Trump Explained, Finally." *Baffler*, no. 36 (September 2017). https://thebaffler.com/salvos/the-art-of-the-heel-edison.

Edwards, Eric Arthur. "Stewards of the Forest: An Analysis of Ginseng Harvesters and the Communal Boundaries That Define Their Identity in an Area of Environmental Degradation." MA thesis, Marshall University, 2011.

Edwards, Grace Toney. "Breece D'J Pancake: A Life Too Short." *Appalachian Heritage* 40, no. 3 (Summer 2012): 36.

———. Guest editor's note on "A Loss of Tone." *Appalachian Heritage* 40, no. 3 (Summer 2012): 36.

Elias, Norbert, and Eric Dunning. *Quest for Excitement: Sport and Leisure in the Civilizing Process*. New York: Basil Blackwell, 1986.

Eller, Ron. *Uneven Ground: Appalachia since 1945*. Lexington: University Press of Kentucky, 2008.

Evans, Walker. *Women Selling Ice Cream and Cake, Scotts Run, West Virginia*. US Resettlement Administration, 1935. Accessed May 27, 2019. www.loc .gov/resource/fsa.8a19561.

"*Fallout 76* Player Count Report." *Gamers Decide*, January 16, 2020. www .gamersdecide.com/articles/fallout-76-player-count.

Fallout 76 subreddit. Accessed July 31, 2019. www.reddit.com/r/fo76.

Fallout Wiki. Accessed April 1, 2020. https://fallout.fandom.com/wiki.

Federici, Silvia. "From Crisis to Commons: Reproductive Work, Affective Labor and Technology, and the Transformation of Everyday Life." In *Re-enchanting the World*, 175–87.

———. *Re-enchanting the World: Feminism and the Politics of the Commons*. Oakland, Calif.: PM Press, 2019.

Fones-Wolf, Ken. "Ravenswood Strike." *e-WV: The West Virginia Encyclopedia*, August 3, 2015. www.wvencyclopedia.org/articles/16.

Fox, Aaron A. *Real Country: Music and Language in Working-Class Culture*. Durham, N.C.: Duke University Press, 2004.

Fraser, Nancy. "The Crisis of Care? On the Social-Reproductive Contradictions of Contemporary Capitalism." In *Social Reproduction Theory: Remapping Class, Recentering Oppression*, edited by Tithi Bhattacharya, 21–36. Chicago: University of Chicago Press, 2017.

Freud, Sigmund. "The Uncanny" (1919). In *The Standard Edition of the Complete Psychological Works of Sigmund Freud*, volume 17, *An Infantile Neurosis and Other Works*, 217–56. London: Hogarth, 1955.

Frost, William Goodell. "Our Contemporary Ancestors in the Southern Mountains." *The Atlantic*, March 1899. https://www.theatlantic.com /magazine/archive/1899/03/our-contemporary-ancestors-southern -mountains/581332.

Gencarella, Stephen Olbrys. "Critical Folklore Studies and the Revaluation of Tradition." *Tradition in the Twenty-First Century: Locating the Role of the Past in the Present*, edited by Trevor J. Blank and Robert Glenn Howard, 49–71. Logan: Utah State University Press, 2013.

Glassie, Henry. "Tradition." In *Eight Words for the Study of Expressive Culture*, edited by Burt Feintuch, 176–97. Champaign: University of Illinois Press, 2003.

Glassie, Henry, Clifford R. Murphy, and Douglas Dowling Peach. *Ola Belle Reed and Southern Mountain Music on the Mason-Dixon Line*. Atlanta: Dust-to-Digital, 2015.

GLOW. Netflix TV show, 2017–present.

Good, Owen S. "West Virginia Is So Ready for Its *Fallout 76* Close-Up." *Polygon*, October 13, 2018. www.polygon.com/2018/10/13/17969452/fallout-76-west-virginia-locations.

Gorn, Elliott J. "'Gouge and Bite, Pull Hair and Scratch': The Social Significance of Fighting in the Southern Backcountry." *American Historical Review* 90, no. 1 (1985): 18–43.

"Gov. Justice Announces New Partnership with Bethesda Softworks, WV." WV Tourism, October 11, 2018. https://wvtourism.com/release/gov-justice-announces-new-partnership-with-bethesda-softworks.

Graeber, David. "The Center Blows Itself Up: Care and Spite in the 'Brexit Election.'" *New York Review of Books*, January 13, 2020. www.nybooks.com/daily/2020/01/13/the-center-blows-itself-up-care-and-spite-in-the-brexit-election.

Hafstein, Valdimar T. "Folklore Talks: Heritage, Folklore, and the Public Sphere." American Folklore Society panel, March 10, 2021.

Hairston, Cora L. *Faces behind the Dust: The Story Told through the Eyes of a Coal Miner's Daughter (on the Black Side)*. Bloomington, Ind.: iUniverse, 2013.

———. *Hello World, Here Comes Claraby Rose: An Adolescent Black Girl Coming of Age.* Bloomington, Ind.: iUniverse, 2015.

Hansen, Gregory. "Theorizing Public Folklore: Folklore Work as Systemic Cultural Intervention." *Folklore Forum* 30, no. 1 (1999): 35–44.

Harlan, Louis R. "Booker T. Washington's West Virginia Boyhood." *West Virginia History* 32, no. 2 (January 1971): 63–85.

Harold, Zack. "Live from Oak Hill." *West Virginia Living*, Spring 2017. www.wvliving.com/history/live-from-oak-hill.

———. "Marmet's Yellow Slaw Offers a Tasty Twist on the Standard West Virginia Hot Dog." West Virginia Public Broadcasting, January 22, 2021. www.wvpublic.org/section/arts-culture/2021-01-22/marmets-yellow-slaw-offers-a-tasty-twist-on-the-standard-west-virginia-hot-dog.

Hickok, Lorena A. *Reluctant First Lady*. New York: Dodd, Mead, 1962.

Hilliard, Emily. "Fat Tuesday: The Many Different Doughnuts of Mardi Gras." *NPR Kitchen Window: A Weekly Peek into the Kitchen with Tasty Tales and Recipes*, February 26, 2014. www.npr.org/2014/02/26/282908382/fat-tuesday-the-many-different-doughnuts-of-mardi-gras.

———. "One Year in Helvetia, West Virginia." *Bitter Southerner.* Accessed August 14, 2020. https://bittersoutherner.com/my-year-in-helvetia-west-virginia.

———. "Something Good from Helvetia." *Gravy*, April 11, 2014. www.southernfoodways.org/something-good-from-helvetia.

———. "'Written and Composed by Nora E. Carpenter': Song Lyric

Scrapbooks, Home Recordings, and Self Documentation." *Southern Cultures* 22, no. 1 (Spring 2016): 66–78.

Hoffman, Nancy. *Eleanor Roosevelt and the Arthurdale Experiment*. North Haven, Conn.: Linnet, 2001.

Holder, Sarah. "'Don't Make Us Go West Virginia on You.'" *CITYLAB*, March 26, 2019. www.citylab.com/equity/2018/03/dont-make-us-go-west -virginia-on-you/555776.

Howe, Henry. *Historical Collections of Ohio*. Columbus: H. Howe & Son, 1890.

Hufford, Mary. "Breaking the Time Barrier: Folklife and Heritage Planning in Southern West Virginia." *American Folklife Center News* 15, no. 3/4 (Summer–Fall 1993): 9.

———. "Carnival Time in the Kingdom of Coal." *Social Identities: Journal for the Study of Race, Nation, and Culture* 16, no. 4 (2010): 559–81.

———. "Deep Commoning: Public Folklore and Environmental Policy on a Resource Frontier." *International Journal of Heritage Studies* 22, no. 8 (September 13, 2016): 635–49.

———. "Ethnographic Overview and Assessment: New River Gorge National River and Gauley River Recreation Area." Northeast Regional Ethnography Program, National Park Service, Boston, September 2007. www.sas .upenn.edu/folklore/center/NGR_report_final.pdf.

———. "Tending the Commons: Folklife and Landscape in Southern West Virginia." American Folklife Center at the Library of Congress. Accessed April 6, 2020. www.loc.gov/collections/folklife-and-landscape-in -southern-west-virginia/about-this-collection.

———. "Reclaiming the Commons: Narratives of Progress, Preservation, and Ginseng." In *Culture, Environment, and Conservation in the Appalachian South*, edited by Benita J. Howell, 100–20. Urbana: University of Illinois Press, 2002.

———. "Working in the Cracks: Public Space, Ecological Crisis, and the Folklorist." *Journal of Folklore Research* 36, no. 2/3 (May–December 1999): 157–67.

Isin, Priscilla Mary. "Moulds for Shaping and Decorating Food in Turkey." In *Food and Material Culture: Proceedings of the Oxford Symposium on Food and Cookery 2013*, edited by Mark McWilliams, 184. Totnes, UK: Prospect, 2014.

———. *Sherbet and Spice: The Complete Story of Turkish Sweets and Desserts*. New York: I. B. Tauris, 2013.

Izaguirre, Anthony. "Teacher Beats West Virginia Senate President after Protests." ABC News, June 10, 2020. https://abcnews.go.com/Politics /wireStory/teacher-beats-west-virginia-senate-president-protests -71181772.

Jabbour, Alan, and Karen Singer Jabbour. "*Decoration Day in the Mountains: Traditions of Cemetery Decoration in the Southern Appalachians*—Author Q & A." UNC Press website. 2010. https://uncpress.org/author-qa/978080 7833971.

Jameson, Fredric. "Progress versus Utopia; or, Can We Imagine the Future? (Progrès contre utopie, ou: Pouvons-nous imaginer l'avenir ?)." *Science Fiction Studies* 9, no. 2 (1982): 147–58.

Jenkins, Henry, III. "Never Trust a Snake: WWF Wrestling as Masculine Melodrama." In *Steel Chair to the Head: The Pleasure and Pain of Professional Wrestling*, edited by Nicholas Sammond, 33–66. Durham, N.C.: Duke University Press, 2005.

Jilani, Zaid. "West Virginia Republican Said Teachers Won't 'Have Any Significant Effect' on Elections. Then They Voted Him Out." *Intercept*, May 11, 2018. https://theintercept.com/2018/05/11/west-virginia-primary -teacher-strikes.

Julian, Norman. "'I Am Going to Tell the Story': Al Anderson of Osage." *Goldenseal* 37, no. 3 (Fall 2011): 33.

Kapchan, Deborah A. "Performance." In *Eight Words for the Study of Expressive Culture*, edited by Burt Feintuch, 121–45. Champaign: University of Illinois Press, 2003.

Kennedy, John F. "The White House's Answer to West Virginia." Remarks delivered in Charleston, West Virginia, Sunday, May 8, 1960. Accessed April 2, 2020. www.jfklibrary.org/archives/other-resources/john-f -kennedy-speeches/charleston-wv-19600508.

King, Bruce. *Hot Dog: A Global History*. London: Reaktion, 2009.

Kirshenblatt-Gimblett, Barbara. "Folklore Talks: Heritage, Folklore, and the Public Sphere." American Folklore Society panel, March 10, 2021.

———. "Mistaken Dichotomies." In *Public Folklore*, edited by Robert Baron and Nick Spitzer, 29–48. Jackson: University of Mississippi Press, 2007.

Klibanoff, Eleanor. "Inside White Nationalists' Longshot Plan to Win Over Appalachia." Kentucky Center for Investigative Reporting, September 20, 2017. https://kycir.org/2017/09/20/inside-white-nationalists-longshot -plan-to-win-over-appalachia.

Knollinger, Corey. "Wild, Wondering West Virginia: Exploring West Virginia's Native American History." West Virginia Public Broadcasting, February 7, 2019. www.wvpublic.org/post/wild-wondering-west-virginia -exploring-west-virginias-native-american-history#stream/0.

Kodish, Debora. "Fair Young Ladies and Bonny Irish Boys: Pattern in Vernacular Poetics." *Journal of American Folklore* 96, no. 380 (April–June 1983): 131–50.

Kurin, Richard. "Presenting Folklife in a Soviet-American Cultural

Exchange: Public Practice during Perestroika." In *Public Folklore*, edited
by Robert Baron and Nick Spitzer, 183–216. Jackson: University of Mississippi Press, 2007.

Kyriakoudes, Louis M., and Peter A. Coclanis. "The 'Tennessee Test of
Manhood': Professional Wrestling and Southern Cultural Stereotypes." *Southern Cultures* 3, no. 3 (1997): 8–27.

Lane, Ron. "Great Bend Tunnel." *e-WV: The West Virginia Encyclopedia*, February 13, 2012. www.wvencyclopedia.org/articles/2154.

Lassiter, Luke Eric. *The Chicago Guide to Collaborative Ethnography*. Chicago:
University of Chicago Press, 2005.

Leins, Casey. "West Virginia Is Dying and Trump Can't Fix It." *US News*,
May 25, 2017. www.usnews.com/news/best-states/articles/2017-05-25
/west-virginia-is-dying-and-trump-cant-save-it.

Lewis, Ronald L. "America's Symbol of the Great Depression in the Coal
Fields." *West Virginia History* 53 (1994): 21–42.

———. "'Why Don't You Bake Bread?': Franklin Trubee and the Scotts Run
Reciprocal Economy." *Goldenseal* 15, no. 1 (1989): 34.

Lilly, John. "An Introduction to West Virginia Ethnic Communities." West
Virginia Department of Arts, Culture and History. Last updated November 2007. http://www.wvculture.org/arts/ethnic/index.html.

Lorde, Audre. "Learning from the 60s." In *Sister Outsider: Essays and
Speeches*, 134–44. Berkeley, Calif.: Crossing, 2007.

Lott, Eric. "'The Seeming Counterfeit': Racial Politics and Early Blackface
Minstrelsy." *American Quarterly* 43, no. 2 (June 1991): 223–54.

Ludke, Robert L., Phillip J. Obermiller, and Eric W. Rademacher. "Demographic Change in Appalachia: A Tentative Analysis." *Journal of
Appalachian Studies* 18, no. 1/2 (2012): 48–92.

Mailloux, Eleanor. *Oppis Guet's Vo Helvetia*. Helvetia, W.Va.: Alpenrose Garden Club, 1969.

Martin, C. Brendan. *Tourism in the Mountain South: A Double-Edged Sword*.
Knoxville: University of Tennessee Press, 2007.

Martin, Lou. "West Virginia Mine Wars." *Oxford Research Encyclopedia of
American History*, February 25, 2019. https://oxfordre.com/american
history/view/10.1093/acrefore/9780199329175.001.0001/acrefore-97801
99329175-e-552.

Maslowski, Robert F. "Indians." *e-WV: The West Virginia Encyclopedia*, October 26, 2010. www.wvencyclopedia.org/articles/841.

McCormick, Andrew. "West Virginia's Coal Powered the Nation for Years.
Now, Many Look to a Cleaner Future." *NBC News*, September 29,
2021. www.nbcnews.com/science/environment/west-virginia-coal
-industry-grapples-impact-climate-crisis-rcna2397.

McCormick, Liz. "'Sense of Place' *Fallout 76* Research to Be Published in New Scientific Journal." West Virginia Public Broadcasting, March 25, 2020. www.wvpublic.org/post/sense-place-fallout-76-research-be -published-new-scientific-journal#stream/0.

Miller, Kiri. "Grove Street Grimm: *Grand Theft Auto* and Digital Folklore." *Journal of American Folklore* 121, no. 481 (Summer 2008): 255–86.

Moore, Catherine Venable. "The Book of the Dead." Introduction to *The Book of the Dead*, by Muriel Rukeyser. Morgantown: West Virginia University Press, 2018.

Murphy, Cliff. "Toward a Bright Future: A Look at the State of the Folk and Traditional Arts." National Endowment for the Arts *artMatters* newsletter, November 2018. www.arts.gov/article/toward-bright-future-look-state -folk-and-traditional-arts.

National Conference of State Legislatures. "Legislators by Generation." Accessed July 1, 2019. http://www.ncsl.org/research/about-state-legislatures /who-we-elect-an-interactive-graphic.aspx#/.

National Endowment for the Arts. "State Partnership Agreements: Additional Information on Folk & Traditional Arts." Accessed June 19, 2020. www.arts.gov/grants-organizations/partnership-agreements/state -additional-information-on-folk-and-traditional-arts.

National Park Service. "Basic Information." New River Gorge National Park and Preserve, West Virginia. Accessed February 22, 2021. www.nps.gov /neri/planyourvisit/basicinfo.htm.

———. "History and Culture." New River Gorge National Park and Preserve, West Virginia. Accessed August 13, 2020. www.nps.gov/neri/learn /historyculture/index.htm.

———. "Places." New River Gorge National Park and Preserve, West Virginia. Accessed August 12, 2020. https://www.nps.gov/neri/learn/history culture/places.htm.

———. "Tourism to National Parks of Southern West Virginia Creates Nearly $70 Million in Economic Benefits." New River Gorge National Park and Preserve, West Virginia. Accessed June 10, 2019. www.nps.gov /neri/learn/news/tourism-to-national-parks-of-southern-west-virginia -creates-nearly-70-million-in-economic-benefits.htm.

"Nora Carpenter Traditional Music Collection." Berea College Special Collection and Archives. Accessed October 30, 2021. https://libraryguides .berea.edu/FellowCollections/noracarpenter.

Nowak, Mark. *Social Poetics*. Minneapolis: Coffee House, 2020.

Noyes, Dorothy. "Aesthetic Is the Opposite of Anaesthetic." In *Humble Theory: Folklore's Grasp on Social Life*, 127-178. Bloomington: Indiana University Press, 2016.

———. "Group." In *Eight Words for the Study of Expressive Culture*, edited by Burt Feintuch, 7–41. Champaign: University of Illinois Press, 2003.

———. "Humble Theory." *Journal of Folklore Research* 45, no. 1 (2008): 37–43.

———. "The Social Base of Folklore." In *Humble Theory: Folklore's Grasp on Social Life*, 57–94. Bloomington: Indiana University Press, 2016.

O'Leary, Sean. "Federal Relief Programs in West Virginia Cut Poverty by 71 Percent." West Virginia Center on Budget and Policy, September 3, 2021. https://wvpolicy.org/federal-relief-programs-cut-poverty-in-west -virginia-by-71-percent.

———. "The Where and the How of West Virginia's Population Decline." West Virginia Center on Budget and Policy, April 29, 2019. https://wvpolicy .org/the-where-and-the-how-of-west-virginias-population-decline.

Olver, Ron, and E. C. Wallenfeldt. "Boxing." *Encyclopaedia Britannica*. May 14, 2020. www.britannica.com/sports/boxing/The-bare-knuckle-era.

Ono, Kent A., and John M. Sloop. "The Critique of Vernacular Discourse." *Communication Monographs* 62, no. 1 (1995): 19–46.

Pancake, Breece D'J. Letter to C. R. and Helen Pancake. September 7, 1974. In Douglass, *A Room Forever.*

———. *The Stories of Breece D'J Pancake.* New York: Owl, 1983.

Pancake, Helen. Letter to Tommy Schoffler. May 18, 2003. In Douglass, *A Room Forever.*

Patrick, Anna. "The Poultry Plant That's Changed the Face of This Appalachian Town." West Virginia Public Broadcasting, August 15, 2019. www.wvpublic.org/post/poultry-plant-s-changed-face-appalachian -town#stream/o.

Patterson, Stuart. "A New Pattern of Life: The Public Past and Present of Two New Deal Communities." PhD diss., Emory University, 2006.

PlayerCounter. "*Fallout 76* Live Player Count: How Many People Are Playing Now?" Accessed June 26, 2020. https://playercounter.com/fallout-76.

Pollard, Kelvin M. "A 'New Diversity': Race and Ethnicity in the Appalachian Region." Appalachian Regional Commission and Population Reference Bureau, September 2004. www.arc.gov/assets/research_reports /ANewDiversityRaceandEthnicityinAppalachia.pdf.

Porterfield, Mannix. *A Man Called Shirley.* Bloomington, Ind.: iUniverse, 2009.

Proschan, Frank. "Field Work and Social Work: Folklore as Helping Profession." In *Public Folklore*, edited by Robert Baron and Nick Spitzer, 145–58. Jackson: University of Mississippi Press, 2007.

Rice, Brad, prod. *Swiss Family Balli*, 2015. DVD.

Rifle Gaming. "Here's Why I'm Downgrading into This Trailer." YouTube, February 25, 2020. www.youtube.com/watch?v=NDCl231xDGc&feature =youtu.be.

Roosevelt, Eleanor. "My Day" newspaper columns. Accessed April 23, 2019. www2.gwu.edu/~erpapers/myday.

———. "Ratify the Child Labor Amendment." *Woman's Home Companion*, September 1933.

———. *This I Remember*. New York: Harper and Brothers, 1949.

Rosenberg, Neil. "It Was a Kind of Hobby": A Manuscript Song Book and Its Place in Tradition." In *Folklore Studies in Honor of Herbert Halpert: A Festschrift*, edited by Kenneth S. Goldstein and Neil V. Rosenberg, 315–34. St. John's: Memorial University of Newfoundland, 1980.

Ross, Phil. "The Scotts Run Coalfield from the Great War to the Great Depression: A Study in Overdevelopment." *West Virginia History* 53 (1994): 21–42.

Rukeyser, Muriel. *The Book of the Dead*. Morgantown: West Virginia University Press, 2018.

Ryden, Kent C. *Mapping the Invisible Landscape: Folklore, Writing, and the Sense of Place*. Iowa City: University of Iowa Press, 1993.

Salfia, Jessica. "How 'Strike Tacos,' Delivery Pizza, and Bagged Lunches Fueled an Activist Movement." *Bon Appétit*, November 6, 2018. www.bonappetit.com/story/teachers-strike-west-virginia.

———. Introduction to *55 Strong: Inside the West Virginia Teachers' Strike*, edited by Elizabeth Catte, Emily Hilliard, and Jessica Salfia, 6–15. Cleveland: Belt, 2018.

Sawin, Patricia. *Listening for a Life: A Dialogic Ethnography of Bessie Eldreth through Her Songs and Stories*. Logan: Utah State University Press, 2004.

Schrag, Peter. "Appalachia: Again the Forgotten Land." *Saturday Review*, January 27, 1968: 14-18.

Scotts Run Museum and Trail. Facebook post, May 23, 2021. www.facebook.com/ScottsRunMuseum/posts/1858816310967207.

———. Website. Accessed April 23, 2019. https://scottsrunmuseumandtrail.org.

Segal, Lynne. *Radical Happiness: Moments of Collective Joy*. London: Verso, 2018.

Seybert, B. R. "'He'll Always Be a Part of Us': Folklore in the Stories of Breece D'J Pancake." *Appalachian Heritage* 40, no. 3 (Summer 2012): 43–49.

Shapiro, Henry D. *Appalachia on Our Minds: The Southern Mountains and Mountaineers in the American Consciousness, 1870–1920*. Chapel Hill: University of North Carolina Press, 1978.

Shoemaker, David. *The Squared Circle: Life, Death, and Professional Wrestling*. New York: Gotham, 2013.

Silverstein, Michael, and Greg Urban. "The Natural History of Discourse."

In *Natural Histories of Discourse*, edited by Michael Silverstein and Greg Urban, 1–17. Chicago: University of Chicago Press, 1996.

Slifer, Shaun. "1970s Activist Publishing in West Virginia: Researching Appalachian Movement Press." *Just Seeds*, July 21, 2017. https://justseeds .org/underground-publishing-in-west-virginia-during-the-1970s -researching-appalachian-movement-press.

Slocum, Audra, Rosemary Hathaway, and Malayna Bernstein. "Striking Signs: The Diverse Discourse of the 2018 West Virginia Teachers' Strike." *English Education* 50, no. 4 (July 2018): 367–74.

Smith, Lora E. "The Household Searchlight Recipe Book." In *The Food We Eat, the Stories We Tell*, edited by Elizabeth S. D. Engelhardt with Lora E. Smith, 9–20. Athens: Ohio University Press, 2019.

Spence, Robert Y. "Aunt Jennie Wilson." *e-WV: The West Virginia Encyclopedia*, December 9, 2015. www.wvencyclopedia.org/articles/1284.

Steelhammer, Rick. "Flood of 2016." *e-WV: The West Virginia Encyclopedia*, August 22, 2018. www.wvencyclopedia.org/articles/2443.

Steiner, Michael C. "Regionalism in the Great Depression." *Geographical Review* 73, no. 4 (1983): 430–46.

Steinkuehler, Constance. "Learning in Massively Multiplayer Online Games." In *Proceedings of the Sixth International Conference of the Learning Sciences*, edited by Y. B. Kafai, W. A. Sandoval, N. Enyedy, A. S. Nixon, and F. Herrera Mahwah, 521–28. Hillsdale, N.J.: Erlbaum, 2004.

Stefano, Michelle. "Folklife at the International Level: Intangible Cultural Heritage Defined." *Folklife Today* (American Folklife Center blog), January 30, 2020. https://blogs.loc.gov/folklife/2020/01/folklife-at-the -international-level-intangible-cultural-heritage-defined.

Stoll, Steven. *Ramp Hollow: The Ordeal of Appalachia*. New York: Hill and Wang, 2017.

Strickland, Derek. "*Fallout 76* Sold 1.4 Million Digital Copies, SuperData Says." TweakTown, December 20, 2018. www.tweaktown.com/news /64245/fallout-76-sold-1-4-million-digital-copies-superdata/index .html.

Sutton, David H. *Helvetia: The History of a Swiss Village in the Mountains of West Virginia*. Morgantown: West Virginia University Press, 2010.

———. "Walter Aegerter." *e-WV: The West Virginia Encyclopedia*, June 2, 2014. www.wvencyclopedia.org/articles/15.

Sutton-Smith, Brian. "Psychology of Childlore: The Triviality Barrier." *Western Folklore* 29, no. 1 (1970): 1–8.

Suvin, Darko. "Estrangement and Cognition." *Strange Horizons*, November 24, 2014.

A Taste of History, with Ethnic Flavor: Recipes from Scotts Run, Published with the 60th Anniversary of the Beginning of the Work. Osage, W.Va.: House, 1982.

Taylor, T. L. *Play between Worlds: Exploring Online Game Culture*. Cambridge. Mass.: MIT Press, 2006.

Thompson, E. P. *Customs in Common: Studies in Traditional Popular Culture*. New York: New Press, 1993.

Todd, Roxy. "Do You Know Where the Word 'Redneck' Comes From? Mine Wars Museum Opens, Revives Lost Labor History." West Virginia Public Broadcasting, May 18, 2015. www.wvpublic.org/post/do-you-know-where-word-redneck-comes-mine-wars-museum-opens-revives-lost-labor-history#stream/0.

Trillbilly Worker's Party. "Episode 73: Tomorrow's People." Podcast. Accessed August 12, 2020. https://soundcloud.com/user-972848621-463073718/episode-73-tomorrows-people.

Turino, Thomas. *Music as Social Life: The Politics of Participation*. Chicago: University of Chicago Press, 2008.

Turner, Kay. "The Witch in Flight." Presidential Address to the American Folklore Society, 2017. Accessed March 5, 2018. www.youtube.com/watch?v=ALw2Zw_4hyl.

US Census Bureau. "Census of Population and Housing." Accessed August 27, 2013. https://www.census.gov/programs-surveys/decennial-census/decade.html.

———. Quick Facts. Website. Accessed September 9, 2019. www.census.gov/quickfacts/fact/table/boonecountywestvirginia,US/PST045218.

———. "West Virginia Population Declined 3.2% from 2010 to 2020." West Virginia: 2020 Census. Accessed October 30, 2020. www.census.gov/library/stories/state-by-state/west-virginia-population-change-between-census-decade.html.

US Resettlement Administration. Library of Congress. Photos, Prints and Drawings. Accessed April 23, 2019. www.loc.gov/photos/?fa=location:scotts+run&q=Scotts+Run.

Valentine, Rebekah. "Bethesda Wants to Bring Humanity to *Fallout* through NPCs." March 9, 2020. www.gamesindustry.biz/articles/2020-03-08-fallout-76-wants-to-bring-humanity-to-the-game-through-npcs.

Virginia Folklife Program. "Joey Mirabile Sr. and Logan Caine." Accessed August 14, 2020. https://virginiafolklife.org/sights-sounds/joey-mirabile-sr-and-joey-mirabile-jr.

Wallace, Emily Elizabeth. "It Was There for Work: Pimento Cheese in the Carolina Piedmont." MA thesis, University of North Carolina at Chapel Hill, 2010.

Washburn, Anne. *Mr. Burns: A Post-electric Play*. London: Oberon, 2014.

Webster, Andrew. "Why West Virginia Was the Perfect Setting for a New *Fallout* Game." *Verge*, October 8, 2018. www.theverge.com/2018/10/8 /17943066/fallout-76-west-virginia-pete-hines-bethesda.

Weller, Jack E. *Yesterday's People: Life in Contemporary Appalachia*. Lexington: University Press of Kentucky, 1965.

West, Brenda. "The Best Curb Girl in Logan County." *Goldenseal* 24, no.1 (Spring 1998): 66.

West Virginia Department Health and Human Resources. "A Look at West Virginia's Population by Decade, 1950–2000." Brief no. 8 (May 2002). www.wvdhhr.org/bph/hsc/pubs/briefs/008/default.htm.

West Virginia Hot Dog Blog. "What Is A West Virginia Hot Dog?" Accessed August 15, 2020. http://wvhotdogblog.blogspot.com.

Whisnant, David E. *All That Is Native and Fine: The Politics of Culture in an American Region*. Chapel Hill: University of North Carolina Press, 2009.

Williams, Raymond. *The Country and the City*. New York: Oxford University Press, 1973.

Wilson, Jill Elizabeth. "1990 Teachers' Strike." *e-WV: The West Virginia Encyclopedia*, July 16, 2018. www.wvencyclopedia.org/articles/696.

Wilson, Rick. "Done Too Soon." Unpublished manuscript.

Wood, Sara. "A Hamburger by Any Other Name." *Gravy*, Summer 2016. www.southernfoodways.org/a-hamburger-by-any-other-name.

Woods, Clyde. *Development Arrested: The Blues and Plantation Power in the Mississippi Delta*. London: Verso, 2017.

Worland, Justin. "Coal's Last Kick." *Time*, April 6, 2017. https://time.com /coals-last-kick.

Wright, Erik Olin. *How to Be an Anti-capitalist in the 21st Century*. New York: Verso, 2019.

Index

Abrahams, Roger, 6

Acevedo, Angel (Cuban Assassin #1), 165, 166, 168, 178, 239n66

Acevedo, Richie (Cuban Assassin #2), 165, 167–68, 170, 177, 178–79

Aegerter, Gottfried, 94

Aegerter, Walter, 94

Alford, Violet, 122–23

Alpenrose Garden Club, Helvetia, 90

American Federation of Teachers, 118, 119, 124–25, 233n37

American Folklife Center, Library of Congress, 3, 6, 188

American Folklore Society, 16, 23, 125, 128

American Friends Service Committee, 31, 34

American Legislative Exchange Council, 118

Anderson, Al, 27, 29, 35, 40–41, 43, 44

anticipatory heritage, 210

Appadurai, Arjun, 194

Appalachia: collaborative ethnographic method in, xiii–xiv; conception as isolated cultural anachronism, 13–14; conceptions of regionalism, 20; culture industry in, 34; distressed areas of, 147, 235–36n25; essentializing meaning of, 10, 15; in *Fallout 76*, 23, 182, 192–93, 194; foodways of, 3; history and identity in protest signs, 125, 128–30, 132–33; immigration of ethnic and cultural groups to, 88; insider/outsider narrative in, 9, 109, 167, 230n22, 238n41; and local-color writers' literary narratives, 191–92, 194–95, 197, 205; and Midwest, 4; narrativization of, 23; romanticism of, 13; stereotypes of, 12, 193; as "tomorrow's people," 192, 193, 241n31; tourism economy of, 14, 15; women's nonprofessional songwriting and self-documentation in, 49, 64–65, 81

Appalachian Food Summit, 123

Appalachian Land Ownership Study, 224n38

Appalachian Movement Press, 105, 229n12

Appalachian Regional Commission, 187, 240n15

Armentrout, Frances, 138

Arnett, Heidi, 94

Arruzza, Cinzia, 231n8

Arthurdale, W.Va., 32–34, 35, 37, 225n19, 225n25

Ashe, Thomas, 158–59